The
MODERN
LOVER

D1115128

Mr. & Mrs. Demopoulos
P.O. Box 184
Anacortes, WA 98221

The MODERN LOVER

A PLAYBOOK FOR SUITORS, SPOUSES & RINGLESS CAROUSERS

PHINEAS MOLLOD & JASON TESAURO

TEN SPEED PRESS
Berkeley • Toronto

Copyright © 2004 by Phineas Mollod and Jason Tesauro

All rights reserved. No part of this book may be reproduced in any form, except brief excerpts
for the purpose of review, without written permission of the publisher.

Ten Speed Press
Box 7123
Berkeley, California 94707
www.tenspeed.com

Distributed in Australia by Simon and Schuster Australia, in Canada by Ten Speed Press Canada,
in New Zealand by Southern Publishers Group, in South Africa by Real Books,
and in the United Kingdom and Europe by Airlift Book Company.

Cover and interior design by Paul Kepple and Jude Buffum @ Headcase Design

Permission granted to reprint material from the following sources:

Page 32. Vladimir Nabokov, *The Annotated Lolita*. New York: Vintage Books, 1991
(originally published 1955). Reprinted with permission from Random House.

Page 69. Song lyrics from Deee-Lite's "Stay in Bed, Forget the Rest," *Dewdrops in the Garden*.
Delovely Publishing, 1994.

Page 84. Ed and Dana Allen, *Together Sex: The Playful Couple's Key to Better Sex Parties*.
Momentpoint Media, 2001.

Page 117. James M. Cain, *The Postman Always Rings Twice*.
New York: Vintage Crime/Black Lizard Edition, 1992 (orig. published 1934).
Reprinted with permission from Random House.

Library of Congress Cataloging-in-Publication Data

Mollod, Phineas.
The modern lover : a playbook for suitors, spouses & ringless carousers /
by Phineas Mollod & Jason Tesauro.—1st ed.
p. cm.
A follow-up to the authors': The modern gentleman.
Includes bibliographical references and index.
ISBN 1-58008-601-2
1. Dating (Social customs) 2. Man-woman relationships. 3. Mate selection. 4. Marriage. I.
Tesauro, Jason. II. Mollod, Phineas. Modern gentleman. III. Title.
HQ801.M645 2004
646.7'7—dc22
2004017634

Printed in Canada · First printing 2004 · 1 2 3 4 5 6 7 8 9 10 − 08 07 06 05 04

To E, my everlasting one-night stand.

—J. T.

To my spinning doll and captivating concubine, G.

—P. M.

ACKNOWLEDGMENTS

◆ ❧ ◆ ❧ ◆ ❧ ◆ ❧

To Mom for teaching me the ins and outs of wrinkle-free Lights & Darks, and to Dad for imparting the birds & the bees, namely for buying me my first thirty-six-pack of condoms; of course, to both for showcasing untired handholding and years of togetherness. To my brother Dan for invaluable counsel on In-Laws, Her Analyst, and On-Time Departures, and to Mike, Grand Poobah of Muckeroo Cookies, LLC, for info on His & Hers and Final Hurdles, as well as single-handedly boosting online sales. High fives to the Weber clan for tolerating this scribbling flâneur while he dates their daughter.

—P. M.

A Jersey-sized dollop of gratitude to Mom and Tom for imbibing love and Lagavulin, eloping to the Love Nest, and proving that a soulmate is just the gift for semicentenarians with youthful spines. Fondest admiration to the longest-standing couplings around the Thanksgiving table: Aunt Jay and Uncle Bob, Aunt Jean and Uncle John, and Auntie Suzie and Uncle Fred. A proper Southern thanks y'all to the Eleys for crocheted support, figgy sustenance, moonshine, and trouble-free in-laws. An especial thanks to my little boy, the primogenitary Sebastion, for impressing and messing upon me the rigors of childcare . . . and for typing most of the manuscript whilst sippy-cupping Chartreuse in my lap.

—J. T.

Phineas & Tesauro bid fondest appreciation to: Beth and Wolfgang for Ringless Carousing 101 over chicken 'n' dumplin's at Perly's and to Sharon and Jason for Belgian concubine dogma and Condrieu. To be perfectly Franc, thanks must go to Donny and Pegula for wine-stemmed debates over Finances & Common Cents. Danke schön to Traci and Rob, Linda and McGrath, and Jennifer and Jeff and their three-tiered cakes for hot tips on Contemporary Nuptials. A fedora tip to Leslie and her green thumb for top-notch topsoil advice. Hushed gratitude to Donna and her tempered abandon for One-Night Stands ne'er taken lying down. Backslaps to E. Kirk and his raw confessionals on Brady Bunch Factor and Daddy Detox.

Ujjayi pranayama and kudos to David and his spiraling chi for Tantric Love and Flurry. A pleasant ouch to Lisa for P-Whipping us into shape. Thanks to the newly emancipated Jessica for her courageous journey from Souring, and to Nancy for Loopholers and an intimate peek into her relationship diary, as well as Becky and her generation-skipping insights and allure for Matrons & Maidens. Eternal naughty regard to our landmark playmates: AP, BE, BH, KR, KW, JP, LM, LS, MC, PK, SG.

Aptly wet smooches to Suzanne, Tesauro's luvin' first, plus Jenifer and Anne Marie for teaching us the fine art of lip lock. Hushed thanks to Nancy and her false address for Guest Room Closet inspiration, and a knowing nod to Sandor on the inevitability of Compatibility. To auteur Dan, 8 mm of gratitude for making us look good, wrangling Ringless, and who, along with Dr. Gordon and his jar of Jif, survived the head-clearing necessity of Celibacy. Ringraziamenti, Enzo, per fornire consiglio sul Pilgrimage to Papa. A lip-smacking *mmwah* to Provocative Friends: Monica, the Googlicious Testarossa; and Christina, the Chilean voluptuoso. A chain gang chantie to the Mississippi Pen and Hendrix for singing the virtues of the Red House. A strand of appreciation to pearly Becky, fair Queen of the Kitchen. Proud papa props to three happenin' padres: Dean, Greg, and Dan-O, for the real deal on New Dad. Hearty toasts of thanksgiving to Faro, Christine, Louie Free, Dickie Molnar, Jones and the Vandy boys, and the Krewe for unbending support and prolific purchases. A fistful of Octagon to Barboursville cronies, Palladian *paesani*, and tasting room divas. An authentically guttural merci to Ethan, the Musical Mensaman, and Charlie, two hip sages, for preaching the gospels of Jonathan Richman and the Modern Lovers. Flaming lips of thankfulness to Sharon and the GED-hopeful Josiah for rolling out Richmond's red carpet. Wicket thanks to the Confederate Hills Croquet Club for spirited roquets in whites on Sundays. Naked hurricane gracias to Augusten for literary *pommes de terre* and wet dreams of wainscoting.

Stealthy appreciation to Stan's Happy Tails and Claire's inner dominatrix for the skinny on floggers, and more of the same to Doris at Dream Dresser Boutique for escorting a gentleman down the leather & latex aisle. *Tutto è delizioso* in the gent's pantry thanks to Chef Grandinetti's toqueful of required reading, plus Nach & Matt, gatekeepers of cook lit at Kitchen Arts & Letters. A 99 percent-cacao kudos to James at For the Love of Chocolate for a melts-in-your-mouth tutorial of a true wonder drug, and to the bibliolicious Kelly and Anna at Fountain Bookstore for cha-chinging registers and sexy reads. To Ed and Dana, thanks for swinging into our inbox. Proper salutations and superlatives to Alexandra, Lizzy, and the English Manner for setting our tea trays without lifting their petticoats.

Awe-filled indebtedness to Paul for another smashbang design destined to land us on the finest coffee tables and hoariest nightstands. Thanks to proofer Mike Ashby and indexer Ken DellaPenta, and especially to Marchelle Brain for waxing and tweezing our manuscript's unkempt brows. Right-to-left-coast appreciation to the Ten Speeders Kristin, Mark, and Gonzalo (thanks too for the cookbook hookup) for shouting us to the masses. A twenty-one-flask salute to Aaron Wehner, master polisher and fellow gent at arms, for his savvy prose coaching. Finally, profuse gratefulness to our luminous agent Kimberley Cameron and her dashing man, David, for ten-plus smitten, trailblazing years of googly eyes over Nebbiolo.

CONTENTS

INTRODUCTION

◆ ♥ ◆ ♥ ◆ ♥

For a language that brings us sleek words like diaphanous, antidisestablishmentarianism, and twit, the English tongue is sorely deficient regarding love. What single word describes a passionate lover, conscientious roommate, steadfast companion, and responsible parent? Partner, spouse, and mate fall short, while "old man" and "the missus" are decidedly unsexy. Though long favored by sassy metrosexuals, "lover" sadly wallows in the bargain bin of seedy affairs. Even musicians serenading about the virtues of love all sing a different tune: Dylan crowed, "I wanna be your lover, baby, I don't wanna be your boss," as Judas Priest growled, "I'm your turbo lover . . . better run for cover!" And while true in 1975, there are now more than "50 Ways to Leave Your Lover" by email alone. Our first book, *The Modern Gentleman*, expanded the breadth of "gentleman" beyond a dandy who brandishes escargot tongs. We now embark on a similar reclamation project for "lover."

Once upon a time, the WWII generation took the leap with quick-draw proposals, but for modern www.up-and-comers, a mortgage and two kids can wait. In this spirit, our initial chapters promote a twenty-something whistle-stop tour of amorous experiences. "Beyond the Black Book" urges a dynamic register of romances and a rich store of fulfilled fantasies to promote a comfortable, regret-free residence within monogamy's confines later in life. The evolving bachelor provocateur cultivates relationship savvy by sowing "Wild Oats" and test-driving the wild "Testarossa," along with confident "Web-Slinging" in the online meet market. Far from vanilla, "Nocturnal & Naughty" is for unshy lovers stoking coals under the sheets, even if it involves "The Red House," leather, or a nine-foot tether.

In the trenches of dating, purposeful promiscuity inevitably leads to scorched hearts, broken commitments, and fiery one-nighters—brash acts that ultimately teach a gentleman the tenets of trust, love, and passion, preparing him for bedding and wedding a soulmate. When "Trouble" rears its head, a tactful mate endures a "Night on the Couch," and when temptation strikes, lovers brave the "Six Danger Zones of Infidelity."

The percentages suggest that none of a gent's first three sweethearts will be a lifelong beloved and the mother of his children (barring a broken rubber and subsequent paternity test). By swinging at the first pitch, a lad is banking that the Fates will magically smile upon puppy love. But once a lady has passed the "Compatibility" battery and is nominated for the starring role, a suitor weighs the benefits of prudently disclosing "Skeletons," considers the "Brady Bunch Factor" (when marrying one means committing to three), and checks Bible-thumping tolerances when "It's Jahweh or the Highway."

After landing "The One," the "Ring Bearer" champions "Contemporary Nuptials." A counterpoint to the advice doled out by starchy wedding guides, *The Modern Lover* is a handsome counterweight that addresses "Altar Ego," "The Dynamic Groom," and such eccentricities as Champagne sabering. We also recognize "Ringless Carousers" and other long-term couplers who conduct themselves outside convention, and that certain "Loopholers" refuse to be pinned down altogether.

The remaining pages detail the particulars of playing in and out of the house—"Lights & Darks & Dishes," "The Gentleman's Cellar," and "Spouseless Carousing"—since no amount of pelvic dynamite will assuage a disgruntled bedmate engulfed by strewn socks, nosy in-laws, or soulless cupboards stocked with junk food. "New Dad" offers a primer on the prenatal prep, the "First Hundred Days" on postpartum coos and spills.

We're not PhDs (though Phineas has a JD and Tesauro once narrowly sidestepped VD) harping on the magic of communication as the panacea for love's ills. Yet, the authors have a rich history of amour, and while we haven't spilled a martini in years, romantic slip-ups still land us in the doghouse on occasion. (Our most dubious deeds and fantastic fireworks are laid out in "Phineas's Phlames & Tesauro's Trysts.") We've trolled our own experiences, hit the library, and gathered data from fellow modern lovers. While no animals were harmed in the making of this book, several relationships unfortunately were torn asunder and then mined for the valuable research ore within. (By the by, should you think wooing and dating, long-distance relationships, and prophyletiquette are MIA, fear not; they are securely housed within ML's big brother, *The Modern Gentleman*.)

So Come All Ye (Un)Faithful: bachelor/-ettes with cheeky résumés; long-term marrieds looking to pick up a trick or toy; advanced singles trading up to monogamy; brides-to-be and grooms-elect concluding bachelorhood and spicing up the wedding; newly engaged couples and other live-ins with or without municipal marriage certificates; or even curious ladies wishing a peek into their beau's boudoir. *The Modern Lover* will not remedy a rotted relationship doomed for divorce court, but for long-termers, bounden ringsmen, and monogamous veterans looking for proactive counsel and a fresh approach, our book is the first one to thumb through to cure cold feet, enliven the bedroom, and process wayward temptation.

PART ONE

The
EVOLVED
BACHELOR

BEYOND THE BLACK BOOK

♦ ♥ ♦ ♥ ♦ ♥ ♦ ♥

ONE-NIGHT STANDS

Badge of sexual savvy or tattoo of indecency? Both camps are right. The one-nighter is an inimitable, wanton pleasure that curdles quickly when lowbrow motives and squalid settings collide. A gent can either bask in a soul-shaking dance with a stranger or wind up in a sheet-tarnishing episode that ends with him fumbling at his zipper and tiptoeing away under the pale flicker of an exit sign. Stigmas aside, the majority of lovers have at least nibbled at this trough, testing the mettle of their sexual ethic and thereby challenging the parameters of love and lust. Whether you're pro or con, one-nighters define the louche days of single life that nonetheless become the most palpable sacrifice of long-term monogamy.

A rookie's pretense of an offered neck massage preserves the comfortable veneer of a social call. A practiced Romeo should skip the charade and move straight to the nightcap, harnessing a high pulse rate of anticipation without the red tape; it was never about the coffee or your collection of etchings anyway. With such mutual candor, a one-nighter is often thrust into something more substantial.

The ONS continuum runs from eternally memorable to instantly forgettable:

Hall of Fame (cherished bachelorhood moments that remain replayable for a lifetime)

♥ **Serendipity Colliding**: Your intersecting destinies and adventurous spirits are in undeniable synchrony. Usual prudence is shelved, and sex becomes one of many connections forged before dawn. This explosive début sometimes spawns a great relationship.

- **Carpe diem**: Seize the lay. With overseas airline reservations or never-see-you-again relocation plans looming, the two of you embrace a rare window of opportunity and form an indelible memory. Like in *Casablanca*, emotions run high, yet revisiting this short burst of love in the future may be impossible. Don't be greedy—at least you had Paris.

Heightened Hookups (casual sex enters like a cat burglar)

- **Setup**: To maintain even table seating, you are appointed escort for the night. Who's to say it can't turn into something else?

- **What-If**: Curious friends ponder what it would be like . . . and later answer that very question lying naked. A torrid fling ensues, perhaps to be later brushed off as a lonesome misstep or scientific curiosity. With sexual tension melted, the friendship becomes 80 percent less tempting, as furtive peeks down her blouse when a pencil drops are no longer necessary.

The Debris of Used Rubbers, Sticky Sheets & Back Alley Fornication (one anagram of "one-night stand" is "ends at nothing")

- **Down the Drain**: Skipping the movie, the wooing, and intrigue, this cheap encounter moves from dinner to bed. After the awkward untangling of bodies, lust evaporates, and the relationship fizzles flat like day-old club soda.

◆ **Baited Hook, Bad Line & No Sinker:** Guilty of scamming in the first degree (with premeditation), you utter whatever it takes to find action, long-term prospects be damned. Ultimately, you are exposed as a shallow used-car-salesman liar selling lemons. This type of hookup besmirches one-night stands, and regrettably, this C-grade fling is also the most common.

▼ **The Zipless Screw:** Masturbation using someone else's body. This bar-room bend-over is not about swirling auras of karmic energy, just selfish release. A sublime one-night stand might last until sunrise, but the zipless screw terminates mere seconds after the effluvium of climax when a torrent of shame quickly overtakes the drunken high and sexual endorphins.

Moreover, not all one-night stands come to fruition. Like in the Pick 3 lottery, all balls must fall into place: motive (attraction + lowered inhibitions), means (moral flexibility + prophylactics), and opportunity (private coupling area + no chance of third-party interference). Every carouser has been struck down by the harsh lights of last call, forgotten birth control, or no vacancy; sometimes such obstacles spare you next-day regret, and other times, you're one borrowed apartment key from Eden.

Incidentally, the *Groundhog Day* of one-night stands is a serial rendezvous with the same bedmate, wherein the chat never delves past the how, when, and where. Despite feeble rationalizations, a standing appointment is not a relationship, merely a one-night stand times ten. This status doesn't change until the duo elevates the superficial goal of a no-strings-attached orgasm into actual public regard.

EQUITY

In real estate parlance, you build equity by paying the mortgage and investing in home improvements that cost you now but increase future value. Eventually, you get out more than you put in. Every one-night stand has equity invested (if only a pittance): from a ten-minute proposition in the back parlor to an entire evening spent in the throes of enthralling conversation. Think of your equity as intimacy, trust, and desire built over time, essentially your "going down" payment. While sex after a month of dating represents the equity of multiple encounters and hours of telephone time, memorable one-night stands depend on the following, even when minutes are short:

♥ **Desire**: Turn up the flame, especially with sexy ambiance.

♦ **Intimacy**: Mine the mind beyond the mundane.

♥ **Trust**: Convey sincerity without hidden agendas.

Trust fosters comfort during a high-equity encounter. You're not a sideshow barker selling snake oil to an unsuspecting dupe, rather both parties are voluntarily buying into a connection built on more than base desire. If it goes all the way, it feels worthwhile, even if circumstances prevent a sequel. Although you might be disappointed without a romp, a sexless close won't sully the buzz and intensity of an otherwise momentous evening.

For a low-equity encounter, there is little regard for names, numbers, or favorite colors. With so little invested, the Zipless Screw is a low-return liaison more likely to yield a feather in your cap than a future sweetheart on your arm.

Nice touch: Go all in. If you're interested in continuing the tryst past the bedroom, skip needless pleasantries. Instead of "I'll call you later," test for a live wire right now and suggest brunch in thirty minutes or dinner the next evening. Your proposition will bolster sincerity, and if you misread your cards, it will garner a curt no-thanks and a tidy snip to last night's business ("All in favor? This screw is now adjourned.").

RÉSUMÉ BUILDING

Despite the lack of familiarity, certain one-night stands are surprisingly vivid when stark-naked strangers break out into acrobatic fetish, even if that's not their usual cup of pee. Somehow, the sixties are reborn and the freedom of experimentation leads to sexual escapade; at these moments, it is imperative to ride high and practice a few antics you have witnessed on video. Oftentimes, the anonymity propels a sexual perversity not ordinarily explored during long-term loving relationships.

STIGMA

Sexy urbanites might disagree, but one-night stands haven't shaken their pejorative label. Especially for women, an ONS is unfortunately linked to promiscuity (regardless of frequency) and to the looser set who major in casual sex and minor in free drinks. This stigma is unfounded, especially for ladies and gents with discerning taste for high-equity amour.

Value judgments aside, standard wooing rituals are indeed eschewed during a one-night stand. The green light of consummation is an express-lane pass through customs. Whether the adventure includes condoms or not, there's probably not a lengthy discussion of family pedigree or medical history; thus, you're getting and giving clearance with only the basic security check. Take extra care: anyone who would agree to bed you on the first night has probably done so before, and it is foolish (or arrogant) to think otherwise.

ONE-NIGHT STANDINGS

Thirty lovers do not equal thirty relationships. One-nighters likely make up a portion of your sexual pie chart, but how many is too many? To determine a reasonable ONS allotment, plot your history on our graph. For up to twenty-five lovers, expect to file 20 to 25 percent under ONS; ergo, if you've had fifteen lovers, you've likely had three to four one-nighters. With a bustling black book, you're probably more injudicious in your exploits. Thus, after twenty-five bedmates, your ONS percentage might rise at an equal rate (one percentage point for each additional lover), topping out at 65 percent (this maximum presumes that even a career playboy with over sixty-five conquests stumbles into lasting affairs part of the time). For example, if your tally is thirty-five lovers, 35 percent will likely be one-night stands (twelve); for 128 lovers (enough to fill two cartons of crayons), your ONS average will probably max out at 65 percent, or approximately eighty-three one-nighters, with the remainder representing major and minor relationships.

Falling below the benchmark is fine, but a restrictive no-one-night-stand clause in your sexual constitution is too Spartan. Unearthing a few treasures is worth the price of inevitable youthful mistakes; for the sake of curiosity and development, your libido should occasionally lead where a rational mind wouldn't normally tread.

Incidentally, when you get into four digits, no mathematical formula can contain your virility. According to our one-night standings, the late basketball great Wilt Chamberlain, with a self-reported 10,000 lovers, would tally in at 3,500 meaningful relationships. At a healthy clip of one

ONE-NIGHT STANDINGS

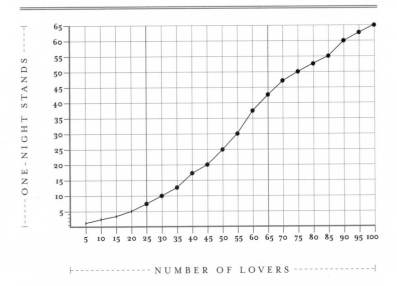

relationship per week, the big man would need 67 years to complete his mission (he died at age 63), all the while averaging 30.1 points and 22.9 rebounds per game during the regular season.

THEORY OF EVOLUTION

Early on, a diet of itinerant couplings is acceptable youthful exuberance, but as goals change from nightlife intrigue to romantic curiosity, the gentleman favors more lasting connections. Whether from daily smoke or the infrequent toke, every pipe eventually clogs with a hard resin; at some point, your heart must process the industrial slag from an active gigolo life. With age comes perspective. At twenty-two, everything is fleeting: relationships, pocket money, temp jobs. The peak of one-night standings likely parallels your greatest era of experimentation, characterized by ever-increasing chunks of salary devoted to leisure, bounced check fees, and communal living with fellow bed-hopping sybarites. Later, when the lifestyle of dodgy affairs becomes unsustainable, you find yourself contemplating long-term lovers, nest eggs, lasting careers, and permanent addresses. In the past, hitting the bottle with friends and then plunging into impulsive decisions was quickly forgiven, but now these frequent flings—once chicken soup for feverish souls—are incongruent with seasoned values. The twilight of bachelorhood is not the time for bulk additions to your sexual résumé, rather a period for productive affairs bookended with solid relationships.

NIGHT CAP

♥ ◆ ♥ ◆ ♥ **Brandy** ♥ **Cointreau** ♥ **Dash anisette** ♥ **Egg yolk** ♥ ◆ ♥ ◆ ♥

PROVOCATIVE FRIENDSHIPS

Some alluring sidekicks are the agent provocateurs who unleash your latent rascality through large-group skinny-dipping, open-eyed dressing room privileges, and late-night, leather-pant gambling sprees. Whether you are married, engaged, or ringlessly connected, when these mini-soulmates cross your path, they introduce the possibility of pulse-quickening innuendo and flirtation without sacrificing integrity. If you are unattached, a provocative friend might become the exclusive object of your affection, but when you are spoken for, you have several options:

- ♥ **Prudish Abstinence**: Avoid all contact with opposite-sex free radicals and limit interactions to couples and unsightly, temptation-free friends only.

- ◆ **Learner's Permit**: Mix it up with whomever you want . . . as long as there's a trusty chaperone in the passenger seat. You're expected to file a flight plan and respect curfew.

- ♥ **Weekend Pass**: Carouse off base, but only with good behavior and prior permission. Clearance is granted for approved gal pals who have passed your partner's battery of tests.

- ◆ **Chastity Belt**: Take your libido for a spin on the town but keep the real means of mischief out of reach. Closely monitor cheek-to-cheek dancing and racy conversation lest your once impenetrable vault be unlocked for a wanton playmate.

♥ **Key to the City**: After a string of good deeds, your mate bestows the high honor of carte blanche, presuming that you won't later deserve a mayoral revoking of privileges.

♦ **Cloak-and-Dagger**: Ditch your monogamy in an anonymous bus locker and sweat up the sheets with a new mistress in every hot-pillow joint in town.

♥ **New Age**: Retreat to a dark, dank cave to meditate and suppress prurient urges over a plate of gruel, stack of incense, and a singing bowl.

Provocative friendships are the earned privilege of evolved bachelors and monogamists who maintain discipline without sating carnal curiosity. Those lacking "No" in their vocabulary ought to recuse themselves from PF enticements. The shadowy delight of infidelity is fleeting and not nearly as inspired as stringing out little pleasures of riveting confessions and scintillating eye contact over many moons. Instead of taking the easy plunge into a moral maelstrom of booze and tawdriness, open the curtains and channel sexuality productively. For example, a new friend who is soft on the eyes might also be a great swing dancer, football fan, or political debater. No two lovers have hobbies and impulses that overlap 100 percent; when your partner does not fancy rave clubs, chess matches, or NORML "Smoke the Vote" rallies, a PF steps in nicely. These friends invigorate flagging spirits, smooth the transition after a break-up, or provide temporary relief from marital dystopia. When homebound blues evoke restlessness and a pining for past conquests, an upstanding PF offers spicy yet guiltless fun, the ultimate release valve for cramped libido and a low-cal alternative to the self-sabotage of motel affairs with closing-time barflies. Yet, don't bogart that babe; PFs offer the heady taste of excess that should be toked but occasionally.

Some acquaintances raise the heart rate, but only a trusty few generate frisson and also adhere to your dictates of monogamy. Here are the likely candidates for your PF shortlist:

- ♥ **Former Fling:** Lacking the drama of a five-year relationship gone sour, this ex-turned-friend surfaced after a short-term coupling was scuttled by circumstance.

- ◆ **Queer Eye:** Uninhibited flirting with this expressive PF is harmless since hetero possibilities are off the table.

- ♥ **Sublimator:** This stimulating conversationalist shares your view that a constructive sassy friendship trumps a regretful one-night stand.

- ◆ **Flame-Retardant:** Despite your roaring fire, this sidekick can be counted on to smother untoward affections in an asbestos blanket of restraint.

- ♥ **Fellow Inmate:** With equal stakes to lose, a married or seriously involved partner in crime knows the rules and the jailhouse consequences.

HELLO KITTY

In your partner's mind, faceless friends can morph into imagined hussies. To preclude wild assumptions, arrange for introductions at home to establish a baseline of trust. Like a parent scrutinizing a tattooed prom date, your partner can then size up a PF and sniff for any scent of mutiny. Instead of harboring jealous notions, your darling shan't worry, even while you primp ("Are you spritzing cologne? Oh, you're stepping downtown with Daphna.").

REBOUND

After the demise of a meaningful relationship, you're in a vulnerable state—the virus of rejection has compromised your love-immuno system—and you rebound with a quick hookup to scare away the lonely, lugubrious ache. Once off-limits, a provocative friend is now the likeliest target of your hungry look. To bolster poise and shed your anguish, sometimes any love is better than no love at all, but leaping into commitment so soon is the rash act of a wounded animal. If a celibate quarantine after a jagged breakup isn't your style, consider a low romantic profile until the black and blues heal. Beware of latching onto PFs and other quick fixes that are softer succor than Linus's blanket or Mama's bosom. Rather than desperately trying to reanimate lost love in a new mate à la Bride of Frankenstein, declare a grace period to process the last lover's impact.

On the flip side, if you are dating a rebounder, mind the onrush of infatuation; your charm is indeed magnetic, but don't equate clinginess with connection. Watch out for the emotional vampire, drained by a breakup, hunting for a fresh transfusion to restore ruddy cheeks. Romance with you will likely prove unsustainable in the heavy undertow of melancholy, new flirtations, or her ex's teary calls. An unsuspecting suitor risks getting blindsided by rebound reality when she whispers, "I need time to be alone." To avoid such a scenario, afford the rebounder space to pursue renewed freedom or an ill-fated relapse with the old beau.

Nevertheless, provocative friendships are still a danger zone of infidelity. Amid spilled secrets and incidental contact, there are typically tempting moments when forbidden doorways creak open. Hold the line and revisit a near miss the next day with the PF so that boundaries are reinforced ("Last night was tasty, but no more truth or dare without a chaperone."). Once a PF cultivates an honest regard for your character and the relationship, thoughts of nest breaking are quashed; innuendo still flourishes, but this overriding respect provides the battery backup of your fidelity.

Nice touch: Instead of broadcasting sins in a blog, invoke the confession privilege whereby a PF absorbs the unabridged blow-by-blow of your peripheral desires best kept away from the breakfast table. As long as you don't inhabit a vast haunted house of a double life, juicy details oft omitted at home can be explicitly aired in the company of a tight-lipped PF.

MONOGAMY TEST

Monogamy doesn't exist in a vacuum. Sometimes another dynamic soulmate bowls you over, providing a field test of fidelity. Going off Tuesday nights to talk photography over pots of tea is fine, but what's a sensible modern lover to do if chemistry is developing in the darkroom?

♥ ◆ ♥ BOOMERANG ♥ ◆ ♥

♥ ◆ ♥ **Swedish punch or spiced rum** ♥ **Rye or Canadian whiskey** ♥ ◆ ♥

♥ ◆ ♥ ◆ ♥ **Dry vermouth** ♥ **Dash bitters** ♥ **Dash lemon juice** ♥ ◆ ♥ ◆ ♥

Is flirtation a harbinger of sweeping change or a trial of button-fly resolve? No one wants to turn down a defining love-life encounter merely out of principle, but a commitment to monogamy mandates sacrifice. A sober gut check identifies the righteous path, revealing whether the new interest is an upgrade or merely fool's gold falsely outshining your current mate's subtler but proven assets.

Less-than-serious daters are eligible to consider a dastardly alternative: the Devil's Choice. In lieu of starting a detestable, protracted affair, two consenting soulmates realize the imminence of desire and sate their curiosity in one ceremonious debauch and then part ways. Like a double agent swallowing the microfilm before capture, months of compelling work is committed to memory, then destroyed and never divulged again.

P-WHIPPED

[collar]

[leash]

"You are so whipped": the ultimate indictment that you have renounced too many rights for too few privileges. The whipping begins innocently with voluntary compliance under the nascent regime of the Carb-Counting Diet Czar and Sappy Movie Despot, and autonomy is further eroded through campaigns for early curfews and preapproved cohorts. When the manacles are expertly applied, even the most browbeaten peons have the illusion of freedom since the free-will takeover is imperceptible. Friends, however, easily spot lost autonomy in your hangdog

look of surrender. Bickering in public is commonplace, and your mate's dictatorial asides and governing manner are sad to behold.

A young buck who falls hard for a fox and subsequently stars in the dramatic role of dutiful robot is laughable, if a good life lesson. Lest you think males are the only hopeless submissives, the "p" in p-whipped also applies, though less frequently, to the lady loveslave wrapped around her stud's finger. Whoever the victim, power inequalities are symptoms of more serious flaws, like a dearth of trust and a fundamental lack of respect. Everyone has played the sycophant, but seasoned lovers reserve bootlicking for role-play night.

Before career confidence and dating acumen are cemented, p-whippedness is a common condition. To the afflicted, a controlling mate, any mate, seems worth the price of sexual security: trading independent thinking for hugs is better than another dry spell on the couch with Pringles and pornos. Freud might say a p-whipped man struck an early deal with his mother, that in exchange for snippets of affection, he'd forfeit large parts of himself; to Jung, he suffers a deficiency of *anima,* or the inner feminine part of the male personality, and emulates his partner to fill the void. Regardless of which iconic psychotherapist you believe, deep-seated flaws in your psyche are easier to ignore under a diet of constant clingy relationships, where the empty calories of sex render you too fat and feckless for real introspection.

It's a fine line between respect and servitude, and except for self-effacing married men, few will admit to being under a companion's thumb. Compare a conscientious partner, who checks in at night, consults on major purchases, and compromises on entertainment, to a powerless serf who consents at the force of a stiletto heel point to a viceless life according to another's bland tastes. Most subjugated men are defensive, especially around the guys after calling it an early night yet again. Some conditioning whips you into shape, and friends note actual improvement (now with 25 percent less profanity). Nonetheless, heed friendly observations that your individuality has been sold down the river for so much ass. Are you p-whipped? Let us count the ways:

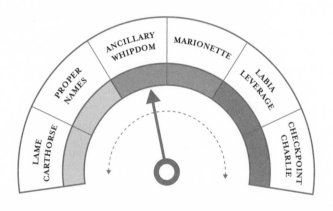

P - W H I P P E D

▾ **Lame Carthorse:** The once wild mustang is now the domesticated beast of burden. You have wide reign over a limited domain . . . like choosing salad dressing for the household. Will it be fat-free raspberry vinaigrette or lite Italian?

♦ **Proper Names:** In a more-than-obvious attempt to play the domineering mother, she uses your proper first name—Maxwell, David, Vincent—despite twenty-five prior years of Max, Dave, or Vinny. The authoritarian tone of hearing your Christian name reinforces your subordinate role.

▾ **Ancillary Whipdom**: Conscientious behavior aside, your good graces shouldn't be whored out past the city limits. Is your back still aching from a four-hour session rewiring her sister's stereo and ceiling fan? Wash up, you don't want to be late for Friday night dinner with her parents.

♦ **Marionette**: You blindly side with your partner-puppeteer and zealously fight irrational battles, losing friends and respect along the way. After growing up in Miami, you adopt your mate's corn-fed allegiances, causing a rift among friends ("When did you become a Colts fan?").

▾ **Labia Leverage**: One partner rations sex like WWII scrap iron. No longer an intimate union or carefree release, lovemaking is meted out based on mercurial moods and your level of compliance.

♦ **Checkpoint Charlie**: Homecoming involves a Breathalyzer, urine test, and corroboration of alibi. Muttered half-truths about whereabouts and hastily bribed friends become status quo to avoid interrogation by the household Stasi. It feels as though you must steal freedoms and fight for every sneaked beer in the basement and smoke in the chilly garage after midnight. Socializing is done mostly with other couples or at "functions." Like Popeye's erstwhile friend Wimpy, you sheepishly propose, "I will gladly stay in to watch *ER* reruns with you Tuesday for burgers and brews with the boys today."

There are four power-wielders within the p-whipping taxonomy stalking weak-willed prey. Like a presidential candidate at election time, the domineering mate scrambles to steal the podium, with the goal of setting the party platform.

♥ **Lorder**: Ruling over big decisions of home buying, vacations, and funeral plots, this undisputed czar seeks an indifferent, biddable partner who places the dictator's priorities first.

♦ **Fawn**: This little deer longs to be cared for and compensates for personal insecurities by seeking out pushovers. Ironically, the fawn longs to feel safe, yet knows her milquetoast cannot ultimately protect her (let alone change a tire). Thus, the control begins, and the feeble man never grows a backbone.

♥ **Control Freak**: This micromanager's fiefdom is based in the minutiae: clothes, food, and final say over color schemes for the den. The relentless onslaught of edicts erodes will until the pummeled mate stops resisting.

♦ **The Black Widow**: This vixen ensnares her mate with the promise and award-winning performance of every fantasy fulfilled. A carnal loss-leader sale, this deal packs in lust what it lacks in heartfelt intimacy. It's total bedroom submission for him, total boardroom control for her.

PROGNOSIS

Infidelities can be forgiven, bad credit can be rectified, but a p-whipped twosome is doomed to metastasize into a cancer of passive denial. Once the tumor has spread, no number of heart-to-hearts can cure this sickly romance. Moreover, upping the stakes with cohabitation or engagement simply postpones the inevitable breakdown. Caught in the early stages, however, mild p-whipping based on appearance or finances is treatable. The initially skewed power balance can swing when the ugly duckling finally molts extra weight and hits the payday, becoming a self-assured mate deserving of respect.

Incidentally, not to be confused with a p-whipping, settling down is the natural progression of a bachelor from the selfish life of a hedonist to the ethos of a tempered libertine who embraces fidelity and restraint. Instead of always looking to score (a late-night party, a clean needle), this evolving gent recognizes that there are times for excess and times for prudence, and that posted limits help distinguish between the two.

WILD OATS

Barring the statistical anomaly of open marriages and swinging fantasies, you'll need to answer the monogamy question well before settling down, and not in the last-gasp panic of the bachelor party. For easy transition into fidelity on your terms, sow your oats before the twilight of bachelorhood lest you become plagued by the what-ifs of casual sex and find yourself peeking enviously out from suburban shutters into the enticing cityscape.

More than a campaign of reckless promiscuity, sowing wild oats is a multidisciplinary undertaking vital to even the most rational male and female minds. This age of whimsy builds self-confidence as the diligent pleasure-seeker samples the many wares of freedom, sexual and otherwise. Before mortgages tie you down, sate wanderlust: take a semester abroad and take a broad for a semester, backpack through Europe, act irresponsibly (youthful misdemeanors can usually be expunged), and master the virtues of being unattached. By exploring possibilities and indulging fantasies now—when wild oats are still regarded as "finding yourself," not slutting about—the evolved bachelor reduces the risk of playing host to a scattershot, ravenous libido in the future.

RALLY, DON'T TALLY

There is no magic number of partners or experiences that satisfies the curious and the testosterone-crazed. Greenhorns equate volume with virility, yet evolved bachelors recognize that, sowed indiscreetly, wild oats can turn into a weed-choked sandlot of regrettable interludes. In early dating, diverse couplings and passionate mistakes transform amorous apprentices into skilled suitors. Gradually, more meaningful lovers begin to smooth out the roller coaster of single life, with the occasional wild ride imparting central lessons about companionship. By the time a mysterious brunette falls from the sky and sets your senses ablaze, you're an all-star attraction flush with romantic savoir faire rather than child-ish hang-ups and carnal cluelessness.

THE SEVEN HEADY WHIMS

Rather than shooting for double digits, here's a checklist of essential experiences to cultivate your inner Casanova. Consider the first three mandatory and choose two electives to broaden your versatility. Lest you think wild oats mean promiscuity, note that one well-chosen lover can satisfy three or four categories.

- ☑ **Purely Sexual Tryst**: Experimentation and education on the finer technical skills without the distraction of formalities, like sending birthday cards or calling the next day.

- ☑ **Intimate Relationship**: The tender side of sex and the emotional art of compromise prepare you for complicated soulmates worth the labor.

- ☑ **Kinky Foray**: The foundation of fetish tolerance without long-term consequences. Before meeting the mother of your children, this is your carefree survey of leather, steel, and toys not made by Fisher Price.

- ❑ **Fantasy**: Test inquisitiveness with a tapas-like assortment of flavors that widens your tastes: foreign rapture vs. office romance, moody actor vs. athletic dancer, tattooed/pierced vs. prim/strait laced, timid virgin vs. blue-talking redhead.

❑ **One-Night Stand:** The chase, the excitement, the satiny strangeness of waking up under an unfamiliar duvet, especially as the climax of a holiday party, New Year's Eve ball, or out-of-town wedding.

❑ **Anonymous Kisses:** First-base encounters that never reach the bedroom. Appreciate the nuances of sensual language: spin-the-bottle lip-locking and necking between strangers in lounges, on sidewalks, at parades, and in house party coatrooms.

❑ **Odds & Ends:** These remarkable acts are often done only once, if at all: public sex and exhibitionism, threesomes, taboo arenas, childhood bed revisits, taxicab/limousine shenanigans, elevator mischief, trains, planes, and manual transmission automobiles.

TEN GROWING PAINS

The ultimate boot camp, these games of amour eventually battle test your constitution and prior learning. If you make it through, your hard-earned stripes will attest to an arduous tour of duty and grant you entrance to the officers' club of higher love.

1. Pregnancy scare, with a dash to the drugstore for a home test.

2. Flat-out rejection, followed by pleading, then further rejection.

3. Ex sex, with its hazardous mix of lust and drama.

4. Philanderer and philanderee, the cheater and the cheated, with extra experience points for getting caught or catching your partner *in flagrante bedsheet delicto*.

5. Performance stress, without a second chance.

6. Smothering mate, who stamps out any flickering embers of harmony.

7. Sexual injuries, including nail marks, hickeys, rug burns, and medical marvels requiring a doctor's appointment.

8. Slumming, when you go shopping for love in the low-rent district during a romantic nadir.

9. Playing all the angles in a love triangle.

10. Dry spell, extended beyond four or five lunar cycles.

PETER PAN

♦ ♥ Gin ♥ Dry vermouth ♥ Dollop orange juice ♥ Dash peach bitters ♥ ♦

EARLY ADMISSIONS

Some high school seniors sacrifice the thrill of Ivy League acceptance letters in April for the sake of an early-decision slot at State confirmed by mid-December. Instead of holding out for the slim possibility of Dartmouth or Brown, these single-minded types prefer to lock in, forgoing the trials of multiple applications, and the unexpected ecstasy of receiving a fat envelope from a long shot. In amour, some steady personalities reach an early plateau of sensibility that carries them into their thirties sans frivolous experimentation. If your libido isn't an untamed force, declare your wild oats sown. Though, early admissions are only awarded to those who had ample opportunity to sample the bachelor platter but declined. Precocious kiddies who settle down at twenty-three ought at least break in their passport to exorcise youthful

FLOTATION DEVICE

When the music stops after graduation or a faraway career shuffle and you are cast adrift into a faraway city, avoid the impulse to desperately grasp for stability at a mediocre love or long-distance flame that you mistake for "the one." Like Chelsea Clinton's puberty, transitional phases are just the awkward emotional storms after you've shed your acne and opened a 401(k). Faced with a full hatchback heading for a new zip code, tread water for a spell rather than forsaking wild oats and importing last year's romance. Today you're a copy-monkey paralegal, but tomorrow you might be a corner-office, Cohiba-smoking partner-to-be. Before too long, leases are cosigned, wedding plans are set, and, at age twenty-four, your bachelor career is at a premature end. Congratulations, that ho-hum college dormmate or business school bitty is now entitled to half your wealth.

demons, test foreign waters, or confirm the value of their commitment by staring down temptation. You can have a successful long-term relationship with but a few pelts hanging from your bedpost, yet make sure your early admission is a conscious waiver, not a suppression of desire that might later resurface as a wanton binge of philandering.

THE BACHELOR PARTY AUDITION

At its most swinish, a bachelor party is a practice run of retiring one's singledom. Assuming the groom has a working moral compass that points "south" concerning infidelity, bypassing a cheap thrill shouldn't be difficult. If there are nagging doubts about the future, however, the wedding chariot halts when the groom's encounter with titillating opportunity leaves him with cold feet and hot dick. Instead of calling off the nuptials, the addled gent should use this scare to drum up reserves of discipline and compel a reexamination of the rewards of monogamy over the lost pleasures of single life.

THE SETTLED MIND

Like a junkie chasing the first great fix, monogamists never regain that first-night novelty of glorious seduction but instead embrace other highs only reserved for a trusting twosome. With kids at day care and paychecks earmarked for family vacations, it's no time to brood for the good 'ol days of all-nighters and newfound nookie. A storied sexual history creates a rich archive of game film that can be drawn upon to help quell cheating urges every time a tantalizing office temp is hired. With wild oats sown, your plush field of wisdom permits you to direct energies toward developing as a loyal lover and respectable flirt.

MATRONS & MAIDENS

[longing gaze]   [coy body language]

"That was my Lo," she said, "and these are my lilies."
"Yes," I said, "yes. They are beautiful, beautiful, beautiful!"

—HUMBERT HUMBERT'S FIRST LEERING GLANCE OF TEENAGE LOLITA,
WHEN POINTED OUT BY HER MOTHER; *LOLITA*, VLADIMIR NABOKOV, 1955

In viticulture, modern winemakers fuss over the age of vines and its effect on a wine's quality. Australians boast blockbuster Shiraz from thick-trunked, pre-phylloxera vines that are fifty or even one hundred years old, while a small minority argue that grapevines, like racehorses, generate their best results in the first years of production. In amour, modern bachelors are similarly divided: nineteen-year-olds have their plucky, youthful charms, but dashing forty-niners aren't just for San Francisco football fans. By twenty-five, desire encompasses comely belles aged eighteen to thirty-five. On the cusp of forty, however, the cut-off date widens to include the spry retiree past her second facelift and third husband. Whether you prefer the mellowness of experienced years or the exuberance of youth, slake your thirst with some of each . . . and always read the warning labels.

Before venturing into the uncharted terrain of fiery young redheads and racy matrons, learn the ropes with your own generation. Skipping a few grades is fine, but make sure you master algebra before sampling the distant vectors and derivative pleasures of the advanced calculus set. When you decide to plug in the numbers and solve for XXX, it's wiser to sign up for a bedroom mentoring program with a matron than to foolishly self-medicate a major midlife crisis with a silly maiden.

THE MAY—DECEMBER

The naked bronze of sexuality is cast early in the fresh, firm mold of teenage skin. Despite the clumsiness of fumbled bra clasps and backseat econo-car sex, a bachelor, receding hairline and all, never unlearns those first affairs. Understandably then, a seasoned veteran's eye is still distracted by the flash of sticks at a college field hockey practice or the glint of glitter from a rave club couch. By the time a gentleman collects social security, he knows better than to mess around with giggly twenty-somethings, but while wisdom warns "no," his Cialis-charged willy says "perhaps. . . ." For men who refuse to grow up, a May—December tryst (even if the relationship barely lasts as long) is just the remedy for aching phobias of Grecian formula and family wagons. As an occasional between-meal snack, a tasty maiden can be as satisfying as a summer melon.

PILLOW PROSPECTUS

Nostradamus peeked into the crystal ball for his soothsaying, but you can scry the future with a tussle on a matron's mattress. How does the body curve after forty? What's news on the far side of marriage, career success, and child rearing? When you were a young cub, perhaps a sassy den mother got your Scout heart racing. Likewise, to a matron, the youthful energy of a fuzzy-antlered stag inspires creativity and coaxes out dormant desires. The butter-soft tenderloin of young lovers is grill-ready, but older game is best left to marinate overnight, in anticipation of a slow braise in saucy allure. Whereas you might surprise young lovers with your wild streak and a penchant for curious positions that warrant a ceiling mirror and a year of yoga training, when you find yourself in the hands of a wise tigress, lie back and enjoy being manhandled.

SKIRTS & SLIPUPS

Perfect for a cruise ship love affair, a rendezvous with a matron or a maiden is arousing for its fiesta deck possibilities, even when warnings of Titanic disaster go unheeded. Aside from the usual challenges of amour, expect to deal with the following pains once the anesthetic of novelty wears off:

Generation Vexed. The younger one digs Michael Douglas's performance in *Traffic;* the older one recalls Traffic jamming on *The Mike Douglas Show*. She remembers FDR pulling the country out of the Depression; he recalls the FDA approval of Prozac. With a generation gap, there is inevitable annoyance of separate tastes and unfamiliar reference points for TV, books, and the like. A well-rounded couple born on opposite sides of a decade narrows this great divide with vintage clothes and timeless albums. Shared modern pursuits of hot bistros, new exhibits, and playoff tickets are a tonic against the awkwardness of flipping through the other's seemingly alien LP and DVD collections. So, if you quote *The Breakfast Club* while she recites *Breakfast at Tiffany's,* rejoice in the exchange of beguiling classics that shrink the distance.

Incidentally, a twenty-year-old may be waylaid by a hangover while an older gent worries that his walnut-shaped prostate will inflame to the size of a boxing glove. The younger lover who knows little of kidney stones and homocysteine levels must learn to deal with the issues of middle age. Being widowed young sucks, but then there's the insurance money, no?

TESTAROSSA

Since the '50s, the Testarossa model has stood for sleek race cars and Ferrari fantasies. In Italiano, *testa* = head and *rossa* = red; Signore Ferrari and his engineers nicknamed their vrooming wonder based on the color of the cylinder heads. Off the racetrack, redheads deliver serious horsepower without wheels and handle quite differently than blondes or brunettes around hairpin curves.

To understand this hot rod, first look under the hood. Little Rosa was a lassie unlike the other girls. She was either instantly revered or else mercilessly teased, left to fend for herself on the playground as grammar schoolers chanted "carrot top" or "Bozo." Things got worse before they got better when puberty set in. Banished from the blacktop, fair-skinned redheads with shaky self-esteem built reputations on intellect or athletics instead of looks. Pluckier gals embraced their freckled misfit status and rebelled with art, poetry, and summer vacation experimentation. Over time, gawky orange traits faded and from the crimson chrysalis emerged a sexy, speckled, auburn fireball.

Once you know the lore, the riddle of redheads is less cryptic. They love the attention, but suspicion underlies the confident facade. "Where were the flowers and chocolates all those lean years?" she wonders, as suitors now appear in droves eyeing her plumage. This sporty coupe goes from zero to sixty in under five seconds, and as for the track conditions, expect brilliant weekends and tempestuous stormy skies that render crashes fatal. Drive a Testarossa because the ride is perilous and inviting, but do it young, while your flesh and pliable heart still heal quickly. Like many things, the danger is part of the attraction: every lover of the Testarossa has gazed a redhead through a black eye.

For more information on the banes and boons of redheads, plus speculation that they are descended from an alien race, dog-ear a copy of Tom Robbins's surreally comedic *Still Life with Woodpecker*.

Public Relations. When the two of you check into a hotel, the desk attendant asks, "Will you and your niece care for turndown service?" Early on, this might be off-putting, but instead of upbraiding the clerk, simply say thank you, ask for a king-sized bed, and then neutralize would-be rumormongers by draping a stocking over the doorknob. Discretion is never impolite, but flaunt if you must. Make-out sessions in diners aren't gentlemanly under normal circumstances, however, and doing so with a young mistress is a tawdry transgression. Should the "cradle robber" stigma become a small-town burden, head to the city where such couplings are everyday sights.

Shuffling the Decks. After a few secret meetings in hotel rooms and darkened cinema rows, eventually your rule-bending twosome will have to be unveiled. Before friends and family go slack-jawed, issue a brief press release ("Just so you know, she's twenty-three") to dispel any awkwardness. Think twice: your friends and her posse might rumble like the Sharks and the Jets, with your poor Maria caught in the middle.

When she trades her leather skirt for a ball gown at the opera, she probably feels like a lady on your arm. On the other hand, when you swap Calvados and cigars for some Mad Dog and spliffs in a smoky basement, you may feel like an old fogey. To overcome the knee-jerk aversion to middle-aged lovers with living wills, make introductions on a bi-generational stage. Both groups groove better at a relaxed lawn party than in some raucous teenybopper hangout that makes buttoned-down elders feel like prom-night chaperones. On the town, stick to venues and activities geared to mixed crowds (a lounge with dinner *and* dancing or a swanky pool hall with beer on tap *and* single malts), and everyone will feel at ease. Consider, too, playing the clock: your grey-headed pals peter out by eleven, but her swinging cronies don't even get started 'til midnight.

The Glass Ceiling. Is it ever going to be all-the-way serious? If one person has already notched a divorce or two, love without marriage may be the limit. Before signing a lease together, at least agree whether the relationship is year-to-year or month-to-month. Is he winding down to quiet seclusion while she's gearing up for an active growth spurt? However precocious, the younger lover's drive for new experience may conflict with an older, already settled spirit who dropped acid with Huxley in the '60s and crashed two Pontiacs in the '70s.

Sugar Daddy. Does the older lover with a pension foot the bill? Opening doors is the gent's duty and picking up the tab isn't amiss, but look out for patterns of expectation that include "loans" for rent, "help" with credit cards, and "petty cash" that feels like a per diem for a kept woman. The one with a CPA on the payroll should certainly cover the cycle of birth control pills, but don't make money a top-three relationship perk. For the poet-artist bedding a matron with a late-model Jaguar, be doubly sure that your hand is in her bloomers more than her change purse.

Nice touch: Respect her parents, even if you're longer in the tooth. Regardless of age, mom and pop still want daughters taken care of by a polite, stable man. What mother wouldn't approve of a suitor with a true heart and a steady job, especially if she finds him handsome, too?

WEB-SLINGING

[monitor]   [SWF]   [keyboard]

Before the dot-com boom, Internet dating consisted of cut-rate chat rooms and paltry pages populated by desperate, pockmarked masses—castoffs left with no place to go when the Dungeons & Dragons fantasy ended, forcing reclusive gamers to open the shades and face the dating world armed with nothing but smudged prescription glasses and a worn *Monster Manual*. In contrast, today's sites are like new shopping malls: inviting forums of carnal commerce teeming with a bright cross-section of young professionals, small town thrill-seekers, and urban hipsters all looking to meet the same or just window-shop. Previously considered "beneath" traditional wooers, online dating's ease and effectiveness have converted the doubting public and now is standard practice for busy singles playing the field.

LOGGING ON

Traditional methods of finding romance—friendly referrals, chats in bars, winks and smiles at the modern-art gallery—remain the most reliable, but web-slinging is a fast, electronic supplement. As long as you don't become a compulsive inbox checker with ten screen names and four different online subscriptions, it's worthwhile for the pure entertainment value of contacting strangers and getting your groin out there. An active nightlife is commendable, but without yogi-like bilocation techniques, you can't be in two places at once, working in the office *and* flirting in public; a posted profile sells your sex round the clock. Moreover, some sites specialize, further narrowing the field: Jewish-only (jdate.com), gym rats with hard bodies (fitnesssingles.com), swingers and the randy set (AdultFriendFinder.com), or friends-of-friends intraspecies dating (friendster.com).

After you plug in your wish list and dating criteria, search results spit out matches; it's like scanning a room of a thousand and pinpointing the ten who share your favorite author and chronic coulrophobia (fear of clowns). Expect some duds, but a few Internet pen pals and blind dates hone courting skills and cushion a Trojan-free month. Likely, your most furious period of serial clicking will be the first fortnight of active pursuit, when new recruits are noted daily as you tweak your profile to widen salability. Ideally, by the time daily interest peters out, your venture will have expanded your black book of three-star possibilities. When the urge strikes again, update your profile and click anew.

The antiquated custom of male as pursuer is inapplicable to Internet dating since both sexes are encouraged to initiate contact. Though, behind the cybertext, traditional wooing rules still apply. Desperate pleas, maudlin profiles, and pushy lines won't win hearts; similarly, bland politeness and mundane pleasures ("I like long romantic walks"; "I love to travel") assure you a warm seat at a cold computer terminal. Cockiness is also a no-no. In person, the waxed fenders of a muscle car, overstyled hair, and an overdose of swagger are unappealing to most potential mates; the email equivalent—puffing, "I'm in the high six figures. How's waiting tables working out for you?"—is equally charmless.

PROFILING

Better than a snazzy pick-up line, your posted profile is your one-meg chance to land a love. Suitors who leave scads of blanks or fill out questionnaires with sentence fragments evince a lackluster attitude and a perplexing ambivalence that suggests they're too cool for online dating . . . yet they've posted a profile anyway. With the ubiquity of digital photography and scanners, there's no excuse not to attach fetching, madcap photos alongside your info. Though old-timers with stacks of daguerreotypes and not one fetching jpeg of themselves should wait instead of posting a glum mug shot. If you've got a full coif or an athletic build, show it off; wooly hats suggest receding hairlines or elephant ears, while baggy pants and winter sweaters falsely signal a pudgy cover-up. Similarly, staid photos and unsmiling passport glossies aren't sexy. Conversely, travel adventure photos or active candids make for a dynamic page (though, avoid group photos, which lead the viewer to wonder which one is you).

When trolling the unattached hordes, search within desired parameters of age, size, education, and vice. Despite perceived love at first click, respect others' caveats; "six feet and over only" means squat munchkins propped into loafers with lifts need not apply; "Republican only" precludes mutton-chopped liberals driving hybrid cars bearing McGovern '72 stickers.

Incidentally, don't overlook the rare enigmatic potboiler lacking a picture. After wooing with choice words, pray for a luscious pictorial reward; that said, males without photos are automatically assumed to be comb-over bald, three-chin flabby, or both.

The answer to the principal profile question "Who are you looking for?" is the spot for crafted wit and specific turn-ons. Avoid the banal ("I want someone smart and crazy, funny but not superficial, sensitive but strong. Someone to laugh and cry with . . ."). Prose spiked with edgy examples trumps empty adjectives and narrows the field of prospects ("You are Mother Teresa, a Russ Myers starlet, and Anaïs Nin rolled into one: a kind, courageous luminary in a busty turtleneck with a taste for exploring the cityscape's back-alley cafés. My car is still a Pinto. No Nader voters, please!"). The true art is inserting endearing quirks and hobbies into the equation without compiling a tedious list. For example, workout hounds might mention jogging shoes and a yoga mat as two items they can't live without; shutterbugs might allude to the smell of fixer in their spare bathroom; or *Simpsons* fanatics might slip in a sly reference to Krusty the Klown. Spruce up your pen and infuse your mission with sharp words rather than boring them with bromides. If you've got creative yens and more eccentric longing than "strolls on the beach," forever banish the following words from your online interactions and profile: *interesting, unique, fun, chemistry, snuggle, cuddle, cuddly, cute,* and *cutesy,* along with the phrases *comfortable silences, the one,* and the limp *I am like no one else you've ever met.*

FIRST CONTACT

Choose wisely and personalize each note by citing common interestsand riffing off the other's profile ("I see we are French-speaking, Tavel-sipping esquires. Let's pick a continent and sup up some ethnic atmosphere over a bowl of olives"). Reusing a few clever sentences is economical, but trotting out a transparent "Dear ___, hello" form letter will stir as much arousal as a cover letter mail merge trumpeting ambitious work habits and your impressive GPA. Most online daters are men, so females can be choosy in rejecting obvious claptrap. Instead, greetings should be rollicking, but not a freakish stream-of-consciousness wordplay; aim for one or two electric paragraphs that purposely ignore yawning topics like your mean boss, rising gas prices, or food allergies. For non-wordsmiths, maintain zing with brevity instead of turning someone off with plodding theses.

There are two types of appeals: sexually direct or cerebral. The former player scans an overtly suggestive profile and then politely, yet firmly, makes it known that this is a cyber pickup, your hard drive or mine. The more common cerebral woo is rife with the double entendre and banter of an enchanted dinner date. Though, after a few volleys, push the agenda into the real world of personal email addresses, phone calls, and a face-to-face rendezvous. Results vary, from a string of bad blind dates and computer eye strain to new provocative friends and budding flings that spring into romance.

SWM SEEKS DELICIOUS PLAYMATE FOR CANDLE-LIGHT CROQUET AND BARBARESCO LOLLYGAGGING.

Must be able to lift Umberto Eco in a single bound and endure bouts of sushi and necking. Serious inquiries only, two references from past lovers waived for short essay or haiku on the art of footsies.

FEBRUARY 14

[silky rose]

[thorny stem]

Before the Church wrung most of the fun out of it, February 14 was the Roman celebration of Lupercalia, an erotic festival honoring Juno Februata, the goddess of *febris*, or feverish love. Today, an exchange of cards and bonbons is charming, but better to commemorate the holiday's orgiastic roots with a dollop of amour and a healthy pinch of lust. Celebrate, even modestly, and turn this manufactured spike into a passionate evening rather than dropping the chocolate heart and risking a romantic blunder.

ELEMENTARY, MY DEAR

There are happy alternatives to playing the chump forced to buy two dozen roses at a 300-percent markup. If you haven't bestowed flowers since last February, don't start now. Once-a-year stems are a blatant admission that the holiday is more motivation than the sweet fragrance of love. Instead of a plastic-wrapped nosegay bought at a stoplight, jump-start floral affections: skip the red roses and express yourself more colorfully with exotic wildflowers or a handsome houseplant that stays green long after petals wilt. Or plan ahead and send lilies to work a few days before so they're fully abloom on Saint Valentine's Day.

Homemade cards are best. For less than the price of a high-gloss Hallmark missive, you can buy construction paper and a pack of chubby crayons. Cut out hearts and shapes like you learned in first grade and tack them up on your Valentine's path: bathroom mirror, coffee mug, and steering wheel. Also, revisit toddlerhood and send close friends and PFs silly little Valentine cards mailed in diminutive envelopes.

HOME-FIELD ADVANTAGE

Celebrate in a manner that befits your personality. Who wants to be the drone making reservations for two in a packed restaurant as eighty other couples clang forks in chain-gang synchrony? Especially if you're light from overspending on Kwanzaa or New Year's, the at-home affair is tender as seared tuna. A regal meal can be had at home for $50 and without a clock-watching hostess monitoring table time and pooh-poohing stolen kisses. For creative types, why leave the props of wooing to profit-seeking restaurateurs? Advocate your own brand of fantasy: dress yourself and the table, arrange a centerpiece embedded with little baubles (beaded necklace, bubbles, Bazooka gum), deftly prepare a gourmet menu or feast of finger foods, and unplug the phone. Queue up the dance breaks, and don't skimp on mood lighting, tapered candles, and unexpected oral pleasures beyond fondue. Artists should use the intermezzo for guitar-strumming serenades, interpretive dance, sculpted Crisco busts, or magic-marker caricatures on placemats. After dessert, ratchet up the kink factor as napkins and inhibitions are left in a heap.

ON THE TOWN

If you must brave the bistro crowd, involve the waiter in gift-giving conspiracies and spice up a card or small gift by planting it beforehand. While making reservations (well in advance, otherwise you'll be seated at 5:45, if at all), inquire about corkage fees if there's a worthy bottle in your cellar for the occasion. Bringing flowers is okay; sending them ahead is better. A few choice shoots are fine, but don't overcrowd a two-top with an ostentatious, view-obstructing flowerbed.

VALENTINE VETERANS

As long as the union isn't jaded, the celebration shouldn't be either, never mind you've bestowed truffles ten years running. Shuffle the playlist. Go dancing first and then coo over a late night meal in an empty eatery; whisper fondly over lunch and go out for mousse and Moscato later, when languid pacing is possible at a sultry café. Even if the babysitter cancels and your best suit is stuck at the cleaner's, reach deep into the troubadour's soul and make a longtime lover swoon if only to the tune of gentle praise or with slow dancing to the living room turntable.

Nice touch: Euros to spare? Go hog wild: spring for her fitted gown and shoes, hire a chauffeured car, uncork a bottle from her birth year, and prolong the love with a morning-after massage and brunch.

LOVE-O-METER

In gymnastics, you can muff a routine and still medal; in love, you can botch January after a stellar (and expensive) holiday season, but you'd better stick the landing in February if you want high scores in spring.

Here's how the judges see it:

♥ If the romance is healthy . . . Valentine's is double-coupon day. No need to overdote; small heartfelt notions reinforce the felicity already abounding.

◆ If the romance is flailing . . . bumbling on the 14th is more bad news. Instead of a sexy smooch session in a darkened boudoir, expect a

CACAO

In *Chocolat*, a Lenten-chaste count tries to destroy the local chocola-
terie on the eve of Easter, only to succumb to its tempting sweets
when a sliver of chocolate lands on his lip. Blubbering in truffle
ecstasy, the count rightly recognizes the lady chocolatier as a free-
spirited savior, not a cocoa-wielding sorceress casting wicked spells
on the townsfolk.

You can rejoice in your own chocolate high without much
care for going to hell, getting zits, staying awake all night, or
aggravating diabetes. Research has proven that chocolate has less
caffeine than a cup of coffee, it won't make you break out, and
moderate consumption won't spike postprandial blood sugar
levels. Cacao is also a rich source of antioxidants; in fact, dark
chocolate contains ten times more of them than spinach or rasp-
berries. A milk chocolate bar is as heart-friendly as a pot of green
tea or half carafe of red wine, plus there's no fuss with DUI check-
points. What's more, the fruit of the cacao tree contains compounds
that activate cannabinoid receptors and closely mimic molecules
found in cannabis, though your boss won't likely fire you for passing around a blunt-sized profiterole during a smoke break.

Trust a chocolatier when you've only got a ten-spot to tempt a
playmate's sweet tooth. Skip the shoppers' club discount sack of
melting junk food and invest your coin in a carefully selected array
of gourmet treats. Looking for a delicious novelty? Try chocolate
body paint or a tattoo set with brushes. There's even a chocolate bar
shaped like soap for a shower-side nosh. When the shades come
down, remember that you can dip more pulse-quickening things
than strawberries into melted chocolate.

You know your lover's dress size, why not your sweetie's choco-
quotient? Before shopping for cocoa confections, gather clues
about preferences. Dark, milk, or white? What about fruit and coffee flavors? Unless you want to rush a lingerie-clad love to the
emergency room with a heart-shaped box in one hand and a swollen

esophagus in the other, figure out if nuts are all right. As for liqueurs, though the alcohol is typically cooked off, nothing will relapse an AA alum like a "Welcome Home from Rehab" assortment of brandy-filled treats shaped like fifths of booze.

Once you've bypassed frozen yogurt for darker delights, follow these six confection directions:

1. Never refrigerate your leftovers; for the long haul, the freezer or a wine cellar works best. With the fridge door swinging open and closed, cocoa reacts to temperature change by "blooming," or separating, which turns the surface whitish and dull.

2. Sixty-eight degrees is the ideal serving temperature for noting color, aroma, taste, and texture. For the fullest effect, hold a morsel in your mouth and breathe out your nose. As for pairings, only powerful flavors can compete: tawny Porto, Tokáji Azsú, Banyuls, and rich, ripe reds. More than a 1953 Peggy Lee hit, black coffee is a ne'er miss with a chocolaty mouthful.

3. Cacao percentage on the label is the surest sign of quality. As cacao content climbs, sugar is reduced and the intense, bitter chocolate stimulates your taste buds. Milk chocolate fans hover around 33 to 60 percent; go higher if you prefer it deep and dark. Don't be surprised by vintage-dated "grand crus." Like tannic wines, dark chocolate mellows with age and stored properly, it lasts indefinitely.

4. White chocolate is the black sheep for no good reason. It's made like milk chocolate, except that cocoa butter is used without any cocoa powder or cocoa liquor. After forsaking the stuff as mere "white confection" for decades, even the FDA finally acknowledged white chocolate as its own legal, cacao-derived product.

ROMANTIC FARE

5. Grandma might still be nibbling bonbons filled with crèmes, jellies, and squirting cherries, but the new wave of chocoholics are as experimental as fusion-entranced foodies. Reconnoiter a Hershey's for Halloween, but for serious consumption, try an exotic bar blended with rose hips, chiles, lime flowers, sel de mer, or lavender oil. Can't-miss boutique brands: Amedei, El Rey, Lake Champlain, Michel Cluizel, Recchiuti, Rococo, Scharffen Berger, Valrhona, and Vosges.

6. Get in the mood: *Baci* chocolates are like cocoa fortune cookies—each one comes with a petite romantic quip. *Chocolove* confections are wrapped like mash notes and contain a classic love poem. Of course, green M&Ms are still the undisputed legendary king of aphrodisiacs.

COUPEZ LE FROMAGE

Little Miss Muffett relished her curds and whey, but cheesemakers producing aged cheeses are interested in the former by granting milk its final wish to become Fourme d'Ambert instead of the delivery method for corn flakes. Though, young cheeses made from leftover watery whey, like feta and ricotta, are light and creamy in their own right. The array of cheeses is daunting to the layman, who is likely to sample only a small percentage of products beyond the diner tuna melt options; furthermore, Americans are denied authentic raw-milk Brie and Camembert, which are pasteurized before import, blasting good taste for all. For shy noses wary of stinky Livarot and Maroilles or distinctive blues like Roquefort and Gorgonzola, there's always the more accessible and mild smelling Emmental, Gouda, and provolone, which also pair more easily with vino.

For cocktail hour or the denouement of a homespun dinner for two, put a cheese plate together. Typically, cheeses are aesthetically arranged on the platter clockwise according to a theme: cow, sheep, or goat's milk cheeses; mild to medium to strong; a medley from a particular country. No one wants to hack at a rock-hard brick of Edam or spoon a soupy mess of Taleggio, so take out the cheeses one-half to one hour before serving to bring them to proper temperature. Rather than circumcising the tip, or worse, thoughtlessly cubing the Stilton, start the presentation with but a thin vertical pie slice.

Garnish the plate with the cheese's natural sidekicks. Brie begs for prunes or cherries; Gorgonzola, figs; strong cheddar, chutney; pair feta cheese with watermelon; mozzarella with basil; goat cheese with bitter greens and roasted beets; and EZ Cheeze with Ritz crackers and Cold Duck. When in doubt, every cheese adores the company of grapes, pistachios, walnuts, pears, marmalades, pickled or roasted vegetables, not to mention wheat crackers and rustic loaves like rosemary or black bread. Epicurean hosts seeking to seduce a like-minded femme should impress by pairing cheeses with their local foodstuffs. For example, complement a grand Provence goat cheese Picodon de Valréas with regional Picholine olives and a Côtes du Ventoux light red. As for uncorking bottles, avoid serving too light a wine, especially with Italian aged cheeses, like Parmigiano Reggiano, which begs for a voluptuous Amarone. Soft cheeses, like Chaource, pair nicely with Champagne or a dry rosé; goat cheeses enjoy crisp whites from Côtes de Provence or Sancerre; and blue cheeses are an ideal match with dessert wines like Sauternes. When in doubt, white wines pair better with cheeses than reds since the wine's bright acidity cuts through the dairy.

Nice touches: Plant a flag or placard to identify the varieties by name and region; employ separate knives for cheeses of differing texture and strength; use a chilled marble or granite tile remnant as a handsome, proxy cheese board; and when your hear moos over the fence, sniff out a local artisanal cheesemaker with handcrafted products far tastier than the freshest government cheese.

ROMANTIC FARE

serious hashing of your shortcomings and ho-hum attitude under unwelcoming lamp light.

♥ If the romance is steady but flat . . . jump-start the winter doldrums. A homerun on Valentine's Day breaks the slump and catapults the twosome back to bliss.

Incidentally, beware of reenacting cheap moves that undermine the joy of an unwitting darling whose heart is aflutter over your supposed original-ity. Don't plan a weekend getaway at that B&B you and your last Valentine brazenly used as a love shack.

CAVEATS

Be wary of love interests who overemphasize the 14th, focusing undue attention on stem count and exclusive dinner reservations. Later, these second-tier turtledoves will equate love with carat size and property square footage. Similarly, ladies must watch out for faux Romeos who only flex their romantic muscles on New Year's, birthdays, and Valen-tine's Day (or worse, can't begrudge even one night of woo). These itty-bitty beaus grow up to be small-minded schlubs who won't be able to summon a hot date or a lukewarm erection ten years from now.

As for sex, indulge in the full array of foreplay, sensual massage, and unbridled romance. This is no time for the three-minute egg; you're not getting off that easy. Whatever the usual, try it at half speed, and like dipping a finger into grandma's marinara, taste what happens when love simmers all day long.

SINGLE'S NIGHT OUT

Escort service fully booked? Grab the boys and take it on the town. What you'll find: couples are gathered elsewhere and unattached amateurs are home wallowing in old photo albums and tired videos. What's left are upbeat youngsters who pay no heed to the hype and the implied shame of being single in the dead of winter. This is the perfect time to meet a snappy lady who's out with clever friends belatedly celebrating Lincoln's birthday (February 12). To break the ice, tote little candy hearts (with edited phrases) and mingle with the singles.

LIVING IN SIN

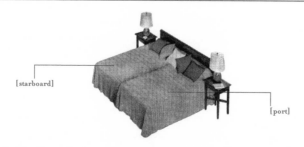

[starboard]

[port]

Sandwiched between adultery and incest in the sex offenses chapter of the North Dakota Century Code, §12.1-20-10 states that, "A person is guilty of a class B misdemeanor if he or she lives openly and notoriously with a person of the opposite sex as a married couple without being married to the other person." In April 2003, the North Dakota Senate defeated a bill that would have repealed the backward 113-year-old anti-cohabitation law, thus living in sin remains a crime against the state (not to mention an affront to the Lord).

Prehistoric parents may disagree, but there is no better preview of marriage success than living together first. (Though, living together is not always the stepping-stone to betrothal for couples motivated by monthly savings and proximity to a wireless hotspot.) Whatever your future plans, the stakes are raised from the moment you record the outgoing greeting on shared home voicemail. Besides surveying morning face and monthly sex drive, it's your chance to find out whether a serious flame is also a conscientious roommate and reliable partner in the business of love. Moving in also exposes the rash decisions and temporary insanities of immature lovers who can't muster the staying power for a ring. Forced to work out issues without repairing to separate pads, you can still slam doors, but this time it's the bedroom door, not the front door. Unlike marriage, where fiascoes at the altar are public and expensive, a living-in-sin arrangement carries the implicit right to walk away in the shadow of a moving van. Should the experiment fail, expect gross change, either a reversion to nonexclusive dating or a wholesale disintegration.

Incidentally, financial disclosure of checking account balances and mountains of debt is recommended but not obligatory. Despite the optional joint account for household expenses, you don't have to talk to her creditors or be polite to the repo men slim-jimming the lock of her underfinanced cabriolet.

CHANGING ADDRESSES

After you've traded apartment keys and taken over a guest dresser drawer, the lingering high from a weekend getaway might prompt the question, "Why don't we get a place together?" Gauge the reaction: is it a giggly, warm coo or an awkward, stony silence? It is not a marriage proposal, but yes or no, the answer offers a reliable relationship review. When the parties differ on the prevailing direction of the relationship, the inevitable "Where do we stand?" triggers a tangential, perhaps thorny conversation about the future. If the move-in is designated a marital test run, the decision ought to be backed by a solid-state union, not just crash-pad convenience.

Will it be her place, your place, or a new place? In a merger, one corporation absorbs another; a consolidation occurs when two companies combine to form a new entity. The consolidation-type move into a new space is ideal, but real estate values, irksome leases, or city living might designate the partner with the best view as the default host. The tricky merger instills the host with an unequal hold over decorating and storage: by the laws of inertia, it is trickier to remove the incumbent's stuff than to make room for the incoming mate's boxes. Most importantly, the current leaseholder holds the death switch and legal authority of ouster. When the carefree times of fire-escape barbecues sputter, this ace card will blacken the mood worse than any garbage strike wafting through the bedroom windows. Get both names on the lease. Should a stormy breakup arise, you'll have the law behind you to prevent a 2 A.M. duffel bag defenestration of your measly possessions into the courtyard.

TERRITORIALISM

Sharing a 425-square-foot studio sounds adorable, but claustrophobic is more like it. A two-bedroom, two-bath pad promotes independence and sanity while providing buffer room. Carve out safe havens for solitary decompression after a squabble. Furthermore, a gent knows which drawer houses her delicates and prerelationship vibrators, but resists the temptation to rifle through and check battery life.

The new space spawns a battle of the sexes as she boldly claims blank walls for her lithographs and he, precious closet space for his suits. Those with ragtag armchairs and fiberboard dressers should gleefully accede to furniture upgrades. When pets are the crux of heated negotiations, either play the "allergy" card or look for a bigger place with a doggie

---

COMING OUT OF THE
GUEST ROOM CLOSET

Living in sin is a mutual decision for two consenting, adventurous lovers to have a go at playing house. For those still hamstrung by meddlesome families and parental lines of credit, are you forwarding phone calls and keeping a sham apartment for appearance sake? Lest you forget, Romeo and Juliet—the tragedy of forbidden love blossoming under the shadows—ends with everyone dead. Come out of the guest room closet, speak up, and declare your adulthood. Inform iron-fisted parents post-move so that the conversation is one of bold declaration instead of wormy pleading.

Does anyone want a live-in automaton whose elders still dictate domestic policy? Is it worth keeping ardor under wraps for the sake of an allowance? If your parents still claim you as a dependent on their tax form, cast off thy yoke—your gallantry won't go unnoticed by your darling. Though, coming out of the guest room closet should be a one-time stand for mature couples on the marriage track, not a rash stunt that jeopardizes your trust fund on a forgettable bozo-of-the-month or fling with a floozy.

When it's not about money, it's about religion and morality. To avoid the family's holy indignation, why is he or she committing a worse sin by living a lie? Cut the cord now or else incur intrusive in-laws who invariably make cameo appearances as the wedding czar, salaried career peddler, baby name vetoer, and perpetual cumulonimbus guilt-rainer.

door; even nonpedigree, fluffy pooches can't be stored in crates like dusty 78s. In general, expect a crash course in refinement as you both fight over shelf assignments and coffee-mug hanging-hook priority. Like heading out west on the wagon train, certain clunky favorites and moldy paperbacks must be consigned to a garage sale to raise precious laundry change. Mourn the bitter end of the following schlock:

♥ Plastic wall hangings bequeathed three roommates ago, unframed domestic beer–themed doodads scored from the Bennigan's dumpster, and swiped street signs that bear your name.

◆ Rumpled nudie mags predating Internet porn and thrice-dubbed skin flicks without a label. Don't fret, you'll never forget that the lovely Fawna (Jan. 1989 Playmate of the Month) was turned on by oysters and Champagne and turned off by housework and taxis.

♥ As for that ratty futon, the lady's queen bed trumps a mattress so storied that any competent botanist could count the rings to calculate the exact number of lovers you've had in the last ten years.

Incidentally, before moving in, reserve a corner in your parents' garage for those keepsakes that didn't make the cut. If the love experiment tanks worse than the '84 Mondale campaign, you'll want a safe place from which to fetch belongings after divvying up the household spoils turns contentious. (Flip a coin for the ficus and Rochambeau for the curio cabinet, but concede the light sax music CD to the incinerator.)

THE FLAK

While 1950s separate-bed prudishness may be long gone, a live-in couple occasionally fields barbed comments from the disapproving conservative wing of the family. The immoral "fornicators" are Amished to death by old-fashioned views; suddenly, the terms "scripture," "jezebel," and "sacred union" are spoken with absurd solemnity. Without acknowledging the growth and sexual maturity borne out of living in sin, some take the slanted view that the man gets everything from the deal, à la "Why buy the cow when you get the milk for free?" In modern times, however, fresh cream is readily available without a cosigned lease, and couples move in together for more sophisticated, less carnal reasons. The best defense against judgmental upbraiding is silent nodding followed by a forbidden screw in your fusty aunt's upstairs drawing room.

Part of dealing with flak is fielding well-meaning calls and dodging passive jibes. After answering a ring from her father early one morning, there is that moment of prescient quiet when Daddy realizes, "That little miscreant is copulating with my baby." Now that you're living together, you can no longer simply pass the hot receiver during future check-ins (though, cell phones and simply ignoring the house line do wonders for sidestepping small talk). In addition, married friends might pull sinners aside in jest to hard-sell a wedding agenda: "When are you gonna make an honest woman of her?" Instead of responding to that tired wisecrack, revel in the rascality of this sinful arrangement and affectionately refer to one another in mixed company as paramour, courtesan, concubine, and odalisque.

Nice touch: With a heightened level of trust, partners can up the ante on kink and fetish and merge respective toy boxes, selling doubles at a sexy tag sale. ("We have two Steely Dans now, good as new . . . only highway driving. For you, ma'am, $10.00.")

DANGER SIGNS

Living together isn't for everyone. Below are four sorts deemed ineligible for a standard-issue cohabitation license:

- **Mooching Slacker:** This vagabond's belongings all fit on your mantel. The real goal is to eat your food, watch premium cable, and invent lame excuses why "I'm a little light this month," despite having a full dope sack and enough scratch for cover charges.

- **Serial Cohabitator:** This career roommate/player boasts umpteen exes and a sin-living résumé that reads like a zip code roll call, raising questions about commitment levels.

- **The White Glove:** A domestic god or goddess on speed. Following the lease-signing, side agreements must be reached regarding maid service and dishwashing detail. The deal may be kiboshed if a clutter accord isn't ratified.

- **Bed Sore:** A recluse whose favored habitat is a teeny basement apartment meets his match. While he composes a manifesto and sups on freedom-fighter stew, the other mends clothes and broods. As the walls close in and the unemployment checks run out, cabin fever poisons the relationship.

NOCTURNAL & NAUGHTY

♦ ♥ ♦ ♥ ♦ ♥ ♦ ♥

BEDROOM ARCHETYPES

[Prince Charming]   [Lady Fair]

The *Kinsey Report* and old nudie mags may open your eyes, but nothing rivals the trial and error of diverse partners or hungry experimentation with a long-term love. Even if you have only one lifelong lover who spells out the XYZs of her pleasure points, your range of lovemaking demands an ever-expanding passionate vocabulary, whether in the Sanskrit tongue of Tantra or the leather purrs of fetish play. More than technique learned through repetition, the magic touch comes from reinventing your repertoire and arousing the other four senses through creativity, bravado, and sensitivity.

Sometimes the bedroom is a petting zoo, other times a jungle expedition requiring a pith helmet. How many roles can you play, or want to play? Unlike the twelve animals of Chinese astrology, the following list of sexual archetypes won't appear on your placemat at the Mongolian barbecue joint. Determine which one best describes your style and which ones belong on your to-do list. First, the male archetypes are spotted on the Wild Safari, and then the ladies are named on the Lovely Menagerie; some pairings are more delectable than Cabernet Sauvignon with a New York stripper.

WILD SAFARI

What's love without the loud? The lion purrs, growls, and roars all in a night's work. When asked, "Your place or mine?" pick the one with the thickest walls or the soundest-sleeping roommate.	**STENTORIAN LION**
Two-year-olds, billy goats, and lusty ravenous sorts want to put everything in their mouth. Whether threesomes, orgies, or bi- or bestial encounters, the horny goat's appetite is never sated.	**INSATIABLE GOAT**
With or without psychotropics, a bedroom wizard can redefine an out-of-body experience and take you—as Puff did Jackie Paper—to a land called Honalee.	**MAGIC DRAGON**
The snake's design hasn't changed since the Jurassic period. No need for fancy toys and instruction manuals: this straight shooter's skills are instinctual and perfectly calibrated.	**PRIMAL SNAKE**
Tickling, bed wrestling, bantering, and nonintercourse romping typify this good-natured beast. Playful sex and naked tomfoolery are the signs of those comfortable with their bodies and unafraid of pleasuring a partner in coltish ways.	**PLAYFUL BEAR**
With props, crops, and edible tops, not to mention the thwack of a flogger and the light clang of cuffs, the sly fox tweaks the power balance and introduces a blue streak of dirty talk that peels back the knickers and peeps into the psyche.	**KINKY FOX**

LOVELY MENAGERIE

FLAMBOYANT BUTTERFLY	A mild-mannered caterpillar by day, but after hours and out of the cocoon, she trades power suits and glasses for funky dress and free expression (feather boa, platform heels, blonde wig). *Best paired with Stentorian Lion.*
CLASSIC TIMEX	Reliable partner who likes to be wound every day to keep on ticking. *Best paired with Insatiable Goat.*
MAUNA LOA	This otherwise tranquil lover erupts with powerful flows of molten lava passion during turbulent spats or emotional highs. The spectacular fire is worth the wait. *Best paired with Magic Dragon.*
KUNOICHI	This female ninja toys with emotions, manipulates with womanly wiles, and exhibits mastery of the amorous arts without ever falling too deeply in love. In bed, she's secretive, multiorgasmic, and dangerous with *neko-te* (cat's claws), *geta* (wooden clogs), and a *nawabashigo* (rope ladder). *Best paired with Primal Snake.*
SACAGAWEA	Guiding her Lewis or Clark, she explores the far reaches of rooms and furnishings, including the ne'er used settee and porch swing. Sometimes the hottest place is off the map in a friend's guest room or woodsy nature trail. *Best paired with Playful Bear.*
FIRESTARTER	Donned lingerie, rented films, or other stimulants are de rigueur when she mischievously ignites your flame. With a run to her toy box, there's rarely a propless encounter. *Best paired with Kinky Fox.*

WILD SAFARI

This impassioned whirlwind, whether in five minutes or five hours, leaves the same wake of overturned lamps, rattled headboards, and unsheeted-bed dishevelment.	**TASMANIAN DEVIL**
Heavy emotions call for more than heavy petting. This intuitive partner senses when tender, soul-fertilizing sex is just what the doctor ordered to fortify the connection. Tears of ecstasy are valued over cries of climax.	**TENDER BUCK**
This 3 A.M. dreamer seamlessly transitions from sexy REM to sleepy sex with a half-awakened sweetheart. Lovers relish the occasional moonlight rendezvous that blurs lines between vivid dream and reality.	**FANTASY OWL**
Why don't we get drunk and screw? This beachcomber squeezes in carnal delights between mai tais and always ends the tailgate party with a slurry rendition of "Margaritaville."	**PARROTHEAD**
Half-drunk and fully aroused, this bird of prey swoops in for a quick feeding. In the best of times, a selfish start gives way to a mutually enthusiastic finish, but at worst, this boorish bird is one blow-up doll away from jerking off.	**PREDATORY HAWK**
Full of surprises with flexible hips and an open mind, this trapeze artist is as comfortable swinging from the chandelier as roosting together in the nest.	**FLYING SQUIRREL**

LOVELY MENAGERIE

INSPECTOR 12	Quite willing, but she's methodical about arousal prerequisites: dishes done, kitchen straightened, dog walked, doors locked, shades drawn, ringer off, pyjamas on. "Okay . . . where were we?" With so much tidiness, she craves disorder in bed. *Best paired with Tasmanian Devil.*
MODEL T	Requires multiple hand cranks to get started, but she'll run all day. The glorious act itself shouldn't take less time than the foreplay since quickies won't satisfy. *Best paired with Tender Buck.*
BUSY ROMANTIC	Overworked and underserviced, she fills the gaps with racy notes and compliments. This harried professional cashes in her rain checks during odd hours and catches up in bunches over weekends and holidays. *Best paired with Fantasy Owl.*
THREE-CREDIT CLASSMATE	This coed observes a regular bedroom schedule: either Mon/Wed/Fri short sessions or Tue/Thur intensives. Optional weekend assignments. *Best paired with Parrothead.*
SHAMPOO QUEEN	This luxurious lovemaker boasts frequent encore performances with pert and suave finesse. For best results, lather, rinse, *and* repeat, anytime. *Best paired with Predatory Hawk.*
GYMNAST	Athletic contortionist who enjoys pretzel-like poses and multiple changes of pace. Eager to chalk her hands for the uneven parallel bars and Kama Sutra's Sporting of a Sparrow. *Best paired with Flying Squirrel.*

ORAL PLEASURE

[nozzle]  [dessert topping]

Despite regional differences in sodomy statutes, oral pleasuring is a noble act. Treated with dignity, it's an intimate gift, but if undertaken like housework, it becomes a loathsome chore. Coercion, forcible head-grabbing, and the "Pearl Harbor" (orgasm without warning) are selfish deeds of the rotten apples who gave Sodom and Gomorrah a bad rap.

Many gents find themselves on the receiving end when their date is skittish about going all the way but will happily venture halfway. Further-more, savvy bachelors learn early on that "talking to the canoe driver" is a gateway that, with perseverance and care, often leads to the promised land. Later, in an established relationship, piping hot oral sex is the Oysters Rockefeller of bedroom appetizers that ushers in three more courses.

Enjoy the versatility oral sex offers since it can be performed mostly clothed, or even upside down. Mix up the trajectory to include: kneel-ing, *soixante-neuf,* prone, supine, and spine-cracking side postures that will satisfy even the finickiest chiropractor. Like coming attractions at the cinema, oral sex can either build anticipation or suffice as a tempting newsreel teaser when there is nil time for the full-blown act. When on the town, lip service offers discreet, neat-and-tidy fulfillment in small confines (fitting room, second-run theatre, business class). Whether giving or receiving, climax is but one desired outcome; tallying orgasms like a PBS membership drive isn't the only way to measure success after "knocking the dust off the old sombrero."

GIVING

Ask fifty women if they'd rather have a mate with a polished tongue or talented pelvis, and the consensus will be the former. Young Casanovas ought indulge in the oral arts as often as prodigies practice scales on the piano. By "facing the nation" early in their careers, bedroom tyros still green at intercourse can at least keep their audience rapt with their oral skills. Diversify your repertoire by studying a pleasure guide in private or turning pages with a plucky lover in the bookstore aisle. With a tongue fluent in trills and arpeggios, budding lovers are equipped to tackle the Rachmaninoff concerto of intercourse.

THE QUICKIE

The microwave of mating, the Campbell's soup of sex, quickies are condensed yet satisfying, and the shortest distance between "A" and a standing "O." Select from two varieties: the Classic and the Long Sprint. The Classic begins without deliberation and ends as fast as it starts, without so much as a bead of sweat. The Long Sprint is a blast off when engines go from zero to intercourse in 5.6 thrusts, but soon after, the stopwatch is shelved and languid pacing takes hold. Quickies should make up a minority of encounters, but these two-minute drills remain mandatory preludes for joint napping and are staunch stand-ins for public sexcapades. Like doing Europe on five dollars a day, sometimes you only have the means for a glimpse of the major sites. The best quickies are furtive couplings when sex interrupts other activities; it's a couple's little secret why his pocket square is askew and she is ten minutes late returning from a smoke break.

Incidentally, during hectic times, you can get by with quickies, but these are not renewable resources. For sustaining long-term connection, heed Ranger Rick: if you cut down one now, you ought to plant two later.

Going through the motions yields dry fruit, so cock your ear to the verbal and nonverbal clues. If you feel your lover's body quiver, remember the where and how fast for next time. For a brief intermezzo, up periscope: surface for air and whisper suggestively; the tone and inflection of the response cue your next move. Before things truly heat up, show off your battery of crowd-pleasing techniques, but when in the homestretch of climax, get down to business and maintain steady, brisk cadence like a metronome set to allegro moderato.

Nice touch: "Go down south in Dixie" with no strings attached—institute a one way oral sex policy that doesn't carry the implied pressures of immediate reciprocity.

RECEIVING

A conscientious lover doesn't leave the other fumbling to guess the right moves. There's nothing condescending about murmuring guidance ("faster," "slower," "higher," "lower," or the affirming, "that's it, right there"). Akin to when a lover scratches an unreachable itch between your shoulder blades, use caressing digits and words to gently nudge your busy darling into the right rhythm and intensity. The soft music of sighs and moans prevent silent drudgery from setting in and provide wordless encouragement beyond the raw soundtrack of wet skin and the whirring ceiling fan. When receiving feels awkward or reminiscent of sharpening a number two pencil, coax your lover toward you for re-engagement of the lips; the polite change of subject diverts attention to other erogenous zones without insult.

APHRODISIACS

[suggestive gaze]

[not-so-subtle hint]

Avocado derives from the Aztec name *ahuacacuauhitl*, or testicle tree. Such was the avocado's purported aphrodisiacal power that virgins were shuttered in the house during harvesttime, and nubile Aztec women would rub avocado oil on their skin to rehydrate and perhaps get in the

KAMA SUTRA

Misperceived as merely a 1,001 sex-position guidebook, the *Kama Sutra* seems as ubiquitous on bachelor shelves as wayward chest hair during the '70s. Written by Brahma the creator and considered divine in origin, the original 100,000 chapters on dharma, *artha*, kama, and *moksha* were condensed by Vatsyayana into the current *Reader's Digest* version with thirty-six chapters in seven parts, with chapters six and eight explaining oral and intercourse techniques: Splitting of a Bamboo, Congress of the Crow (sixty-nine), and Forcible Mounting of an Ass, plus the nuances of biting, striking, and scratching with nails.

Women are classed according to yoni depth: a deer, a mare, or an elephant. Men are divided into classes according to lingam size: the hare, the bull, and the horse. Apparently, not much has changed from third-century texts to twenty-first-century spam, because the final chapter includes several surefire methods for supplementing lingam thickness and length, though magic Internet pills sure beat Vatsyayana's dictate to "rub it with the bristles of certain insects."

mood. Ever since Aphrodite emerged from the foam of the sea splash caused by the castrated member of Cronus (Zeus's father), people have ascribed sexual powers to seafood (scallops, oysters) and, later, to rare victuals (sarsaparilla, licorice). Moreover, the ancients' "law of similarity" attributed sexuality to phallic fruits and objects such as banana or rhino horn. Not just suggestively shaped, certain foodstuffs contain verifiable chemical zing: the phenylethylamine in chocolate, the capsaicin in chile peppers, and the zinc in oysters have documented effects of stimulating the nervous system or providing nutrients for testosterone production. Other purported aphrodisiacs—like the renowned Spanish Fly, prepared from dried beetle remains—are medically dangerous despite significant sales at the Quickie Mart counter. In any case, the goal is epicurean delight that stimulates the brain's pleasure center, which then sends neural signals to the pelvis and enlarges genital blood vessels, thereby welcoming an onrush of blood to phallic tissue and a surge of all-natural, opiatelike dopamine to the body. Voilà, it's time for dessert and a prodigious erection.

For spicier romance, indulge in succulent foods and erotic placebos whether dining out or in. Imagine: shapely asparagus; plump figs and juicy grapes; eggs with basil, white truffles, and new potatoes; angel hair pasta with baby artichokes and rosemary sprigs; powerful dashes of nutmeg over pumpkin soup; foie gras with raspberry vinegar glaze; polenta with maple syrup and mascarpone; berries with lush mint leaves and careful drips of honey. *Buon appetito.*

TANTRIC LOVE

I like it when you show me
The endurance of a Tantric yogi.
You got your chocolate in my peanut butter
Spreading love with your eyelash flutter.
—DEEE-LITE, "STAY IN BED, FORGET THE REST"

When your love needs a kick in the ashram, turn to Tantra (Sanskrit for "expansion"). More than parlor tricks meant to land studs instant action, Tantra is the Hindu spiritual system in which sexual love is also a healing sacrament that elevates intercourse to the level of art. In this "yoga of love," the ultimate goal is unity, not a mere Matterhorn-conquering of the G-spot. Tantra invigorates partnership with meditation, breath control, and conscious techniques easier to learn than swing dancing. Not every screw has to be a chakra-on-chakra frolic, but when your twosome needs a tune-up, a dose of high-octane Tantric sex sets the bed ablaze.

YONI: LOVE AT THE ACROPOLIS

Athens has its ancient Sacred Rock, and Tantra, too, has its own tourist attractions. The clitoris and the Grafenberg spot—technical terms more befitting white lab coats than sumptuous red satin bedsheets—are known in Tantra as the Jewel in the Crown and the Sacred Spot. In the West, the penis is nicknamed pecker, prick, and wang, while the East refers to the man's lingam as Jade Stalk, Wand, or Scepter of Light. Likewise, Eastern goddess worshippers describe the woman's yoni as Precious Gateway, Flower Heart, and Pleasure Field of Heaven. Recite these phrases mid-embrace to shift focus from lust to mindfulness.

Nice touch: When a partner is out of sorts, try the Nurturing Position: spooning on your left sides like two parentheses, ((. With chakras aligned, the inside person is enveloped in a tender pose that restores synchronicity and can turn randy in an instant.

SEXY STRATAGEMS

Once you've mastered Tantra's ongoing love meditation, it's time to get down to the nitty-gritty of the Tantric sex techniques listed below. You'll know you have your Sanskrit mojo working if you tap your lover's Amrita (the woman's divine nectar). Released only at peak levels, the essence of a woman's sexual awakening nourishes both partners in an aura-cleansing tonic. For Tantric lovers, there's nothing more spiritually nutritive than a little come in the third eye.

- ♥ **Non-Movement:** Amidst a spirited bout of sweaty love, sometimes the sexiest thing to do is nothing at all. Pause. The ensuing call of "Don't stop!" is well worth the brief hiatus. Combine this technique with long, deep breaths to back off the throttle when orgasm threatens ahead of schedule.

- ◆ **Internal Movement:** Pulse and release the love muscles in a rhythmic beat. Encourage a partner to answer your *bandhas,* or kegel contractions, with her own. If you both know Morse code, talk dirty without using your mouths: - - - - - . - . . = MORE.

- ♥ **Trajectories:** Unlike a returning lunar flight, your angle of entry can vary widely for titillating effect. Likewise, vary the exit; you don't have to leave by the same arc with which you entered.

• **Higher-Chakras Focus:** Better than visualizing baseball standings or your grandmother's visage to slow the onset of orgasm, turn your focus away from lust by retreating to loving manners of stimulation. In Tantra, touching is "kissing with hands."

THE TRUST FUND

The Tantric system suggests that you ought to save for retirement—not with dollars, but seed. Over the course of a young man's development, he can either squander his Tantric fortune on meaningless one-nighters or grow his currency with investment in worthwhile encounters. By separating orgasm from ejaculation, energy is dispersed throughout the body, not just spilled upon a lover's belly. Plus, semen conservation shortens refractory periods, prevents fatigue, and reportedly leads to vigor and youthful skin at old age so that you'll be able to chase around maidens when you're eighty without wrinkly, flapping jowls.

YABBA DABBA YUMMY

Experiment with Yab Yum, a sexual posture unique to Tantra. Lovers sit facing one another, the woman atop her cross-legged man. Supported on his thighs, she wraps her legs around him and touches her soles together behind his back as their nipples press in concert. In this position, as one partner exhales and the other inhales, chakras and beloved hearts align. In the afterglow, let the lingam lie in repose to absorb the yoni waves like an antenna receiving radio signals.

Incidentally, during her orgasm, a woman's crown chakra radiates massive energy through the roof of her mouth. Though mom's chicken soup used to be medicine enough, it's now finally clear why a little sick-day head can really lift a man's spirits.

TOYS & TOLERANCES

[bullwhip]

[thigh highs]

[high chair]

Unlike the turn-of-the-century meat packing industry justly reviled in Upton Sinclair's *The Jungle,* sex toys and fetish gear have been given an unfair shake in mainstream culture. Most people are quick to admonish the unfamiliar, and advanced props like bullwhips carry deviant associations when removed from the context of the big top. Nevertheless, it is quite beneficial to explore the curiosities of sexual adventure openly with a like-minded lover. Kink is going to creep out somewhere, and four out of five leatherettes say it's better in the home bedroom than the rest stop bathroom.

The topic of fetish offers a peek into your partner's psychosexual development. Does she fancy socked feet, hot wax, plastic wrap, soft fur, or pony play, or is it nurses, needles, nettles, and neurowheels? Some fetishes—diapered men wearing bonnets shaking baby rattles—are Freudian fixations that escaped the purge of therapy and a healthy dose of Seroquel. In short, when venturing into the realm of extreme fetish, ensure you have an extreme understanding of a partner's boundaries before laying down a plastic tarp for scat play.

TOLERANCES

Understand your lover's tolerances before going shopping to outfit the bedroom. Next to nipple clamps, openness and love are the fetishist's best friend. If your partner blanches at the thought of whipping cream or a creamy leather crop, work slowly and make fetish tolerance a gradual compromise. Usually, there is nothing stopping experimentation other than a fear of revealing one's inner self ("Honey, I want you to dress like an undertaker and throw me in a coffin while singing Lyle Lovett tunes. After that, I promise to do the dishes."). The more experienced lover adjusts to vanilla tendencies and slowly sprinkles exotic flavors over the bland plate of missionary. An obliging partner can accept anything that isn't unduly painful or so advanced that it requires UL public safety certification before powering up. Certain *objets de fétiche* might never fit right, though others, lubricated with underlying trust, make a comfortable match.

You can't grumble to buddies that your sex life is boring until you've attempted to introduce a few reasonable props into the mix. Best times to experiment? Link it to the we-cycle: if your home life is in traction, don't hook up the harness; if the prevailing winds are favorable, try something new. A romantic getaway may not be the optimal time to premiere the red ball gag; though, elegant restraints are just the thing after a sexy tuxedo-and-gown affair. Capitalize on your lover's extraordinary states—dance floor ecstasy, anniversary highs, frisky hormones—to introduce a pleasure heightener. Be proactive and stock up ahead of time, so the paddle can come out to reprimand a ready mate (or you).

BROWSING

Scouting props for the toy chest is a task best reserved for a couple's outing when mutual wide eyes and hesitant stares at the merchandise are indicators of tolerance. Peeking into a sex shop or fetish boutique can feel as awkward as strolling through a wine store before you know the difference between sherry and Shiraz. However, a top-flight clerk loves a virgin and the chance to initiate a newcomer, whether to a bottle of German Riesling or into a collar of German steel, so speak up and ask for the grand tour. If you still think B&D stands for Black & Decker, get out of the wood shop and start at the beginner's sex shop, where basic props like dildos are sold under flashing neon next to bachelorette party novelties and adult greeting cards. Serious clients should skip this rookie way station and head straight to a more sophisticated fetish boutique where high-ticket items like molded-latex catsuits are presented in refined surroundings akin to a custom clothier.

Once you and your lover finish dancing around talk of toys and map out one another's lusty leanings, furnish the basics for the home dungeon. Like building a wine cellar, start with those everyday consumables, plus a few once-in-a-while gems, and then augment as appetites dictate. Review our SINventory below before removing the rear seat from the minivan for an all-day fetish-a-thon when you and your honey shop till you crop.

TOYS & TOLERANCES SINVENTORY

To help guide nymphs and neophytes alike into obliquity, *The Modern Lover*'s Toys & Tolerances SINventory demystifies the trimmings of erotica that turn an ordinary screw into a spanking good time. Just as every dish on the menu might not be to your liking, every last bit of fetishwear needn't excite you or your partner. Not sure of your mate's tastes? As a rule, start slowly with eye-catching costumes and playful props before venturing into items that go thwack in the night.

Clothes. You dress for dinner, why not for dessert? Marquis de Sade was as finicky about his wardrobe as he was his perversion: one simply does not masturbate with a pair of crucifixes into a chalice without being properly attired. Instead of showing up under the sheets in your every-day boxers, invest in lingerie meant for play. Especially for those just dipping toes in shadowy waters, looking the part is a first step toward act-ing the part. Cross-dressers know the transformative powers of garters and demi-cups, and corsets are a splendid addition to the cedar chest, especially for Rubenesque types with curves to spare.

Leather. In the dungeon, silk is for sissies. Leather pants are so mainstream now that they work for rock stars *and* sexy soccer moms. At the after-hours club, cowhide is a kind of advertisement for frolic and mischief; in the bedroom, leather turns any strapping lad into an author-ity figure. Leather belts aren't just for holding up trousers, and gear likely found in a Harley-Davidson motorcade works nicely off the bike, too.

Latex. Leather brandishes rebellious leanings and summons animalistic urges, but feels downright baggy compared to the reptilian second-skin fit of latex. Latex doesn't breathe, but shouldn't fetish be breathtaking? A shiny garment is a sign of commitment to the lifestyle, as latex develops a sheen with use. (Although the same effect can be achieved with Armor All, spare the tongues of your admirers who'd rather not suck a dashboard.) When you're ready to put your money where your mouth is, Skin Two is the foremost fetish fashion brand. Whatever your bedroom fancy, latex is the difference between a cuddly kitten and Cat Woman.

Jewelry. An appetizer for the uninitiated, nonpiercing fetish jewelry is a way to test-drive the lifestyle without the skid marks. Belly jewels are available for pierced and unpierced navels, while body chains require nothing more than sexy hips. For veterans, nipple jewelry is downright titillating for women and men. Nipple shields and stretchers are orna-ments for pierced people and halftime-show performers.

Collars & Chokers. Body jewelry is often discreetly worn, but steel collars and spiked chokers are front and center. Lawyers have their neckties, and submissives have their collars—often attached to a master's tether (when out prancing, obey all leash laws and always curb your pet). For fun and sheer costumery, nothing says "We're attached" like a couple in matching collars gyrating on a dance floor to the goth du jour.

Gags. For the latent librarian in us all, balls, bits, and rings can be used to help keep the quiet. Breathing is the big issue for those new to gags, gagging, and being gagged, but there are designs that limit discomfort and look more fashionable than a roasted pig garnished with a red apple. Even a gagee with a head cold can wear a ring that keeps the mouth open without blockage. Tube gags have all the *mmmpphh* of the regular variety, but there's a large hole drilled through the ball for breathing. If these gags are too intimidating, simply use a scarf or blindfold.

Restraints. Anything that moves can be restrained: wrists, arms, ankles, etc. Restraints empower one person to revel in pleasure without the implied obligation of reciprocity. Even proclaimed nonfetishists probably own a pair of furry handcuffs, which are a fine opening act before stainless steel shackles or asylumwear is donned by kinky Houdinis. For starters, employ silk scarves to bind your partner to the bed corners. Even if all that happens next is a bout of erotic tickling, the trusting experience of restraint shifts the power relationship enough to stir loins in both the restrainer and the restrained.

Hoods & Masks. Dominators use hoods and masks as a kind of release mechanism to set aside identity and summon the spirit of bandits and highwaymen of yore. For those not up for playing the gimp, even a feather Mardi Gras mask brings the excitement of anonymity to a darkened room. To conjure WWF old-timer The Masked Superstar, play dress-up with partial or full-headed leather hoods. Steel eyelets and black leather lacing on a mistress make quite the impression on her restrained lover (often outright horror).

Dildos & Harnesses. Dildos and vibrators are tame toys in comparison to professional-grade stirrup sets and cargo nets. Still, they are indispensable bedroom accoutrements that are satisfying to bedfellows on a rainy night. Chest, full-body, or lower-body harnesses can be worn as sexy fetishwear all by themselves or used to attach someone to your sturdy Sears & Roebuck dungeon rack. Other harnesses accommodate a dildo, turning a simple accessory into a strap-on. Typically associated with lesbian sex, hetero couples can use the harness and dildo to explore backdoor fantasies with the female as the starting pitcher. Batter up?

Paddles & Slappers. Paddles are hard, slappers are soft, yet both are made to thwack lovers and frat boy initiates alike. Among the most underrated fetish toys, they are devilishly versatile—ping-pong by day, kink at night. A graceful hand can paddle without smarting and slap without ever leaving a mark. Many are double-sided with contrasting textures (wood and fur, hard leather and soft rubber) to suit bedtime cycles and tushy sensitivity.

Whips. Faster than a speeding bullet, the crack of a whip is actually a mini sonic boom as the tip, traveling over 1,400 feet per second, breaks the sound barrier. Like skis and surfboards, shorter whips are easier to maneuver. Can't quite commit to the whip? Test-drive a riding crop first, if only to sate an equestrian fetish.

Role-Play Gear. There are clothes that set the mood and costumes that set the scene. For intrepid fetishists, gather the gear for at-home fantasies better simulated than real: striped jumpsuit and sheriff's badge; monk's cloak, convent habit, and Ten Commandments for a Sunday sermon of naughty nun and penitent priest; or exam table, stethoscope, and white nurse cap for portraying a randy bedside manner (urethral sounds and speculums for severe medical kinkophiles).

SIGN OF THE KINK

When Mercury goes retrograde and Mars trines Jupiter, head to the toy shop to find just the right thing for your astrological playmate. Six zodiac-inspired favorites:

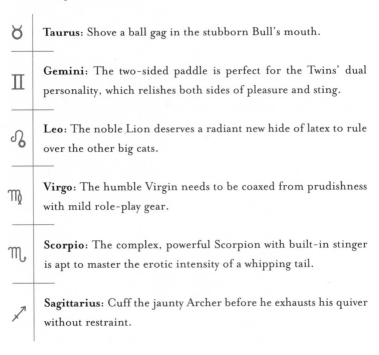

Taurus: Shove a ball gag in the stubborn Bull's mouth.

Gemini: The two-sided paddle is perfect for the Twins' dual personality, which relishes both sides of pleasure and sting.

Leo: The noble Lion deserves a radiant new hide of latex to rule over the other big cats.

Virgo: The humble Virgin needs to be coaxed from prudishness with mild role-play gear.

Scorpio: The complex, powerful Scorpion with built-in stinger is apt to master the erotic intensity of a whipping tail.

Sagittarius: Cuff the jaunty Archer before he exhausts his quiver without restraint.

DEMYSTIFYING THE FLOGGER

The unknowing public associates the flogger with bullwhips, Singaporean justice, and S&M reprobates (just SM, for those in the know), but the adept lover knows this leather scoundrel as a sensual handheld PDA (personal discipline accessory). The flogger has soft or firm leather strands for mischievous caressing and spirited spanking on the derriere; in skilled hands, it is a foreplay prop for tantalizing a lover. While it may not be the first toy out of the chest during early dating, the flogger is the Pearly Gates of Class II fetish for couples gliding deeper into sexual exploration. After serious relationships conquer the vibrator, purchasing a flogger is a sly way to introduce kink without the stigma of cross-dressing or expense of installing a sex swing in the playroom.

Not to be confused with a cat-o'-nine-tails, a standard-issue flogger has twelve strands, though tails can number twenty-four or more. The greater the number of strands (or falls), the less whiplike the sensation. Also, unlike the unforgiving cat-o'-nine's tightly braided tails, floggers feature flat strands that vary in width and texture, like fresh pasta, from tender vermicelli to strappier fettuccine (wider and thicker equals less sting). Put the right snap in your slap: horsehair delivers a healthy thump, thin leather and cowhide impart more bark than bite, and kangaroo hide's high tensile strength inflicts quite a sting. If bison or moose sound like too much smack, consider a soft elk flogger or a supple doeskin model for sensitive skin; kinky hunters might purchase a matching trophy mount. There's nothing softer (or luckier) than rabbit fur for beginners who want fun without the tears.

For those with cramped closets, today's flogger takes up no more space than a spare flashlight and fits nicely in a sweater drawer or hung on a tie rack. Like the studded black belt, it's not a regular workweek accoutrement but more like a melon baller, a handy tool for special occasions. Pony up the dough for something special from a fetish boutique, not a cheapie from the novelty shelf in a discount sex shop. Quality floggers incorporate artful craft into the handle plaiting as well as the falls. Down aisle five, test-drive that new flogger on a bare arm or leg to approximate its sting. Buy a brand-spanking-new one together as a couple; like certain toys ("I've had these anal beads for ten years"), a flogger shouldn't be recycled for future lovers.

Akin to a well-oiled baseball glove, a stiff flogger loosens up with care and use. The same can be said for the floggee. Draped sensually over erogenous zones, a flogger inspires frank discussion of fantasies with even the coyest lover. The flogger can be foisted lightly as a tool of arousal, of course, but it is also a bold device capable of feisty discipline and good old-fashioned subordination. Employ a safe word, just in case, as an audible cue to soften the blow. Explore the surge of endorphins associated with flails and tails as the flogger becomes a force to be beckoned with at bedtime. The primary target area is the *gluteus maximus* (think frolicsome spanks on the rear, not a back-lashing). Learn to swirl in the motion of an omelet-fluffing whisk, whereby a revolving wrist alternates between loving smacks and soothing strokes. Like your kitchen blender (pulse, whip, grind), the flogging hand should have a dimmer switch; temper force according to body language and clues. At its mildest, the

WHIP

♦ ♥ **Brandy** ♥ **Dry & sweet vermouth** ♥ **Splash Cointreau** ♥ **Dash Pernod** ♥ ♦

flogger is a velvety tool, whence the flurry of soft leather sweeps over the skin like scores of fingers plying a tender neck.

Nice touch: To punctuate mischief after midnight, unfurl the flogger amidst intimate friends. As a conversation piece, it's more hip-shaking than a coffee table book and, as a saucy photo op, more bawdy than sitting for a boardwalk caricature.

DIY

[easy clean up]

"The habit of self-abuse notably gives rise to a particular and disagreeable form of insanity . . . failure of intelligence, nocturnal hallucinations, and suicidal and homicidal propensities."

—George H. Napheys, A.M., M.D.,

The Transmission of Life: Counsels on the Nature and Hygiene of the Masculine Function, 1874

You retreat into the basement, purportedly to locate the WD-40 to repair a squeaky garage door. Instead of foraging in the toolbox, you dig up other lubricants hidden under the hamper and unearth your secret skin mag stash of the Sierra Madre from behind the water heater. With your partner in the shower, there is just enough time for "a little five-on-one" to work out a nagging fantasy you've had since lunch.

During the marathon of a committed relationship, even the experienced jogger occasionally stops at the water station to grab a banana and a liquid pick-me-up. Far from the desperation of being sexless and single, you're "waxing the Buick" to add sheen to an otherwise gratifying sexual relationship. Given time and space constraints, the quality of the experience varies: sometimes "sanding the banister" is like taking yourself out for a white tablecloth dinner for one; other times it's like eating with the refrigerator door open. Yet, whether it involves multiple props and silenced telephone ringers or is simply a sperm-of-the-moment "She's out of town and I've got five minutes before *Law & Order*," play it safe and don't oversnack between meals.

COURTESY

Conscientious partners respect privacy and silently acknowledge a busy mate, instead of needlessly confronting them with the telltale evidence of uncapped lube and a loaded VCR. If you come home early and the crisper is light one green vegetable or the magazine rack has been raided, tiptoe around the pad to avoid barging in on an occupied sweetie.

SPEED LIMIT

In a monogamous relationship, you can no longer turn barroom fantasies into reality without consequences. Self-love cranks open temptation's pressure-release valve and filters from your memory banks the impurities of lustful visions and surrendered opportunities. Within a cultivated fantasy life, racy thoughts aren't destructive, and it is not scandalous to picture someone else when you're with your partner. Lest your bedfellow become a warm shell servicing your fantasies, however, it's best to keep the bulk of such imaginings to DIY time. If you overdo it, you may lose the ability to become aroused without the crutch of secret longing.

Moreover, an overindulgent mate permits self-pleasure to impinge on intercourse and intimacy. When a spate of slaphappy hand-jives siphons sexual energy away from the relationship, it's low-grade cheating. During periods of heightened sexual biorhythms, don't hoard those ravenous desires all for yourself. Sexual healing is important to any couple, but you shouldn't self-medicate too often; your lover is the primary care physician for chronic cases of horniness (hopefully charging a low co-pay). At the least, honor the following occasions by going hands-free to build up a seventy-two-hour reserve tank: birthdays, anniversaries, and any celebrations where a tapped-out root inhibits a special evening or romantic getaway. On an away trip, enjoy a little freedom early in the week, but save the rest for sweetheart sex upon your triumphant return.

PARTING SHOTS

No need to swing at the first pitch; rather, extend your arousal and work on stamina. Even though it's an exhibition game, this is a stress-free moment to practice Tantric breathing and hone recognition of your personal point of no return (an important technique when *coitus interruptus* is the prevailing birth-control method). For added spice, employ

LEAVE IT TO ME

Gin ♥ **Apricot brandy** ♥ **Dry vermouth** ♥ **Dash grenadine** ♥ **Dash lemon juice**

ambidexterity and bring in the rookie southpaw for a few innings during a blowout.

When both partners are extra frisky, mutual masturbation is a routine-breaking, B-side play. For some, it is more intimate than intercourse since this private act reveals much when facial contortions and fluttering fingers are shared between sweethearts. Like laying down a bunt, mutual masturbation is a squeeze play for special situations, particularly when intercourse is out of the question: it's perfect for phone sex, dual porn watching, and between nurse shifts while in adjoining hospital beds.

Following a breakup, a replay of the failed relationship's hot points can dominate your daydreams, making you feel like a fifteen-year-old single troglodyte on a Friday night, ferociously tugging yourself into the land of yank-believe. After a fortnight stint as a slave to your schlong, challenge yourself to a ten-day masturbation sabbatical to clear the head.

THE SWING SET

Swinging is often criticized for its lack of "meaningful" emotional involvement. Is a bridge club to be condemned because its members don't develop deep emotional commitments before leading trump? Couples who share sex with each other are just as likely, if not more likely, to share dinner, movies, family picnics, conversation, recipes, and birthday presents as couples in any other group.

— *TOGETHER SEX*, ED & DANA ALLEN

Swinging calls to mind 70s key parties, mounds of blow, pyramids of pills, smoking jackets, and toasters in the tub, à la *Eating Raoul*. Group splashes may always be a hit, but this orgiastic venture is still a dicey topic, even for liberated adults. Nevertheless, thriving regional and international "social sex" communities suggest that modern marrieds and other long-termers are upping the stakes of playtime. Much more than a swap meet for wicked husbands, swingers aren't chattel but allies in naked adventures that may or may not involve exchanging partners. With the advent of Internet personals, online party pals are as easy to order as a gourmet cheesecake with your choice of topping. The days of fuzzy Polaroids printed in cheap newsprint "contact" mags are replaced by digital pictures posted on sleek websites that match like-minded couples according to location, body type, smoking preference, and fetish leaning, not to mention hot tub make and model.

Nonswingers would do well to drop prejudices. In general, swingers are not sleazy malefactors likely to slip you a downer while belting your lover or wife with leather comeuppance. To the contrary, the practice of neighborly openness lends itself to honesty and civic responsibility. In fact, many lifestylers are champions of personal freedom and G-string-toting members of the ACLU, along with NASCA, the North American Swing Club Association (add an R for extra raciness). When they're not lobbying pro-orgy politics, swingers flock to theme parties that showcase creative recreation. For example, safari night unleashes inner tigers, and body-painting parties set a tactile mood for budding Pollock splatterers. Discerning hosts create an environment of sexual versatility and tend to wine and gender pairings as carefully as condoms and coats, temperature and towels, and lighting and lube.

PLAYGROUND PERKS

There might not be a monthly newsletter or roadside assistance, but there are plenty of tangible AAA membership benefits to swinging.

♥ **Arousal:** Even for soft swingers (no penetration with others), a roomful of writhing bodies is like a live-action porno and is an undeniable natural stimulant.

♦ **Adventure:** Looking to test-drive a new fantasy? A carnival of delights presents mischiefs that are logistically impossible to replicate at home without moving the furniture, such as: King of the Mountain/ Queen of the May (stimulation of one by three or more people), Pretzels (salty clusters of partygoers around a central person or couple), and Daisy Chains (a conjoined group of four or more; called "perfect" when a circle is completed).

♥ **Acceptance:** Tired of wearing the scarlet letter of B/D or crossdressing? Amongst a crowd, the probability is high for bumping and grinding into fellow fetishists. Plus, instead of hoping for a dance club come-on, curious women and their voyeuristic mates can rejoice that it's always ladies night at a swing party. Eighty percent of swinging women are either bisexual or bi-playful; the other 20 percent say, "Bring out the hardware."

PLAYGROUND PITFALLS

What may sound like paradise for some is a shortcut to crack-up for couples hardwired for jealousy. To most people, swinging, like communism, looks better on paper than in practice. Before you give up your lover to the people, don't be afraid to call the whole thing off if either of you gets cold feet.

♥ **Jealousy**: Swinging exposes incompatible tolerances when one partner feels threatened by the arrangement. Smart couples make home life priority one and step away from the scene before a twinge of envy escalates to finger-pointing rage. First-timers might establish parameters so that nobody gets hurt: "Only if I'm watching," "Only if I can do the same thing."

♦ **Shame**: Sanctimonious co-workers and clergy unduly label swingers as deviants. Condemnation is nothing new to progressive spirits accustomed to browsing for dildos in tinted-window storefronts. Still, no one wants a showdown over ethics with the boss or the PTA if word gets out. Be liberal but discreet, and forgo the front-and-center Associate of the Month parking spot if your rear bumper proclaims, "I Brake for Swingers."

♥ **STDs**: While these are never popular party favors, VD and its ilk are valid concerns. Condoms are commonplace at swing clubs with open membership, but as party rosters tighten with familiarity and trust, rubbers are decidedly optional. Since monogamous couples present a lesser risk of disease than an active bachelor, antisingle attitudes abound. For added safety, stick with married partners or dyads going steady.

Not-so-nice touch: Like gate-crashing a wedding and consuming all the Krug and cocktail shrimp, the dubious practice of toting a "ticket" is seriously frowned upon. Parties are for swinging couples and unescorted ladies only, not horny bachelors. Sly, single men who fake their way into a soirée by passing off a nonswinging lady as their admission fee ought to expect a silk-robed, be-moustached host to shoo them off unceremoniously.

CELIBACY

Celibacy . . . it's not just for Jesuit missionaries and Poindexters anymore. Despite a bulging black book, killer threads, and perfect posture, you make a staunch decision to temporarily suspend amorous ambling about town or Internet clicking for dates. Then, active flirtation with strangers is shelved with alluring commuters on the bus and even that pretty enema salon attendant helping with your internal cleanse. As time passes, meeting friends out unshaven or in grunge-rock flannel bears an air of being above society's mating rituals. Little do you know, one errant wink or flattering smile may foil your carnal fast. Perhaps you'll even attract a co-celibate lady whose triangle and leg hair have grown rainforest wild under winter leggings, with no short skirt or mate in sight until the spring thaw.

After an agonizing breakup, take a little me-time away from the dating scene; following an intensive Latin lesson at the doctor's office (i.e.,

---

FLURRY

After a long relationship with all the trimmings (intense passion and a ridiculously protracted split), some wounded lovers seek celibacy. Other casualties of love, however, find immediate solace in a multitude of beds, propelled by that vulnerable, post-breakup glow, which attracts lovers like ladybugs. Free of restraints, the gent on a Flurry indulges in a whistle-stop tour of seedy bars and seedier flames, spurred on by the ravenous libido of someone who's just awakened wide-eyed from a cryogenic freeze. Despite a Flurry's rapid turnstile of bedfellows, you're essentially alone, sleeping with everyone but emotionally invested in no one. Fortunately, the mending heart usually slows the pace, and the slew of indiscretion eventually wanes into therapeutic me-time.

Chlamydia trachomatis, Neisseria gonorrhoeae), stay on the sidelines for a stretch. Similarly, after a string of regretful mating choices leaves you exasperated, a cooling-off period can be just the thing for looking inward and focusing on the future. For most socially active gents, celibacy seems unnatural, as sex is a biological imperative on par with the play-offs and sleep, but are a few weekends home alone curled up with a good book and cup of green tea really going to jeopardize a studded reputation? Too much hermit seclusion hints of major depression and asexuality, but once in a while, declined flirty advances or sexless Saturday nights are therapeutic, not emasculating.

CELIBACY VS. DRY SPELL

There is a vast vas deferens difference between celibacy and dry spells. A dry spell is a rough patch—you're off your game or on the disabled list due to an unspeakable case of eczema or a mall haircut that hacked off your bangs and your dignity. Celibacy may start with a dry spell, but eventually you take ownership of it and focus on hobbies and nonlibidinous leisure. If a dry spell is going 0 for 4 with three strikeouts, then celibacy is not even coming to bat or dressing for the game. Though, involuntary celibates (or incels) shouldn't try to rationalize a dateless season or pass off sexual awkwardness as virtue; instead, embark on a new gym regimen or expel pleated plants from your wardrobe to invigorate dating possibilities.

OFF THE DL

Like a crackerjack résumé, some love lives lack serious gaps of dead air between gigs. Some people require an accomplice, even a rebound fill-in, to sort through a painful episode. So, if a month of celibacy begins to feel like three months in the maximum-security hole, step back into the dating world. Celibacy isn't a compulsory form of self-punishment, but should feel like a pleasant stay at the Clinic for Recovering Romantics. Like a stint in the steam room, celibacy brings clarity, and the detox opens the possibility of sexual redux. Upon emerging from the haze, you'll find that your standards have inched upward. Thus, if a soulmate or a high-equity one-night stand beckons, file the discharge papers and declare yourself rehabilitated.

TROUBLE

♦ ♥ ♦ ♥ ♦ ♥ ♦ ♥

SKELETONS

Every mate has embarrassing tidbits housed in credit agency databases, sealed police files, and a jilted flame's memory banks. At a moment's notice, that pesky information can be dashed off to any interested party with access to your social security number, or to a grudge-bearing ex with a motormouth. Even light packers bring baggage to a love affair—hope that your mate travels with but a slim carry-on. Regardless of who has the larger karmic debt to pay, disclosure of past sins before engagement should preempt fine-print flare-ups after the proposal is volleyed. Like having the opportunity to run an automobile title search, an unsuspecting lover deserves to know whether you're a new roadster or a banged-up jalopy salvaged from a wreck.

New relationships present each partner with a clean slate. Nonetheless, unpleasantries have a way of outting, whether by chance run-ins on the street or scandalous search-engine results. To avoid bumbling through an impromptu explanation, thwart disaster with measured disclosure ahead of time. Like a vaccination, your past ills should be doled out in safe doses to inoculate a mate without overwhelming her with toxicity. Once the matter of your street-walking history is confessed, you will have eliminated a potential land mine down the road. Though, bottomed-out souls who reinvent themselves on an opposite coast or European shore may mask their former life until talk of cohabitation and dream houses.

There is no statute of limitations on discovery of hurtful things. For instance, if your spouse hears that you bilked old ladies in a stock scam at twenty-six or poked a duck in the eye at age six, either will dampen your pristine image. If you have much to tell, get busy so friends aren't left wondering if high jinks predating the engagement are still classified. Disclosure empowers: a catty opponent's smear tactics are rendered impotent when your mate has already washed, dried, and folded your filthy laundry.

TACTFUL CONFESSION

There is a kind of selfishness in deep confession since it can dump a heavy load of shady deeds onto an innocent partner. Revealing prior incarceration (or other public-record transgressions) may be sensible, but purging tenebrous tales of deceit and disgorging a tornado alley of strewn exes can burden your mate, implanting unsavory images in her mind. *Penthouse Forum*—worthy narrations of debased, fleshy encounters are best trotted out only for boys' night, although certain advanced dabblings (swinging, sex across genders, diseases beyond the clap) and their legacies should be disclosed as a moral imperative. After an ample but abridged recitation of your bohemian biography, store the remaining sludge in the landfill of your soul. Other confidants might get a limited tour of your dark matter, but for the most part, a mature psyche can comfortably coexist with a small counterbalance of undisclosed shadows.

TIMELINESS

In early wooing, you may be reluctant to reveal yourself too soon for fear of queering the deal. Prompt honesty carries the risk of rejection, yet a frank exchange of priors fosters intimacy between lovers who are unafraid of the rap sheet. Whereas an indiscriminate blatherer vomits secrets because he can't hide the truth any longer, an adept self-monitor oversees the floodgates of confession and knows that gradual disclosure promotes honesty without busting the dam of mutual respect. The shrewd sharer waits for those times when each party has ironclad regard for the other's character. Reverence is not easily damaged by a few rakish tales of petit larceny recounted during an arm-in-arm stroll, but confessing your former jones for hookers and huffers after a knockdown fight will indelibly paint you a low-down, wretched scalawag. Ideally,

GOOGLING

Before stepping out blindly for a date or online encounter, today's savvy revelers perform the ultimate five-minute due-diligence check. Googling, or entering a person's name into a search engine, is the ultimate social prophylactic, with results organized neatly for your pleasure. Completely aboveboard, Googling (web *and* image search) is a quick public dossier that can be digested over a few nibbles of raisin scone; though, poring over more than the first fifty results might label you a nosy Nellie. Before committing to the profundity of a third date or certainly a marriage proposal, ensure that future romantic mornings won't be spent posting Megan's Law flyers informing the neighborhood about your new love's former stint as a day care diddler. Most search results are harmless, confirming corporate affiliations, alumni activities, or publishing credits. Occasionally, saucier listings emerge in the form of local police blotters, shady memberships, or low-res frames from a "Girls Gone Wild" video.

Googling is fair fodder for mutual conversation. Little black marks, like her arrest in Toms River for equine humbuggery in the fourth degree, are delightfully explained as a Halloween reenactment of Lady Godiva's ride through town. Veteran socialites always stay one step ahead of the prying public by periodically self-Googling to scout for embarrassing tidbits. Lastly, though long slandered for saddling you with a run-of-the-mill autograph, besieged parents should now be thanked, as ordinary monikers like William Johnson are so ubiquitous as to render the namesake impervious to Internet searches.

both partners come away more closely bound after hearing about tough truths or reading unflattering passages from one another's diary. As romantic expectations rise, lovers who accept each other's skeletons have a future together.

Incidentally, a last-minute omnibus confession soils prenuptial joy. Long before asking for her hand, relate your prior fall from grace, though not necessarily as a Homeric catalog of your rotten odyssey. With enough salacious bits revealed, your partner can respond to the "Will you marry me?" question with an informed answer.

SKIRTING TROUBLE

"Measure twice, cut once," sayeth the astute carpenter; though, when it comes to hot topics, adept lovers follow the vital maxim of "Confess once, reference never again." Remember the molten froth that poured forth the last time your evil ex's name was mentioned? Speak it again and risk another night of misery on the couch. Long whiskers and keen ears spot impending trouble when conversation tilts toward unsettling, memory-jogging references that recall taboo topics; stave off danger with deft changes of subject.

BLACK MAGIC

Are a covey of failed loves, business partners, and roommates sticking pins into a voodoo doll with your likeness? Your sweetheart should know which archenemies she has inherited long before an old flame or bitter foe sends a packet of photos that brings to light acts best forgotten. So, too, should you beware of assuming too much bad credit from a mate's emotional bankruptcies; unlike financial slates that are wiped clean after seven years, past calamities and undying rancor remain aboil for decades.

To avoid the voodoo-doll nightmare, tidy up your messes. Insensitivity and jilted exes leave unavoidable residue that can quietly pollute subsequent relationships like pesticides in the groundwater. A Superfund site may never bloom again, but at least try to mitigate the toxicity: aim to downgrade your site status from carcinogenic to rehabilitated. Short-circuited loves from your teens and early twenties heal more easily than adult train wrecks in which money or monogamy was a casualty. A sincere out-of-the-blue letter or email is an unobtrusive way to broach an apology. Conversely, your most appalling transgressions are best left alone; just because you're prepared to clear the air doesn't mean the other party is ready for a makeup hug or even a hello.

NIGHT ON THE COUCH

[headboard]

[limp pillows]

[lumpy mattress]

A pointless argument in bed about money used to warrant a march back to your own apartment; now the walk is a lot shorter (to the living room). A handful of nights on the couch is nothing to be ashamed of; though, if you develop shar-pei-like face creases from the upholstery, couples counseling might be a better solution. Once you've been ejected, the ultimate goal is to be reinstated to the bedroom before sunup, if only for a reassuring cuddle before the workday alarm sounds.

CUSHIONED OCCASIONS

There are eight likely scenarios when the sight of your face or bellow of your snoring is unwelcome until morning:

♥ **Punt**: After a calamitous blunder of words, you volunteer to vacate the bed before a nightstand lamp is hurled at your head.

♦ **Black Flag**: Despite your pleadings of innocence, a feisty mate kicks you out of bed, mandating a to-be-continued blowout the next morning.

♥ **No Trespassing**: As punishment for prior gaffes recently discovered, you are relegated to solitary confinement the moment you walk through the door.

♦ **Dawning**: Reeking of vice, you slip onto the couch at sunrise to prevent a 5 A.M. "Where have you been?" interrogation. When awoken, profess that you passed out during a 2 A.M. *M*A*S*H* rerun.

♥ **Contagion**: After three days of phlegm-hacking flu symptoms, your sorry state jeopardizes a bedmate's bill of health, obliging an immediate quarantine.

♦ **Detour**: Instead of spreading insomnia to a sleeping lover, shoo your troubled mind to the La-Z-Boy for a little me-time.

♥ **The Soft Landing**: A mild argument prompts makeshift bed-making in the rec room, but before settling in for the night, you're summoned back for a full a pardon.

◆ **The Dreaded Double Duty**: After treaty negotiations break down, it's
  back-to-back nights in the sofa crack.

It's the fourth snide remark and a long time until daylight. Call in
the Punt team. Instead of feigning sleep under tense sheets, get productive shut-eye on the couch and let hours apart soothe last night's sharp
words. A kiss on your lover's forehead before dragging out your blanket
augurs tomorrow's reconciliation.

When the Black Flag is waved, you've been cited for an infraction
and pulled off the track. Appeals to racing officials must wait for business hours, so grab your jammies and make a pit stop in the medicine
cabinet for an Ambien. Respect the restorative power of the sofa bed:
instead of passive-aggressive sheet yanking, errant elbowing, and mattress jockeying, both mates can soberly reflect on miscues before lobbying for forgiveness at daybreak.

If the spat happens at lunch, it will probably be cleared up by sup-
per, but when arguments get a late start, No Trespassing saves tears and
lost hours of soothing rest. When the P.M. burns away without reconciliation, use the sofa as a rear-window defroster to clear the foggy mind.
Men can sleep with their head on a rock, so for the sake of chivalry and
your lover's morning mood, surrender the bed. Don't violate the sanctuary of the master bedroom, even if it means curling up in your button-
down and using the tablecloth for warmth.

If your mate stirs at the creak of floorboards, crash in the easy chair
to forego the scorn of dashing under covers past the witching hour.
Dawning conceals actual homecoming time: snooze on the loveseat until
first light and then glide into bed at dawn. Returning home from a serious bender, take measures to prevent the relationship bends by detoxing

in the sofa drunk tank. Turn a post-curfew violation into bonus points by supplementing your slip-in with a Sunday paper and continental breakfast for two waiting in the breakfast nook.

Ah-*choo.* Your bed-quaking cough has kept you both up for a week, and she has a big board meeting tomorrow. To quarantine the Contagion, deputize the sectional as a sick bay.

Instead of subjecting your partner to your unending pillow flipping after an unwise double espresso, unfold the guest Murphy bed. A Detour to the pullout settles a restless mind and gives a cramped body space to starfish. The occasional at-home all-nighter has its attractions: read an entire page-turner, phone foreign time zones, or special order late-night TV goodies. Should pay-per-view become personally inspirational, it's okay to drive the skin bus after hours. Can't muster the fare for the ride home? After hiking up your drawers, turn off the engine, pull over to the sofa rest area, and dry out before heading to bed.

After a tiff, you storm out to let off steam. Upon your ignominious return home, slither to the davenport. If you're lucky, you'll wake up with her snuggling at your side, two forgiving souls teetering on the ottoman. With troubles falling away like so much loose change lost between the cracks, The Soft Landing is ushered in by the five magic words: "Honey, come back to bed."

The cushions are stacked neatly in the corner, the alarm clock sits on the coffee table, and you're only a duffel bag shy of passing for a weekend guest: it's official, you're now pulling Dreaded Double Duty in the rec room. Two nights in a row signal rusty conflict-resolution skills, so use this time to brush up on techniques such as tempered tone of voice, active listening, and a strict ban on hurtful blurts of ancient history. In the heat of rage, remember that you love each other, even if you don't particularly like one another at the very moment. Without the salve of sincere communication, you'll soon be packing a garment bag and retreating to a friend's bachelor pad, or worse, she'll cart her suitcases to her meddling mother's house in the next county. Let things further deteriorate with nary a contrite phone call and she'll come back only to usher you out to a rent-by-the-week economy motel with a view of the interstate.

Nice touch: To avoid waking up to a huffy wife and slamming front door, catch her under blankets while she still has sleepies and an unbrushed mouthful of compassion. Spooning speeds healing and is rarely wrong, though whether to instigate sex after a night on the couch should be determined on a case-by-case basis. There are times when you can go right from the couch to the carpet, but for the most egregious errors, bottle up libido until a proper union presents itself.

FIREWALL

Intracouple communications, like those of an attorney and client, are privileged, a policy that encourages honesty and juicy jaw-flapping among a committed pair. Divulging your sweetheart's sensitive history, sexual appetite, or sappy-movie favorites is the swiftest route to wrath; even your best friends shouldn't have full access to touchy, embarrassing data. Once information is released, the damage is done, and no amount of horse-trading or offered secrets in return will mollify a slighted lover.

Defy this sacred trust once, and in retaliation, the entire neighborhood may learn that you wet the bed until age ten.

When squash buddies prattle on in the steam room about recent party conquests, a devoted man can be made to feel utterly dull. It's tempting to add your own spicy kindling to fuel racy dialogue, but before a groundswell of pride has you revealing your partner's fancy for French ticklers or her howling endorsement of doggie style, zip your lip. Otherwise, months later, expect a tipsy flub from an oafish pal, followed by a stiletto heel jabbed at your shin: "What student loans, Heather? Why, Dean told me you paid your way through college by stripping at the Private Dancer." If necessary, retell declassified escapades of gymnastic ex-flames who received 10s on your judge's scorecard, but keep state secrets under lock and key.

TELLING TWO

While household privacies are hallowed, outside confidences from friends and acquaintances frequently cross the relationship membrane. However, your role as confidant shouldn't be abandoned—a chum's respectful request for silence can be honored without raising trust issues at home. Before spilling secrets in your ear, speakers should assume that telling one lover is telling two bedmates; in order to secure privacy, they

YOU NEVER KNOW

♥ ◆ ♥ **Blackberry brandy** ♥ **Green crème de menthe** ♥ **Dash of nutmeg** ♥ ◆ ♥

should make a personal appeal for a bedroom gag order. As a conscientious friend, ask whether dubious data is on or off the record ("Is it okay if I tell Simone and no one else?"). Wickedly good tales from minor acquaintances or co-workers far removed from your spouse's social circle are hardly protected and can be retold with gusto.

Other retellings demand closer attention. Are you violating another's trust and rationalizing it as *sharing* with your mate? While exchanging confidential info with your sweetheart should be the default, at times, you must erect the relationship firewall. Marriage and live-in love doesn't trump all, and some loyalties ought to override burning desires to rumormonger. Close comrades and friendships that predate your relationship garner strict confidence, especially when a story expressly transmitted on the down-low could irreparably mar perceptions. For example, telling your spouse that Eli had an affair with a chorus girl at the Shriners convention will forever label him an infidel, even though his marriage survived and blossomed after months of counseling.

Incidentally, akin to days when setting up a pal earned you a blow-by-blow review of the first romp, couples are granted secret-trading privileges in matchmaking scenarios. As a finder's fee for being set up, new lovers submit to separate debriefings. The matchmakers are then free to swap saucy stats with each other, but in exchange, they are sworn not to pass such communiqués back to the lovers in question.

DAY ON THE COUCH

She's just come home from therapy with a smirk of contentment, the kind you only wish you could inspire in the bedroom:

"I had a good session."

"What did you talk about? Me?"

"We only talked about you for a few minutes. Though, my shrink says that since you like me on top, you're adopting a negative oedipal position."

"I see. But you didn't talk about that other 'little problem' I had under the covers last week, did you?"

Chances are she did, and there's nothing you can do about it. A little jealousy over her psychotherapy is normal, but rampant suspicion smacks of insecurity. Therapy is a weird animal, as patients share intimate memories and weaknesses that remain unspoken elsewhere. The intimacy between exclusive lovers is formidable, but so is the bond with a therapist, and this shouldn't be disconcerting. Therapy is a process of uncovering, and you needn't hear all the small considerations that precede a breakthrough of personal confidence or sexual openness; perhaps her confession of fantasies involving a bed of balloons and a pillow of sour cream is just a phase and shouldn't leave the analytic couch. Then again, don't you wish, just once, she would share her lesbian-sex dreams with you first?

Don't hold back your lover's mental health; restrain her in other, more furry-handcuffed ways. Tracking improvement isn't as easily measured as ten dropped pounds on the grapefruit diet before summer bikini season. As each month progresses and insights filter inward, offer an active ear, behave yourself, and refrain from uttering any trigger words that revisit upset anew. Treat a head shrinker's work-in-progress like a construction zone: only step in with an invitation and never without a hard hat.

Her therapy is good for you since someone else is doing the heavy psychic lifting of the often-tumultuous psychoanalytic method. As long as she is not becoming a sparkless pharmacological robot, spending

---

NAME THAT NEUROSIS

The *DSM IV-TR,* the principal diagnostic reference tool used by mental health professionals, lists clinical disorders such as schizophrenia and depression by code. Below, see if you can distinguish the real disorders from our fictitious afflictions, which we hope will make it into the next edition (answers follow).

a. 314.9 Undifferentiated Nagging

b. 300.4 Unsexy Winter Clothes–Wearing Dysthymia

c. V71.01 Adult Antisocial Behavior

d. 302.73 No Oral Fixations

e. 305.00 Gin and Catatonic

f. 307.9 Communication Disorder Not Otherwise Specified

g. 314.8 Bushy Pubic Mound Dysmorphia

h. 312.32 Cash-in-Wallet Kleptomania

i. 315.89 Parallel Parking Disorder

j. 317 Checkbook Balancing Apraxia

k. 625.8 Female Hypoactive Sexual Desire Disorder

Real neuroses: c, f, k.

a pinch of the household's discretionary golf income on therapy is a sound investment. If wedding bells toll, you'll have forty-plus years to contemplate your mate's growth, so pony up for preventative maintenance to ensure a smoother ride. Moreover, knowing what meds your partner is on (especially antidepressants, which often affect sex drive) will obviate an awkward telephone confrontation with her doc about a recent spate of rebuffed advances.

Curb easy assumptions about what happens on the couch and avoid getting personal. When her therapist is a woman, you might falsely presume that those two conniving skirts are plotting a *Thelma & Louise* caper against your scurrilous self; with a man, there's always a sense of intrigue. Brief hellos in the waiting room or in the parking lot after your mate's appointment are standard, but if you bump into her shrink shopping for pâté at the local charcuterie, restrain yourself; desperately asking for the "real dirt" on your bedmate's sexual hang-ups is deliciously tempting but wholly inappropriate. Jealous hubbies shouldn't worry about transference, or a lover's little schoolgirl crush on a therapist, unless her eminent shrink's latest book jacket photo boasts a handsome smile, $1,000 horn-rimmed specs, and a sharp Armani sport coat.

Incidentally, the quickest way to the doghouse is to hit her with anti-therapy sarcasm during a bad mental health day: "Group therapy? At least you get to meet people you have something in common with."

FAMILY PLAN

It is not uncommon for the entire household to be in therapy. With each partner as familiar with the *Diagnostic and Statistical Manual of Mental Disorders* as their own datebook, petty jealousies and nagging doubts about weekly appointments evaporate. However, just because you have the analytic couch in common, don't obsess. Therapy becomes all-consuming when pillow talk, once dominated by winsome coos, unravels into a Woody Allen–esque show-and-tell of neuroses and imagined break-throughs that renders eroticism suddenly complicated. (Remember that Annie Hall, even after all the laughs, eventually tires of the dry-witted Alvy Singer, despite his accumulated wisdom from sixteen years of therapy.)

IT TAKES TWO

Marvin Gaye sang, "Two can really ease the pain like a perfect remedy." Actually, with the presence of a couple's therapist, sometimes it takes three. Couples counseling is one option for a formerly buoyant, loving connection that's become hopelessly stuck in a cycle of ill feelings. Before sashaying into the office together, be prepared for spirited wordplay and heretofore unspoken revelations about the relationship. Couples therapy brings out latent feelings, so don't be shocked if you get angry at new criticisms about your shoddy apology skills and cunnilingus technique. Skeptical and defensive? The prospect of one ordinary forty-five-minute session shouldn't prompt you to smoke up in the parking lot beforehand. As for who pays, there is no easy solution. The most neurotic? Least actualized? In truth, like Ed O'Neill, go Dutch, or else you'll have to find another counselor just to sort out billing issues.

To find a good psych referral, use the same word-of-mouth advice you would for another professional. Any thirty-two-point-font advertisement for a marital/couples counselor should be given as much consideration as shady quacks' cards or uninsured–moving company flyers thumbtacked to the local sub-shop corkboard. Instead, search for a well-regarded, board-certified doc with a thriving practice who also counsels couples. Unless it

INTIMATE HYGIENE

Medicated powders, gooey ointments, enema bags strewn out like deflated bagpipes on the bathroom counter: during early wooing, such imperfections and embarrassing ailments remain behind the scenes, shrouded in euphemisms like "under the weather," "a little redness," and "tummy ache." The first time she picked up new eyeliner at the drug store, you silently headed toward the aisle of infamy, that lane of unnerving tonics abutting the prescription counter—remedies so humbling that otherwise ethical gents would rather pilfer the dastardly creams than shamefacedly admit an itchy problem. No one wants a new flame to see dandruff shampoo on the first weekend getaway, but after moving in together, are you going to secretly pour it into the Prell bottle after midnight? At some point, the body's machinations cease to affect regard, and crossing the thirty-minute mark in the bathroom necessitates a concerned knock for signs of life, not a breakup.

The open-bathroom bazaar of long-term relations means that you no longer have to brown bag over-the-counter unmentionables. At first, minor cosmetics and asthma medicine appear, then brace for the cavalcade of maladies: hair plugs, botox, prostate, infections, hammertoes, athlete's foot, rashes, and dry spots. Yet, as a testament to love, there is no need for full explanation or hands-on application ("We know everything about each other. I've sprinkled jock itch powder down his shorts myself!"). Like porn discreetly stored in the armoire, certain liniments (which thankfully come in diminutive sizes no bigger than lip balm) should be stowed on a low-traffic shelf in the medicine cabinet. Likewise, a lady might conduct home pregnancy tests with negative results that are never spoken about.

is for an isolated visit or two to resolve a distressing crisis, don't tote your partner to your own shrink for an extended run of dual sessions. Although your mate won't be pelted by AA batteries like a Bosox outfielder in the Bronx, your psychic home turf isn't friendly confines.

The majority of couples resolve their own hang-ups in-house (or in court), so exercise muscles of adaptability and compromise before carting your broken relationship to the psychic gym. Counseling shouldn't be the first recourse; rather, it might become a viable option after three months of icy stares and rattled household peace stir thoughts of sprinkling rat poison in the casserole. In the end, couples counseling won't miraculously mend doomed relations, overcome rampant incompatibility, or alleviate one partner's serious condition (addiction, unsightly bunions). After years of false starts and little progress, couples counseling can eventually run dry. Recognize the point when therapy becomes a crutch propping up a condemned twosome that will never stand on its own four feet.

Nice touch: If you're still civil before the first appointment, savor the togetherness of anticipating the unknown office dynamic. Make a wager on which of you will be the first to get lambasted as "the insensitive one."

ALCOHOL & PHARMACOPOEIA

[tamper-proof cap]

[mother's little helper]

If your idea of a leisurely Saturday picnic together involves hypodermics and cooking spoons, perhaps your relationship has *too* much substance. At twenty-five, the party girl who can sniff you under the table and bake a Bundt cake is a temporary allure, but thinking ahead, a pill-crazy mother of two isn't so appealing. Before getting serious, establish an explicit understanding of each other's escapist pursuits. Money problems may be a relationship bugaboo, but unchecked booze and drug issues are often an outright kill switch.

GROUND RULES

Courtship allows a glimpse into your partner's drug habits, which you hope don't involve pawning furniture for smack. Even when one partner is an experienced tippler, the other a carefree sipper, both should recognize what's destructive and what's permissible, and then agree on a level of moderation. Jolly Beans or Frisco Speedballs may be out, but a smidge of Acapulco Gold or California Sunshine might be tolerated in measured quantities. Outside of addiction and heavy narcotics, blanket prohibitions are excessive. In the 1980s, the feds instituted buzz-killing "zero tolerance" policies and sought to impound seacrafts caught with any quantity of drugs onboard. Such unpopular policies won't endear the voters in your home either; better to set commonsense ground rules, such as no smoking inside the house or no inviting dealers over for tea and a toke during business hours.

DOUBLE SHOT

Savor the memories of a night of rare abandon together. The shared surreal experience of a psilocybin trip is the closest thing to having the same dream, and it's nice to know the loving bond endures even at half-consciousness. When you're not included, don't later harangue a mate about an unusual instance of fathomless vice. On top of a rum punch hangover, a sermon about the evils of firewater or lack of self-control is worse than a drumming headache with cottonmouth. As long as no one was humiliated in the name of good, clean fun, let your partner's distressed body be punishment enough. In the end, there'll always be that time you held your darling's hair over the bowl after too many tequila shooters at her thirtieth birthday party.

OPEN CONTAINERS

Healthy curiosity coupled with a healthy liver transforms wine and spirits exploration into a vibrant hobby for two: getaways to vineyards, invite-only tastings, and the joy of sharing sips from a remarkable vintage. The more experienced imbiber needs to cultivate the other's palate. If you're going steady with a beer swiller, open your throat to microbrews, but along the way, why not verse your lover on the virtues of Rioja or Ribeiro? Pouring double magnums at dinner parties won't summon Cary Nation and her keg-smashing temperance troops, but when alcohol routinely serves as chemical impetus for evening-ending public squabbles, it's time to monitor intake. If weekend mornings after brown-bagged malt liquor binges are hazy and toxic as a tire fire, consider hitting the movies next

Friday night, not the sauce. To paraphrase an old fortune cookie, a fool at thirty with a forty is a fool indeed.

Druggie practices come to light when contraband once concealed in toilet tanks and false-bottomed valises emerges in the semipublic stash box. An innocuous-looking sachet housing light sundries is acceptable, but do you really want your significant other stumbling into your basement drug lab as you vainly attempt to boil poppy seeds or render nutmeg into hallucinogens? Hushed habits pollute the relationship as much as the body and taint financial trust. If you have to fudge the grocery bill to pay the man, you can forget about regular installments to the vacation kitty or to every graduate's favorite mistress, Sallie Mae. For modest recreational drugs, light consumption isn't worrisome, whereas upper-tier synthetics need be meted out carefully for singular occasions of law-flouting indulgence, if at all. As for Schedule I narcotics, stolen prescription pads and nearby resuscitation kits are more indicative of pathology than cloudy adventures. Complete disclosure is the default, though the rare capsule can slide under your tongue as long as other consumption is far below posted limits.

EMERGENCY BRAKE

Overheard whispers about your staggering sweetheart ideally concern her beauty, not her vodka habit, and when friends speak of you as a great provider, pray it's about your earning potential, not your supply of dime bags. A compatible mate is the bulwark against excess, not the enabling force for the other's runaway intake ("It's no big deal, she just drinks like that on the weekends"). Whether by red noses or slurred speech, an astute lover discerns the danger signs and actively keeps the other inbounds, without playing the drink-counting fun-vacuum. Hence, nudge a glassy-eyed mate toward the club soda at a cocktail party and expect the same temperate elbow in return on another night. Unless it's a two-way street, the relationship will sour, as one partner resents the starring role of the indentured weekend chauffeur and twenty-four-hour janitor for an incorrigible sot. When underlying issues are left unaddressed, the gap between partners widens as one drinks more and woos less, wasting away and boasting a sex life about as vibrant as that bloated bag of empties sitting at the curb.

POST-NUPTIALS

After tying the knot, most couples have moved beyond the giddy drug-experimentation phase; those with leftover hankerings should have snorted them out pre-engagement. Daily dazes and all-too-frequent blurs are incongruent with the role of good husband. Mutual plans carry the promise of undivided—meaning, sober—attention, even if it's a mind-numbing hour of rummaging through carpet remnants looking for the perfect doormat. Rare treats with long-lost buddies and social usage pass muster, but starting weekend brunch in a Special K–Hole or inhaling all the nitrous from the whipped cream canister before your wife's book club is a fair predictor that you'll be celebrating the next anniversary alone in rehab, wearing paper slippers.

A heap of loose stems and seeds on the writing desk or bongs higher than a cat's back spotlighted in a curio cabinet are not indicative of a balanced lifestyle. Unlike the bachelor pad with its instruments of vice housed like ripsaws in a toolshed, the marital space is discreet. With illicit leanings now considered privileged information, the couple's pharmacological candy dish isn't automatically proffered to untested guests right after the vintage Port.

Incidentally, despite the neatly tied bow and ribbon, bestowing drugs—even designer pentobarbital—as birthday gifts isn't romantic. A monogrammed flask is handsome, but for most couples, a sterling silver drug scale isn't even proper for odd-numbered anniversaries.

SOURING

Encased in red Tupperware, last night's leftovers sit squarely in the refrigerator. A few days later, the vessel is shoved aside, upstaged by fresh groceries and a chilled six-pack. By the following week, hidden in the milk carton's shadow, old leftovers grow moldy like a bowl of bruised fruit. You forget it's there, see it again, and then ignore it once more. You put off the unpleasantness of peeking inside and washing it out for another day, but deep down you know that the shiny plastic veneer hides rotting insides. Finally, in a fit of filth-inspired adrenaline, you open it up, recoil with repulsion, then jettison the entire mass—container too— and drop the bag down the chute. This is not only how people misman-age meatloaf, it's how they bungle love.

EXPIRATION DATES

Souring is when good relationships go bad. Numerous warning signs (nit-picking, quarreling, idle bedsheets) must be ignored before a vibrant love sputters out of gas. When romantic ennui settles over a twosome like pollen on windowsills in springtime, the dynamic duo seems allergic to flirtation, dress-up dates, and sweet, sexy nothings whispered over chocolate mousse. Lingering malaise can fester into numbness and unshaven apathy, as vitali-ty is anaesthetized without a reinvigorating weekend of Tantric lovemaking.

Putting on a few pounds, watching too much TV, and spending late nights in chat rooms are symptoms of an expiring relationship.

Love is work, yet it shouldn't be backbreaking labor that mandates daily upsets, weekly fights, and constant counseling just to eke out a decent year. After exhausting a reasonable supply of *we-can-work-it-out* patience, consider a clean cut long before souring spoils any chance for an affable breakup. Show some stones and stamp out lame rationalizations (nonrefundable plane tickets for an extended trip together, the start of a new semester) that conveniently prolong a lukewarm coupling for a few more moons. Souring is Mother Nature's way of giving you one last chance to split gracefully. If you survive the flagging joy, fight off the sexless months, and maneuver through a forest of near-miss flings, the reward is long-term mediocrity. Once you declare yourself the type who is content with half-assed passion and rickety mates, it's no big jump to a so-so career, pot belly, and regular tryst with the ladies' bowling league runner-up.

It's easy to slide into a personal slump as the relationship tumbles. Before misdiagnosing your depressed funk as genetic disposition, see if a stagnant romance isn't to blame. When in denial, souring is easier to bear than the heartache of untangling shared belongings, beloved pets, and mutual friends. Besides, no one wants to believe they've wasted the last five years on a doomed twosome. Thus, sign off from a good thing before it drags ad nauseam like *Police Academy* parts IV–VII or even the inimitable Bubba "Hightower" Smith won't be able to strong-arm soured lovers back together.

BREAKING POINT

In a common souring scenario, an optimist courts a diamond in the rough, but the jackpot never comes. Paycheck-to-paycheck living might have been acceptable fresh out of college, but eventually, the surging partner tires of supporting a stagnant mate jogging in place. One does yoga religiously, while the other is a sloth; one ponders crystal wands, while the other maunders on crystal meth. As the epoxy of love loosens, financial, wellness, and spiritual disparities can augur a final breakup.

With so many shared arteries, separation surgery is daunting. When the perks of a rent-controlled, prewar apartment hang in the balance, nothing short of a jarring bonk like infidelity or an act of God hastens a final divide. Often, it takes getting turned on elsewhere to realize how much you've been turned off at home; similarly, a new job offer in a foreign land can expose fault lines and provide a handy sayonara. Akin to finally parting with your banged-up '87 Cressida and its cracked flywheel, the souring becomes clear when you realize that getting a new love is less costly than fixing the old one.

ENDGAME

There comes a season in every soured romance when you know the end is near. For Cubs fans, it's called September; for curdled lovers, it's when good-heartedness succumbs to decisiveness. Be the pioneer that initiates the endgame, not the pushover who's afraid of confrontation, content to play for a draw. There is no victory in sensing the sour first, but there is wisdom in sparing both souls the life-sucking pain of further erosion. Once identified, sign the DNR-release forms and pull the plug on a comatose relationship that's been on life support for too long.

RUNNING THE OBIT

In the fat part of upset, you have no responsibility to tell anyone. Private processing time relieves you from reliving the hurtful tale as each friend asks what happened. Yet, once you've moved out, a timely "just-soured" news flash, akin to the joyous "I'm engaged" call, is a headline that shouldn't be buried on page 10. A relationship obituary brings pals into the loop, eliminating any unexpected calls to your former address that begin and end with the curt reply, "He doesn't live here anymore." Huddle with close allies and deputize a few mouthpieces to spread the AP summary of the tumult; the details can trickle out in time. If necessary, a group email can eventually unfurl the backstory to satisfy (and shock) the masses.

After cohabitation or marriage, the tangle of mutual friends is messy. The truth is polyhedral, so it's best to tell your side before six alternative versions paint you as the wretched villain. Delay and risk the victim's smear campaign that seeks to puncture your reputation with a wild triad of allegations: appalling insensitivity, prodigious duplicity, and erectile dysfunction.

When asked to take a side in someone else's soured break, prove long-standing loyalty and observe a temporary communication blackout

♥ ◆ ♥ ◆ ♥ **FIREMAN'S SOUR** ♥ ◆ ♥ ◆ ♥

♥ ◆ ♥ ◆ ♥ **Silver rum** ♥ **Grenadine** ♥ **Juice of one lime** ♥ ◆ ♥ ◆ ♥
♥ ◆ ♥ **Powdered sugar** ♥ **Spritz of soda** ♥ **Garnish with cherry** ♥ ◆ ♥

with your friend's ex until emotions settle. Sticking in your altruistic nose to mediate the fray is inflammatory, doubly so for single friends who should never be the cuddly shoulder an injured party leans on, and trebly when the spirit of litigious rancor is in the air.

RENAISSANCE

After conducting a relationship autopsy and tox screen to pinpoint the cause of death (and which complications were brought on by your hang-ups as a lover), it's time to reinvent yourself. Update courtship manners and get your body off cinder blocks and into running shape, perhaps during a purifying stint of celibacy. If you are facing an empty bed for the first time in years, expect aftershocks and tears of regret, especially on glum afternoons or solitary holiday weekends. However, grief gives way to a renewed spirit when you rechannel the energy you used to invest in fixing, fighting, and brooding. After shedding the old skin, don't be surprised when dormant pastimes and compromised beliefs, once taboo under the previous regime, reemerge, along with an uncontrollable wanderlust to visit Spain, run with the bulls, and wash away tart memories in a fountain of sangria and señoritas.

SUPERNOVAE

*[S]he had a sulky look to her, and her lips stuck out in a way
that made me want to mash them in for her.*

—JAMES M. CAIN, *THE POSTMAN ALWAYS RINGS TWICE*, 1934

Some relationships collapse like deflating balloons; others detonate into supernovae. In the cosmological phenomenon, the core of a star collapses, thrusting a cosmic wave of interstellar energy into space. In the relationship equivalent, star-crossed unions are built around radiating hearts that are one donnybrook away from a nuclear meltdown. Ungoverned passion culminates in too many hard drugs, squad cars, crashes, evictions, and tearful reconciliations. Unlike the stalling motor of a soured love, a supernova spins so fast that the wings fly off and the love snaps in two. Last week it was a black eye; this week you roam the streets all night, too hyped for sleep. For the dizzying highs, follow the example of F. Scott Fitzgerald and find your codependent Zelda, but beware the inevitable crack-up. This colorful spectacle is exhilarating, but eventually the fallout is unmanageable. Supernova couplings often end not with an emotional hug by the fire but in waiting rooms, psych wards, or on the dotted line of a restraining order.

THE RED HOUSE

In the clink, five "alternative" diets are typically offered besides the common gruel: kosher, halal, vegetarian, a medical soft diet, and a liquid diet. Yet, when tin-plate rations can't satisfy the most primal hunger pang, it's time to requisition a conjugal visit. When the we-cycle is on decline for a long period (say, three to five in the state pen), air kisses and synchronous palm touches against the Plexiglas partition are a poor substitute for real intimacy. Forget bunkmate Chester and step away from the barbells—there's a red house over yonder, and that's where your baby stays. Strip-search your partner as desired; a burly guard will return the favor when you head back to C-block.

Conjugal visits were cinematically immortalized in the 1989 Stallone classic *Lock Up* (aka Rocky goes to prison), where our protagonist is granted weekend sex furloughs with his pouty B-movie blonde whose other Oscar-snubbed role was in *Darkman III*. In reality, it all started in 1918, when the Mississippi State Penitentiary unveiled an intrepid program for inmates. Warden and plantation manager James Parchman allowed prostitutes to freely roam the prison camps on Sundays, exclusively for the pleasure of black inmates. The "enlightened" policy makers presumed that by sating promiscuity, more cotton would be picked during the week. White inmates, perceived as having greater libido control, were not granted conjugal visitation privileges until the 1940s. By the time of the Reagan administration, women were also eligible for trips to the "red house."

These days, instead of a painted red lean-to, tonk houses provide detached cottages with kitchenettes, living space, and room for a family meal with refreshments so you don't have to ferment your own batch of "pruno" brew in the toilet. The Department of Corrections promotes conjugal visits to maintain family units and encourage rehabilitation, thereby lowering recidivism rates. More than sex, conjugal rights refer to those acts that define marriage and hold the union together: confiding, sympathizing, minding children, and sharing a home. Some institutions even provide sundries for lovin': soap, condoms, tissues, sheets, and even a small fenced-in yard for barbecues and a modicum of privacy.

WARDEN

♥ ◆ ♥ ◆ ♥ ◆ ♥ ◆ ♥ **Gin** ♥ **Pastis** ♥ **Dry vermouth** ♥ ◆ ♥ ◆ ♥ ◆ ♥ ◆ ♥

THE SEXY SIX

Horny would-be criminals should limit their felonies to jurisdictions with liberal visitation policies. If you must get sent down the river, book your passage to one of these six states with a "bone yard": California, Connecticut, Mississippi, New Mexico, New York, and Washington. In particular, the western three have red-house policies nearly worth the plea bargain.

California. Apartment-type settings are available for up to forty-three hours. Families may review menus and purchase provisions from the institution. Despite Governor Schwarzenegger's food and wine appreciation, foie gras and Napa Cabs are still verboten except for last meals.

New Mexico. In the Land of Enchantment, those within twenty-four years of discharge or parole eligibility are granted visitation every eighty days (forty-five for minimum security). The jail provides no-frills cooking, refrigeration, and bedding facilities; chocolate-covered strawberries and Isaac Hayes's erection-inducing LP *Chocolate Chip* must be supplied by the couple.

Washington. Offenders who qualify can visit the red house every thirty days, hence the state's Chinook motto, "Al-ki," meaning "hope for the future." Apparently, naked is okay once the warden approves, but a stringent dress code keeps visitors from teasing hard-luck–and-horny prisoners who lack a marriage certificate: no cleavage, cutoffs, thongs, bralessness, or skirts more than three inches above the knee.

ETHIC OF INFIDELITY

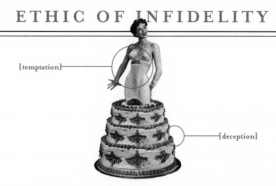

[temptation]

[deception]

The scent of sin blows in long before the foreplay begins. Proving an affair in divorce court might require racy pictorial evidence, but the court of monogamy maintains a more liberal interpretation. For some, a mere soupçon of flirtation directed the wrong way is considered cheating; for others, only skin-on-skin sexual relations cross "the line."

The line is a self-appointed boundary of behavior, the maximum tolerances of one's code of faithfulness. You know where your line is, and during courtship, you'll discover what your partner will comfortably permit. Though each mate ultimately draws his or her own line in the sand, hopefully it's on the same dune. Out of respect, a wild mate rounds down and adjusts behavior in the direction of the more conservative partner's tolerances.

When out together, you're both on your best behavior. It's easy to know which acts stir up hurtful or jealous feelings; all you have to do is read the disapproving sneer and frigid body language. In an ideal world, both partners would observe the same restrictions when out alone. In reality, however, partners gravitate toward their own line when no one's watching. Trouble follows when these two lines differ dramatically, and there's no mate around to police the other.

What's a flirtatious, fun-loving, yet loyal modern lover to do? Fidelity is a self-governed freedom of choice, not a sentence of house arrest. The goal is to maintain independence and come home from carousing with a clean conscience to a mate that trusts your judgment. Hitting the town alone is like a friendly golf game: no one but you is counting your extra strokes out of the trap or recording those lost balls in the woods. Lesser gents use a veneer of daytime respectability to conceal the nocturnal liberties they are stealing behind an unsuspecting lover's back. These repeat offenders with itchy ring fingers ought to flip through the wedding album and renew resolve instead of exploiting loopholes in the household rule book. Advanced monogamists, on the other hand, have an internal guidance system that obviates the need for a tablet of commandments codifying each forbidden sin.

THE LEASH

Certain players parade around the line, embracing the thrill of possibility without seriously entertaining an affair, while dutiful blokes keep three steps back from the electric fence of temptation. A proven history of unsupervised flirting sans incident reinforces the faithful but active man's self-governing ability, engendering trust with his mate. Sometimes, such spirit-of-the-law adherents can even report salty adventures above the tan lines without fear of flare-up. However, bad boys and repeat offenders compel justifiably leery mates to employ a short leash to keep their partner's behavior within the household line. With a short leash, you're guilty until proven innocent, and beepers, blacklisted friends and places, spending limits, and curfews are all employed to curb violations.

Sweethearts who unjustifiably afford each other no wiggle room display a distrust and possessiveness that call the relationship's soundness into question. Like a rebellious teen with a 10:00 P.M. weekend curfew, a tethered mate becomes more concerned with bucking authority than being loyal. Moreover, a shortened leash enforces limits without promoting the overriding virtues of self-control. No matter how short the leash, on occasion the subdued man finds himself with a lengthy stretch of rope when his partner is away for the weekend. Without on-site punitive measures to keep him honest, the liberated mutt typically experiences an onrush of inner demons: uphold the commitment or binge at the strip bar?

A long leash offers more opportunities for trouble, yet it builds a solid foundation of respect within a relationship that ultimately subdues temptation. Without mandatory protocol or a full-time chaperone, you are given slack not available to the unproven partner. Check-ins are to say "I love you," not to report exact longitudinal position, and you enjoy wider berth with provocative friends because of your reputation as a steely mate resistant to juicy propositions. In the end, long leashes allow each partner to embrace sociality and field-test long-term prospects by weighing fidelity against lesser but ever-present temptations.

DOUBLE STANDARD

Are you grossly indulgent with your own liberties while mandating an abstemious social life for your mate? Human nature and possessiveness dictate that there's a difference between where you set the line for yourself and the standards you expect a partner to uphold. When the gap approaches the hypocritical, this is known as the Double Standard. One effective method of self-policing is to picture a mate in your most compromising position and ask yourself, "How would I like someone's lips on *her* neck?"

BENCHING YOURSELF

Look at the word *libido: id* is a solid third of it. In fact, ensconced among the letters are *li(e)* and *do,* with a strong showing of *bi.* A jumbled *libido* is appropriately an *id boil* that conjures the steaminess of affairs and the blanching of monogamy. In any case, an unchecked libido spells trouble.

Certain party hounds with soft spots for dark strangers simply can't be trusted, and they know it. Those at risk should steer clear of captivating dens of vice, especially when trouble is afoot (emails get too suggestive, dancing gets too close, or cell phones vibrate too late). To gauge whether you should grab some pine, assume the whole evening is on closed-circuit television the next time you're out canoodling in mixed company. Before heating popcorn and inviting your honey to view the game film, how much editing would be necessary? A few saucy bits may hit the cutting room floor, but spouseless carousing shouldn't be a shadow world of Nixonian splices and lost tape.

SIX DANGER ZONES OF INFIDELITY

The convergence of vulnerable moments, hormones, venues, and intoxication can land even the truest mates in sticky spots. Below are the six zones where extra vigilance is required to squash mischievous possibilities, followed by six aggravating factors that empower the devil on your shoulder. In police parlance, ex-lovers present the strongest motive to cheat; the fever, the best means; business trips, the finest opportunity; and her temptress friends, the most serious offense.

🛑 **HER TEMPTRESS FRIENDS.** She would be an enviable mate if you weren't already taken. You've heard her secrets and she knows enough of yours, and by default, the infrastructure of opportunity is in place: her cell phone number is programmed, close dancing and public affection are sanctioned, and you have a track record of heart-to-hearts. When the dynamic soars during a group getaway by the shore, it is easy for you to confuse magnetic connections and an innocuous tanning oil rubdown for desire. On the other side, beware of friends displacing romantic notions onto your safe lap after a breakup. Ensure that the shoulder they're crying on doesn't become the chest they're nuzzling.

One of the privileges of monogamy is the backstage pass into the female inner sanctum. Once inside, however, a stalwart gent doesn't dissolve into a horny delinquent sneaking peeks and pushing innuendo. There is a vast difference between courteously zipping up a gown and getting tented by wanton leers up her skirt. Only the stupid, lustful, and greedy will abuse this intimacy with beady eyes and busy hands. Getting nabbed with this illicit cargo is the death knell; rarely can a duo recover when the crime is an inside job. Lipstick smudges on your collar from a barfly in Denver? You might survive. A brief affair with your darling's childhood friend, with whom she's shared Easy-Bake Oven recipes, denim minis, and shoplifting confessions? It's over.

🛑 **CO-WORKERS.** Commuters spend more waking hours with their "second family" in the office than awake around the house. This insular environment contains built-in excuses to account for lost time, encouraging a false belief that playing loosey-goosey with your undersecretary is untraceable. The workplace teams you with kindred souls who share career aspirations (or disenchantment). When deadline frenzy leads to overtime in close quarters, creative energy can unknowingly morph into conference table passion or happy hour advances. Moreover, following a day of tittle-tattle around the color copier, you're less inclined to discuss workaday politics with your sweetie, reinforcing a church-and-state-like separation that widens with every fiscal year.

🛑 EXES. Even if all your exes live in Texas, slipping back into that old comfortable slipper is dangerously appealing, and cheating nearly feels legally grandfathered as a non-sin since no new strangers are involved. After three days of slammed doors and locked horns at home, the rosy picture of an ex looks appetizing compared to the ups and downs of monogamy.

Unlike an unstable co-worker who might threaten to dial your home phone (or tell your boss), a predictable ex bypasses the headaches of a wild-card mistress, especially if you've conspired with this accomplice before. An unusually complicit ex squelches your pangs of guilt by distracting you with freewheeling sexuality and dismissing infidelities as mere trifles. However, familiar trysts risk triple the heartache when whispers of getting back together turn one lonely encounter into an uncontrollable wildfire fueled by renewed emotions.

🛑 BUSINESS TRIPS. Pretzeled inside a janitor's closet of a far-away convention hall, two traveling sales reps ignore the droning seminar and their vows. Without framed family photos keeping a gent honest, distant locales are cheaters' havens that tempt even upstanding mates with the prospect of a squeaky-clean getaway. Upon entering another time zone, you jettison routine and responsibility, and bachelorhood instincts reawaken in the mise-en-scène of foreign beds, pay-per-view movies, and freedom of opportunity. It's the perfect crime: the combined buffer of anonymity and geography leaves no residue or memory cues. Just pray a vacationing neighbor doesn't spy you holding your lead pipe in the hotel lounge with the leggy Mrs. White atop your briefcase.

🛑 **LA FIÈVRE.** This fugue-like state is a cagey feeling of insatiability erected on the throbbing bass beat of raw energy sourced from the intensity of elation or depression. Anger is another discharge of energy and can be a turn-on; a desire for anonymous sex is not too far away. The Fever is no ordinary booze-induced, Friday high where frosty mugs and warm-weather flirtation bubble into risky territory. Impervious to the drag of alcohol or fatigue, you step outside yourself and reemerge a one-man vigilante of vice. With quick acceleration that blinds you to consequences, you're launched into an extended interlude of irreverence, and getting caught is immaterial. In fact, a fevered encounter can happen with your unsuspecting other half in the next room.

This feral dissolution of your superego is an open bazaar of sin—speeding cars, substances, kink, and exotic cohorts—swathed in the febrile flaunting of law and ethics. Craving action over sleep, you harbor ravenous wanting despite the peril, and your activated X-ray vice vision instantly pinpoints uninhibited souls under the same feverish spell. A smoky bar isn't the only venue, as even a late-night visit to the supermarket turns bawdy when a saucy glance down the dairy aisle lands you and a blonde shopper in the stockroom, pants around the ankles.

Other than an interloper or act of God, there is little defense once fever pitch strikes. The best security is a chaperone to splash you with cold-water reality before you've recklessly bounded over the line. At the onset of symptoms, summon a late-night confidante for bar-side assistance to jump-start stalled sensibilities (or shuttle you back home). Like an unpollinated flower, the fever withers if left unconsummated, far from the nectar of stimuli.

🛑 CYBERLUST. When hours tallied in adult chat rooms outnumber paltry minutes invested in the bedroom, you're bleeding intimacy out the cable modem. Moderate fantasy expression and online experimentation shouldn't be punished, but nightly downloading quests and IMed orgasms are spineless infidelities. Fetish forums and traded jpegs are a safe way to field-test untried kink (even if you never intend to get biblical with borzois). Although, trouble starts when fantasy excess leads to impossibly advanced and degrading sexual expectations that are at odds with your tender union. Your dick never leaves the desk chair, but your lover's heart is still bruised when the lusty litter of adult memberships and naked webcams upstage daily attention.

AGGRAVATING CIRCUMSTANCES

Intense moods and gnawing dissatisfaction leave you more susceptible to the eye candy of temptation. When aggravating circumstances meet an infidelity danger zone, the odds are stacked in the louse's favor. Like procreation and Chernobyl, there are certain perilous combinations,

such as an out-of-town trip with a toothsome, free-loving co-worker
after a three-month drought of home-brewed sensuality.

♥ **Dissatisfaction:** On its own, ordinary horniness is no excuse for
straying; by age thirty, you should no longer have trouble keeping it
in your khakis. Yet, a stone-cold mattress, while not a short-term
trigger of infidelity, presents a long-term threat. Just as your unful-
filled partner is more likely to fall into an organized affair with a
comely ex than to jump the butcher's mortadella in the heat of the
Fever, in this case your likeliest candidates for infidelity lurk nearby.

♦ **Midday Idleness:** The late afternoon sun heats the pavement and,
with it, your libido. After you arrive home early from work, daydreams flit about your head amid pre—rush hour quietness. With
everyone else still in their office cubicle, the only prospects for mischief are the sparse suburban population of adventurous freelancers
and longing housewives. The porno portal widens: you're one
breathy phone call or neighborly cup of borrowed sugar away from
slaking a fantastical itch. Luckily, the mood subsides with the onset of
twilight, a round of chores, or a clarifying jog in the park.

=========================| **TEMPTOR** |=========================

♥ ♦ ♥ ♦ ♥ ♦ ♥ ♦ ♥ **Port wine** ♥ **Apricot brandy** ♥ ♦ ♥ ♦ ♥ ♦ ♥ ♦ ♥

♥ **Stimulants**: Substances are social lubricants that blur the line of sound judgment. If you've decided to do a line Saturday afternoon, then crossing the line Saturday night is less of a leap. Drugs bring you in contact with a let-loose crowd of eight ball–bearing ravers who have deposited temperance in escrow for the evening.

♦ **Bacheloritis**: Moving in together or getting hitched dials up intimacy but nips at autonomy. In the monogamous aftermath, independent spontaneity wanes, stirring a yen for solo carousing and bachelor-era debauchery. Acute bacheloritis is the uncontrollable craving to forsake the rules for just one more night of condom-forsaking, devil-may-care indulgence. Not necessarily looking for a screw, you hanker for freedom from check-ins, curfews, and curbed flirtation.

♥ **License to Ill**: The we-cycle is far out of whack. One partner is laden with career setbacks or family turmoil, while the other swims in good fortune and shoulders the burden for two. After a dreary fun-free fiscal quarter of imbalance, the surging party contracts a false sense of entitlement to a guilt-free dalliance.

♦ **Nostalgia**: Like the tiny thermal exhaust port of the *Death Star*, everyone has a weak point that could unleash a ruinous chain reaction. The frisson of running into a long-lost friend or roomie charges the skin and weakens your previously impenetrable virtue from the very first hug. You hadn't planned to stray, but this alluring nymph that got away sparks a turn to the dark side. Despite your well-guarded loyalty, these bewitching storm troopers carry a key that will be your undoing.

PHINEAS'S PHLAMES & TESAURO'S TRYSTS

A breadth of experience provides the romantic bedrock for later relationships, whereas a repeat of the same old safe couplings is like soft quicksand, leaving you little firm ground on which to manage more demanding loves in the future. The emotional highs and amorous dead ends of schoolboy crushes and chemistry-gone-wild are carnal rebar of a modern lover's foundation.

Some amour is worthy of a plaque and a private suite of memories in your pleasure-sensing lateral hypothalamus, but others weren't such shining interludes. Plot a love continuum and look hard into your loveliest Lucky 7. Where are the big jumps and the ill-advised backtracks, and how has upset or selfishness glossed into wisdom and compassion? After plotting your triumphs and tumbles on paper, you can resume repressing the regrets about losing Jeanine, the lovable nymph who caught you in bed with Katy, the flaxen goddess who still stirs up a loin storm years later.

PHINEAS'S PHLAMES

PUPPY LOVE	The all-day giggly of a teenage crush. You are smitten by the newness and the everlasting PG-rated phone calls.
#1 SPECIAL	The first serious love that is the crash course for coping skills, experimentation, and the first taste of monogamous stability and jealousy. At once glorious, yet bound for failure, it eventually cracks despite several reprises.
CASTING CALL	The mid-twenties overly confident serial dating imperative. With a few exes under your belt and a burgeoning career, you judge prospects against an impossibly perfect literary/Hollywood fantasy of being swept off your feet (not surprisingly, most cannot meet these exacting criteria). Potentially great relationships are tossed due to small quirks (stuffed animal jamboree, disliked the cat).
COMBUS-TION	This irresistible "interlewd" of mind-blowing sex and volatility lures you to the flame. From the ancient days of Jason and Medea to Jimmy Stewart's Scotty Ferguson in *Vertigo*, men have been helplessly drawn to the foolhardy pursuit of crazy, unstable ladies.
INTERSTATE COMMERCE	A long-distance love that hones the cerebral and verbal spheres since the physical benefits are sensational but rare treats.
THE ONE THAT GOT AWAY	This pinnacle soulmate connection couldn't overcome dastardly, practical obstacles (geography, timing, age difference). It's perfect poetry on paper, but alas, it can never be. This love burns eternally for both parties, settling at a low simmer, with occasional flare-ups during nostalgic moods.
VIXEN	The gorgeous, out-of-your-league surprise that affirms long-held thoughts that a hip personality and Italian shoes eventually win over high-minded beauties nearing their thirties who are finished with their bad-boy phase.

TESAURO'S TRYSTS

CATEGORY	
F-4 TORNADO	A blitzkrieg of passion leaves hearts splintered worse than a trailer park in twister season. Whether a tempest of three years or three weeks, little remains in the wake besides bite marks, therapy bills, and thongs strewn at the bottom of your closet.
BATTERED ANGEL	Fragile, innocent souls are no match for a bachelor's steamrolling selfishness. Before a clumsy gent learns sensitivity and compassion, delicate lovers are squeezed to death like Lennie's puppy and Curley's wife in *Of Mice and Men.*
GROUPIE	She loved you so much, you had to give her a try. Without mutual chemistry, however, this one-sided affair left your former number-one fan ashen and alone in the bitter cold fire pit of rejection.
SUGAR MAMA	During your dark ages, an unconditionally loving, open-pocketed demi-love bails you out of hock. All you give in return are the scraps of your heart . . . and no interest. Your credit score might improve, but so do your chances of ending up in hell.
OPEN TRIANGLE	For six remarkable months, you successfully manage two distinct romances with full disclosure. Unfortunately, like an alien abduction story, even if it actually happened, no one really believes you.
PLATONIC	You never screwed it up by screwing, though you considered sleepwalking across the hall on many occasions. Without the messy detour into a physical relationship, you learn accountability, respect, communication, and how to be a swell roommate.
PATIENT SAGE	You resist and resist, but this true love is patient. In her divine perspicacity, she knows you'll wise up when Cupid's arrow strikes pay dirt and a low cost, fixed-rate mortgage. Take heed—after stops and starts and at least one trial separation, you might wake up driving a minivan and thanking your lucky stars.

CODA

After all the lessons, lost loves, and hot flings, now what?

The one that stays, the marital love. It may start out giggly, but it develops a professional sheen; the sex begins steamy, plateaus at stirring, and then slowly gains staying power as trust and intimacy foster deeper explorations that compensate for lost novelty. The benchmark relationships of your early days are quintessential fertilizer that make this plot grow plush, ensuring that the ruinous mistakes of the past aren't repeated. Instead of visible fireworks, the ideal partner draws you in with traits beyond cup size and keeps you enraptured by enabling freedoms and spurring your gray-haired goals. A great beloved that got away may be a smoldering candle in the corner of your mind, yet it illuminates the reality that lifelong partnerships aren't solely about love but the grounding practicalities of compatibility and integrity beyond the temporary highs of ecstasy and orgasm.

The
TRANSITIONAL
MAN

Chapter Four

THE ONE

♦ ♥ ♦ ♥ ♦ ♥ ♦ ♥

COMPATIBILITY

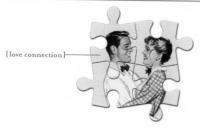

[love connection]

If you could cruise into the Pick-a-Mate-for-Life drive-thru, what would you order? Would "DD with cheese" or "flame-broiled PhD" be the first words out of your mouth? To some gents, surgically enhanced sex kittens top the list, leaving a worrisome second act of divorce when the skin wrinkles and the libido subsides; a few seek a fellow brainiac with a lifelong helping of sass. Still others hunt for someone who tolerates their bad habits and nonsense, a coconspirator for a long, smooth ride into the Medicare sunset. A smaller number of melodic hearts with perfect pitch hunt for the true clincher: a sharp mate who coughs in F major, swoons to the fourth movement of Sibelius's Second Symphony, and can whistle "(Sittin' on) The Dock of the Bay" on key.

Before long-term futures are contemplated, an inexperienced suitor might find succor in the saddle with a one-trick pony. Instead of running a complete compatibility battery, this beginner settles for satisfaction with only the cosmetic attributes, lauding sex appeal over character. For example, that summertime sweetie Bridgette, who owns a Harley and two helmets, is also dim as a refrigerator bulb, and his Sunday school crush Christina, looked wonderfully penitent kneeling in the moonlight, but was more high-maintenance than the International Space Station. Eventually, he institutes wiser standards and overcomes such hedonistic tunnel vision. Thereafter, despite fetching curves, darlings with Greek tragedy—caliber flaws that would turn Sophocles' head are quickly deemed incompatible, often after the second kiss but before the third date.

COMPATIBILITY FORECAST

Until Love Potion No. 9 is perfected and marketed, a flood of pheromones and a good aftershave tonic are your only chemical weapons in the game of love. Once courtship has advanced beyond innocent smooches into tough reckoning over long-term compatibility, however, the modern lover can employ a device of another sort to confirm his intuition that a current mate is the One. More accurate than a Ouija board and less expensive than a pilgrimage to the Oracle at Delphi, our Compatibility Forecast is an empirical method for gauging relationship simpatico. First, narrow down the list of twelve attributes by choosing the one you consider most important from each of the four groups, then pick an extra from the field to round out your top five. For example, under Group IV, if you deem sexual performance more appealing than supermodel looks or edgy pleasures, sexuality would qualify for your top five. Next, using the five-point scales, rate your mate (or mates, for Utah polygamists) and then yourself; for most accurate results, have someone else plot your own scores. Our scoring analysis follows.

GROUP I: DAILY MIEN

MANNERS ✓

Polished & Attentive   vs.   Boorish & Inconsiderate

Skilled hostess with introductions at the ready or a flailing cocktailer with no name recall? Underlying personality is either a foundation of etiquette or a core of thoughtlessness manifest in near-empty milk carton orphans in the fridge and an unappealing crudeness. Unfortunately for dawdling dish-soakers and the perpetually tardy, punctuality and house chores are important to household sanity. Besides overall grace, how tolerant are you of personal foibles such as soup slurping and turbulent driving? Overflowing profanity can be endearing at the ball game, but will it and other peccadilloes be bearable until the silver anniversary?

SELF-RELIANCE

Savvy & Do-It-Yourself   vs.   Hapless & Delegating

Proficient with the power saw and socket wrench or ready with the yellow pages? Takes initiative or waits for instruction? Needed or needy? Some lovers want a fellow carpenter and kitchen confederate, as handy with the whisk as the circular saw. Are you craving an independent feline sweetheart or a naïve puppy who can't read a map?

EXPRESSION

Edgy & Creative   vs.   Buttoned Up & Unimaginative

If physique is Mother Nature's gift, this continuum measures how one works it through hip duds, artistic nature, and cosmopolitan attitude. Mod and dolled up or hand-me-downs behind the trends? At home in downtown cafés or content to traipse the mall food court? Would you prefer a long-term love bearing a splattered easel or a phony gallery goer who just guzzles free wine and then leaves? Do you envision a home adorned with eclectic art and furnishings or a color-by-numbers, Rooms-To-Go scheme found in a thousand other dens?

GROUP II: CHARACTER

CULTURAL LITERACY

Discerning Mind & Worldly   vs.   Half-Hearted Intellect & Simple

What's upstairs: poetic and cinematic appetites, fiction aptitude, travel experience, and political awareness? Is a sassy bluestocking versed in the classics a necessity, or is a B-movie babe with fewer literary interests more enticing? Regarding conversational rigor, do you favor an excitable, colorful talker; a measured, soft-spoken presence; a chatterbox, *like*, plagued with Valley Girl–isms; or a gossiping yenta who stops yakking only to breathe? As for an invaluable sense of humor, if you have a big nose, you better have a funny mouth.

INTEGRITY

Honest & High-Minded   vs.   Unethical & Undisciplined

Some traits can change within a year—finances, style, maturity—but integrity is the cornerstone of character. Are you bedding a snake-in-the-grass with unscrupulous business practices who is given to double-dealing and secret-spilling? Or the waffling chameleon whose opinions vacillate according to the listener? Ideally, the modern lover hits the jackpot with a straight shooter who cares enough to suffer the occasional moral dilemma.

SPIRITUALITY

Yoga Mat & Freethinking   vs.   Scripture & Fundamentalistic

Do you favor a pious sort who knows which way to Mecca or a devout agnostic on the slick, paved road to purgatory? Downward-Facing Dog or kneeling at the Blessed Sacrament? With family fortunes, surnames, and baptismal rites at stake, if Spirituality is on your hit list, make sure both parties' beliefs jibe, lest a wedding be scuttled in the eleventh hour on account of irreconcilable religious differences.

GROUP III: HUMOUR

MENTAL HEALTH

Stable & Well-Adjusted   vs.   Mercurial & Uncontrollable

Reasonable moods and reliable decision-making or radioactive passions and ever-changing conditions? Grounded and sensible or a raving basket case? Committed to monthly therapy sessions with plush Central Park view or committed yearly in a padded room at Bellevue? Hopefully, your companion has no more than a valise of guilt and a fanny pack of melodrama that would otherwise block the Aisle.

TEMPERAMENT

Mellow & Patient   vs.   Histrionic & Choleric

Do you like to live on a fault line of raised voices and quarreling tremors or in harmonious pastures? What is the ratio of consoling hugs to hurled dishware on a monthly basis? Some lads love the hot-blooded, snapping tongue of a fishwife, while others choose an even-tempered vibe over short fuses and theatrics.

ADVENTUROUSNESS ✓

Outrageous & Provocative   vs.   Predictable & Reserved

Is everything yes until proven no, or do all daring acts require prior clearance and a signed permission slip? Master of public spectacles and skinny-dipping tomfoolery or the risk-averse lover content to dine at the same three restaurants? Whereas reserved sorts shy away from spontaneity, adventurous types crave action and seek out a willing sidekick.

GROUP IV: SKIN & SIN

SEXUALITY

Experienced & Kinky   vs.   *Virginal & Vanilla*

A carnal angler with more sex partners than lures or a career monogamist with nary a one-night stand? A mature lover well versed in sheets shenanigans and fetish play must be gentle with a chary newbie who missed the bus to experimentation during and after college.

PHYSIQUE

Centerfold & Healthy   vs.   *Homely & Sedentary*

Appearance and wellness, involving guts, busts, and vitamins. Burns calories on the treadmill daily or burrows to the greasy bottom of a bag of chips nightly? Despite the risk of cavities, are you looking for a sweet bite of arm candy or content with a marshmallow softie whose subtler sex appeal doesn't necessarily fit in a slinky cocktail dress?

VICE

Hedonistic & Rule Bending   vs.   *Teetotaling & By the Book*

What sets off your mate's dopamine pleasure centers? Will it be alcohol and spirits or stronger; bookies and OTB, or more sedate vices like gardening and Bakelite figurine collecting? Around-the-campfire spliff roller or skittish, tattling narc? Whether or not your mate participates, know whether to expect solidarity or major riffs concerning your preferred vice.

0 = CLONE	You've found your long-lost twin, but are you in love with Dolly the sheep?
1–5 = SOLID MATCH	You'll never run out of shared interests, though maintain what little contrast you have to avoid homogenization and routine.
6–10 = HEALTHY DISTINCTION	Outside the home base of common ground, there is plenty of unexplored territory to keep things fresh.
11–15 = OPPOSITES ATTRACT	Disparity makes for exciting conversation and impassioned debates that translate into bedroom sparks, but will the lively dynamic stretch across years?
16–20 = STRIKING POLARITY	What's holding this unlikely twosome together besides prepaid couples counseling?

The Scorers' Table (above). Calculate the difference between partners in each area. For instance, under Integrity, those with unswerving principles earn a 1, while larcenous liars rate a 5, scoring a difference of 4—while two equally felonious or ethical bedfellows garner identical scores, resulting in a difference of 0. Total these differences across the top five attributes and the sum is your Compatibility Forecast. What's the tally tell you?

Wild Card. Outside of your top five, there are intangibles, bonus traits that distinguish the One from the also-rans. Like turnovers and weather conditions in football, game-changing qualities such as courage, ambition, posture, pizzazz, sultriness, and intuition shouldn't be overlooked. Furthermore, a shared childhood geography can link you to familiar highways, dialects, and local delicacies. Sharing a streak of New York City neuroticism or Bay Area liberalism can enhance a connection. Of course, a singular, loving gaze—à la blue-eyed Paul Newman—also goes a long way.

BALLAST

A compatible partner bolsters your prevailing character just like a bottle of Burgundy elevates simple chicken and wine into coq au vin. Once you've calculated compatibility scores beyond mere bedroom thunderclaps, measure the long-ranging impact of a mate on your strong suits and shortcomings and then examine how it all ENTICES the couple. For "solid matches" and "clones," there's plenty of harmony, but how is compatibility being harnessed? Sameness should be a springboard to mutual development, not a stifling of individual accents—similar hobbies and habits should "improve" or "nudge" both partners, not just make video rental choices that much easier. As for opposites that attract, diverging traits should "temper" or "edify" lifestyles in the balanced equation of love. Vast differences that aren't constructive merely sow the seeds of discontentment.

How would you fill in the blank, "My mate [_____] me"?

▾ **E**dies: Instead of registering for night school classes, you tap into your mate's expertise. Besides learning how to merengue at night, enroll your lover as your private docent in museums and assimilate some art history without ever picking up a textbook.

◆ **N**udges: An inspiring partner spurs an underachieving sort out of the comfort zone and into realized goals. Rather than allowing half-finished novels to flounder on the hard drive, this prodding mate helps to edit your drivel and mail out manuscripts.

▾ **T**empers: A bombastic partner is softened by an even-keeled soul with the fortitude to rein in the other when the volume gets too loud.

◆ **I**mproves: Flighty mates require a grounded counterpart who imparts real life responsibilities without compromising childlike enthusiasm. Transcending a party persona, the thoughtless libertine is finally taught to clean the gutters, plan for retirement, and walk lovable Tawny, the Portuguese water dog.

♥ **C**ontrasts: The bookworm is rounded by an athletic spirit who insists on mixed doubles after library hours. Recreational contrasts and varied social circles expand the couple's leisure options.

◆ **E**xacerbates: Rather than showcasing one another's strengths, partners sometimes magnify mutual flaws. When two bargain hunters embark on a no-frills, penny-watching lifestyle, instead of sniffing out extra income and enjoying small pleasures, the couple degenerates into a stingy pair of scrooges.

♥ **S**tifles: One partner's boorishness flattens a creative flower. Sidelines deemed nonessential (orchids, oil paints, continuing education) are snubbed out.

SOUL KISS

◆ ♥ **Dubonnet** ♥ **Dry & sweet vermouth** ♥ **Orange juice** ♥ **Slice of orange** ♥ ◆

THE AMBITION CONDITION

Career ambition includes what you're hoping to gain from your job (money, mastery of a craft, and/or sense of fulfillment) and how hard you're willing to toil. Your lifestyle ambition reflects the kind of life you want to lead in terms of material goods and leisure time.

Ideally, your career ambitions are higher than your lifestyle ambitions; otherwise, you'll never be satisfied with what you have, and you'll never be willing to work nights and weekends to change it. If you have moderate ambitions, you'll wisely marry someone similarly inclined or face the nagging prospect that neither mate will bring home enough imported bacon to sate the household appetite. A gross imbalance of ambitions can lead to pining over the wishing well or, worse, give rise to a life of forged checks and white-collar crime. Financial tendencies are easily assessed during dating: if a Galileo five-star dining extravagance and Georgetown shopping spree are the keys to her lockbox, you'd better ask for a raise or take a few weekend shifts at the lumberyard. With high lifestyle ambitions, once the bank balance drops and the market tanks, the Jazz Age party is over, and then the relationship's true mettle is tested. Are love and affection enough once you're eating cold pizza and ground chuck for dinner?

Spendthrift or tightwad: which one best describes your way of life? What about your leading lover?

CA = Career Ambition, LA = Lifestyle Ambition

❑ HIGH CA + LOW LA = **Workaholics with a gargantuan nest egg and glut of vacation days; these sorts find sick days to be morally reprehensible. This is the realm of self-denying skimpers who smuggle their own Sanka into restaurants to save the buck and a quarter for decaf.**

❑ **LOW CA + HIGH LA** = Gold diggers or trust fund kids who want the best of everything handed over immediately to fuel their rock 'n' roll extravagance. Self-worth is tied to net worth, not to a life calling or hard-earned career.

❑ **MODERATE CA + HIGH LA** = Cosmopolitan twenty-somethings who eat sushi at least three times a week, sip single malts, and go trekking in Chile on borrowed vacation days.

❑ **HIGH CA + MODERATE LA** = A solid place to settle after you've balanced leisure and family with career goals. The perfect temperament to live a rich life with a milder degree of materialistic decadence.

❑ **LOW CA + LOW LA** = Guilty of asceticism in the first degree, these slackers hardly have money for lunch but always have enough scratch for a pack of smokes.

❑ **MODERATE CA + MODERATE LA** = Balanced personalities, with little savings, though no looming mountains of high-interest debt. When the holiday gift tree is fat, January rent gets a tad dicey, but when spending normalizes in spring, shopping for new summer duds is guilt-free.

❑ **HIGH CA + HIGH LA** = Corner-office-seeking, status-conscious, chained-to-the-desk power brokers likely found in NY, NY (or LA, CA). These juggernauts build empires and work harder for bigger yachts, faster wheels, and Malibu retreats, yet leave little time for kids until semiretirement at age seventy.

THE BRADY BUNCH FACTOR

[garage]

[manicured lawn]

[ranch-style home]

Winning the love of one is hard enough, but what about a party of two or three? The genial architect Mike Brady kept a poker face while seamlessly absorbing a new family, calling Mrs. Brady's bet with three boys of his own, then raising the stakes with a saucy live-in maid named Alice. For this lovely family, everything turned out groovy, but in reality, it's not that easy, especially for younger gents without a wealth of wisdom and sporty new station wagon. In the Brady Bunch scenario, partners must reconcile their love for each other with the fear that existing children will complicate the romance. Step-parenting is less daunting when both partners have street cred as mom/dad, but for childless gents auditioning a lady-plus-one as the One, there are multiple hearts and variables to consider. Brace yourself for commotion, exasperation, and uncertainty, even from well-behaved, complaisant tots cuter than a box of buttons.

The Brady Bunch factor is tricky: as much as you want it to work, it probably won't be the perfect fit like Cinderella's slipper, and it may well chafe into unsightly corns. Even if you're a balanced, understanding man (possibly a finer replacement than the biological dad), the children still might consider you second-best. What are you prepared to do about it? How will the dynamic affect your love relationship? Will you patiently adapt or instead reenact the role of Jerry Blake in the horror flick *Step-father*, about a complex man who'd rather hack his loved ones to pieces than face failures in child care?

FIRST & LASTING ENCOUNTERS

At the outset, most footloose gents are unaware of the bedlam they are walking into. Every time you get it on, you're one thin doorframe and two timid knocks away from prying eyes and untimely interruptions. The mattress feels alien when waking in your boxer shorts, she in her nightie, and suddenly, it's a frantic Sunday morning *Romper Room* free-for-all, with toddlers scampering about the boudoir clamoring for pancakes, hugs, and new animated DVDs. Moreover, for joint-custody arrangements, routine is elusive. Just when you've romantically bonded for three days, the kids come home, having unlearned last week's good behavior. Then, after a week of hide-and-go-seek, off again they go to dad's, where their pliable minds are once again shaken Etch-a-Sketch clean, and meanwhile you try to reheat the bedsprings before Monday.

Get involved with the kids early but don't expect immediate results. Before marriage is contemplated, it's all hellos and backyard barbecues, as wonderfully innocuous as flipping through a *Highlights* magazine in a pediatrician's waiting room. Initial bonds are formed with polite "What did you do in school today?" exchanges. The mood is chary; the footing, wobbly: the parent is proud of the kids, and you're wary of them, but any uneasiness isn't yet pressing. Infants and babies without halcyon memories of dad respond more naturally to an affectionate stepfather during this feeling-out period. On the other hand, when the kids are headstrong toddlers or latchkey teens, establishing the bond is more difficult. In attempting to connect with an older kid you may frolic like a sibling, but eventually the solemn proclamation comes: "They don't need a big brother, they need a father."

When an interim replaces a head coach midseason, the team's respect doesn't automatically transfer to the new boss—it must be earned over time, based on new breakthroughs and dynamics. Similarly, morphing into an instant stepfather cannot be done without adequate groundwork. Like winning a sweetheart's best friends over to your corner, lobby for the children's sincere affections, lest a veto from the playroom scuttle blossoming relations. The newly appointed stepfather will fail if he's more *au pair* than a parent (Enzo wants an algebra whiz; Ethan is lonely and needs a drinking buddy), or if he attempts to be a robotic replacement of the real father. Besides weekly visits to the park to teach the kids how to throw a perfect spiral, hitting it off also entails hashing out unpleasant issues and resolving ordeals together. Weathering a medical emergency, school crisis, or police matter will prove whether you are fair and understanding or a distant disciplinarian only interested in what's under mommy's nightgown. If your aim is true, the children will respect the authentic bonds of trust that you've built.

THE KAL-EL COMPLEX

Just like living in sin preludes a marriage, living *en masse* previews stepfather issues. Previously, the household was run on a fragile system of rotating babysitters and stretched work schedules. When you see that mom is alone and the children need stability, idealistic visions of swooping into the house like Superman stir your heart. Quick changing in a phone booth from carefree bachelor on weekend duty to full-time on-site proxy dad can be messy business, though. The supersavior role is hard to fill as you shoulder all the former household job openings. The first month brings out unbounded energy to impress—chauffeur, handyman, school-project diorama constructor—yet pace yourself or risk creating unreasonable expectations. Instead of overdoing it and feeling underappreciated, speak up and identify those household duties for which you can and cannot be accountable. Without compromise, your lost freedoms of hitting the corner pub or playing in the neighborhood softball league stir up acrimony. To help prevent frustration from souring the relationship, carve out blocks of guilt-free leisure time to ensure that important hobbies and overall sanity aren't lost in a sea of kindergarten pick-ups, doctor's appointments, and parent-teacher conferences over little Roberto's ADD.

STEP-BOTHER

After playing nice and making trips to toy stores to grease young palms, a familiar rapport develops. Notwithstanding your recent gains with the kids, their lingering resentment can ignite your reflexive response to resent them in return. Cries of "Who's in charge?" leave you scrambling to define a role. Beware, the bond of blood runs deeper than you think; when she's faced with an "It's either them or me" decision, you'll lose every time. Declare early on: "I'm not your father, but I have three things to offer: advice, resources, and friendship." No matter how benevolent, though, you may still face rebellion against sensible ideas and glimpse disapproving smirks when you nuzzle your sweetheart. Even your newfangled music choices will be pooh-poohed if nosy Lizzy catches you listening to college radio in the study while puffing clove cigs ("My real daddy listens to Bob Seger. He says those angst-ridden alternative bands are fruity. Are you fruity?").

Despite your good deeds, the immutable truth stands: the biological father is on a pedestal, and his name will be venerated, even if he's a rye-swilling, check-bouncing deadbeat. Pep talks, sit-downs, and other rallies meant to eliminate resentment won't wash. Most young children are egocentric and won't appreciate their stepdad's value until

well into adulthood. This petulance triples when the stepfather is
anointed king of the household. Assigning chores and nixing sleep-
overs pit you as the villain, especially when bedtimes, television, and
video games are concerned. During visitation, the biological father
garners all the laughs at the circus or pizza parlor; as the interloper,
you haven't a chance when you're haranguing them to eat Brussels
sprouts and clean their rooms.

WORRY LINES

Is someone with a checkered marital history and multiple children fated
for future relationship failure? Lurking thoughts of losing yet another
lover potentially fuel a self-fulfilling prophecy, especially when sighs of
insecurity spur the other mate to question the withering partner's wor-
thiness. The damsel with a nursery full of baggage—and few courageous
suitors—occasionally pinches her Lancelot and inquires, "Why do you
stay with me?" To some, this doelike attitude is a selling point suggest-
ing that devotion and fidelity won't waver. Others, however, worry about
damaged goods and drowning in the same quicksand that swallowed hubbies one and two.

FREEZE-DRIED FAMILY

Want to get away from the flightiness of youth? The Brady Bunch scenario can be attractive if you've been burned before by a failed young
love. A partner with children is much more accountable than a twenty-
something libertine. If you want to step beyond nightly carousing and
plant roots in the business community, then marrying into children
provides an instant source of stability. Plus, for older gents looking for
fatherhood but limited diaper duty, inheriting toddlers is like purchas-

ing a house-trained pooch, granting you dad privileges without having to endure the tumultuous early years.

Nevertheless, the Brady Bunch scenario isn't recommended as your first important relationship or live-in situation; it's like asking to test-drive a thirteen-speed tractor-trailer before mastering the automatic transmission of your rider mower. Before signing this contract, make sure all bachelor leanings are satisfied. With kids in the mix, you're anchored, and cashing out your stock options at thirty-one to jet-set the seven seas won't be an option. Career sabbaticals and transcontinental relocation clash with expensive ballet lessons and the legal constraints keeping the kids near their biological father. However, if you've already been up and down the ropes of modern love, then a settled woman with a C-section scar won't make you squeamish.

RINGLESS CAROUSERS

The long-term ringless relationship is a two-sided coin. On one hand, there's no question that the couple is held together by more than habit and a thin wisp of 14K gold. On the other, the IRS, the Pope, and many parents typically dismiss these "ringless carousers" as posers who haven't sealed their bond, at least at the drive-thru chapel. While marrieds tout the sacred institution, ringless carousers point to escalating divorce rates and skyrocketing catering costs. To RCs with messy divorces behind them, the marriage ceremony has justifiably lost luster. If two veterans already experienced their fantasy wedding with all the satin trimmings and caviar station, they might now pass on the pomp. The opposition argues, however, that an RC is not battle tested since wedding plans alone can expose an unstable relationship or certify one that withstands in-law housing issues and an eleventh-hour floral breakdown. This is one reason why marriages earn more public laud: they prove the couple survived a tough growing season without being overrun by weevils.

Whereas married couples live with two keepsakes (wedding album and marriage certificate), RCs live according to two tenets (free will and trust), by which their ringed counterparts may or may not abide. With exits unobstructed by lawyers and mothers-in-law, it's not legal or logistical impediments that keep lovers together. Rather, couples wordlessly reinforce mutual regard by coming home to the same bed night after night because they want to, not because they are contractually bound. Healthy marriages enjoy this same fundamental quality, but after breaking in the silky trousseau, there is indeed a license, a ceremony, and witnesses' signatures formalizing the boundaries of free will.

"For richer, for poorer, in sickness and in health" are public pronouncements of expected lifelong decency. Since RCs have no such formal guarantee, they must resort to the honor system, like actually paying the correct amount to a cup-shaking blind man for the daily paper. RCs self-govern, and as long as both parties agree on the ringless arrangement, the privilege won't be misused as an excuse for unreported mischief or line-crossing liberties. Trust is further cemented when key

===================| S A T U R N ' S   R I N G S |===================

♦ ♥ **Vodka** ♥ **Chambord** ♥ **Orange juice** ♥ **Cranberry juice** ♥ **Splash soda** ♥ ♦

future issues like children are resolved. While pregnancy and subsequent marriage are still a hot shotgun combo, those drawn to ringless relations often have little ones already or agree to remain childless.

SCATTERGORIES

Before digital cable, love advanced linearly: you met, you frolicked, you proposed—usually after telling Momma, and certainly without living in sin. For modern wooers, relationships must be plotted along a more complex continuum. The short list of classifications—boyfriend/girlfriend, fiancé/fiancée, husband/wife—is outmoded because these labels can't cover every possible twosome permutation. This dearth of terms leaves RCs ever fumbling with the awkwardness of naming their relationship in three words or less. Everyone knows what "fiancée" means, but expressions like "lover," "live-in," "concubine," and the quirky census term POSSLQ (Person of Opposite Sex Sharing Living Quarters) are imperfect translations that don't convey sanctity. If you say "partner," listeners assume you're either gay or in business together. Add children and it's even murkier ("I'd like you to meet the son of my daughter's boyfriend of fifteen years"). Even the law rubs it in, as most property deeds state, "Holly____, a single woman, in joint tenantship with Wolfgang _____, a single man . . ." Ironically, it's easier to label a relationship after the breakup, when the blanket term "ex" refers to spouse and nonspouse heartaches alike.

SURROGATE RING

Some would suggest that without conjoined accounts, shared keys, and home equity, RCs are no better than Billy Joe and Suzie goin' steady during sophomore *and* junior year. To solve the credibility gap, RCs grasp the surrogate ring. Instead of tossing the nest egg into the glamour and glitz of a wedding, RCs surround themselves with honorable spoils: homeownership, life insurance policies, small business ventures, family pets, orgy dens, and other loving credentials more steadfast than engraved wedding day bev naps.

For ringless carousers who decide to build with Sheetrock rather than a 1.2 carat engagement rock, real estate is a harbinger of growth. A house eventually becomes a "home" and the formerly dubious relationship gains value in the public eye, as guests and new acquaintances assume that the couple is for keeps. However, RCs should beware the surrogate ring that shines falsely: is all the effort to finance, decorate, insure, and maintain that Berkeley duplex just an elaborate distraction from wedding plans? Like Dorian Gray's portrait, does the beautiful veneer of window treatments hide a decrepit core? During periods of distance and disconnect, lovers should sink hours into real home improvement: salsa lessons and romance, not new bay windows.

LOOPHOLERS

Thanks to dubious legal loopholes, you can dodge a massive tax bill or claim an acre of the moon from a company selling extraterrestrial green cheese. Not to be left out, selfish bedmates can exploit love's loopholes whereby they enjoy a lifetime of benefits with neither a promise of marriage, nor a firm pledge of even ringless commitment.

While ringless carousers are united by monogamy and mortgage payments, loopholers take advantage of a living-in-sin arrangement that's stagnating in the haze of a big proposal that never comes. Loopholers favor rentals and the transient nature of the lease, a yearly document

lacking the punch to put a scare into anyone. On-again/off-again cohabitation and engagement promises are a shoddy foundation upon which
to build a future; without a shared vision of tomorrow, an ungainly past
becomes the only thing holding the couple together. Lovers are entitled
to know where they stand and what they can expect, but in the typical
loopholer scenario, a magician who excels at pulling excuse after excuse
out of his hat dupes the ready and willing partner into a life of dashed
hopes. In the absence of definitive answers, the stonewalled partner con-
tests the other's integrity and fidelity with exasperated "Where is this
going?" and then the suspicious "Where are you going?"

CLOSE, BUT NO VEIL

Loopholers, like congressmen, are up for election every two years, and the
relationship referendum either gets quashed, or you are reelected by a bare
majority for another short term. Regardless, electioneering and poll taking
are constant activities in this tense, highly contested district. When playing
house, yearly paperwork (lease renewal, tax time) is a thorny reminder of an
unstable status quo, leading one partner to debate why a justice of the peace
or joint filing wouldn't make things simpler. Despite good intentions, such
bureaucratic convenience is a poor justification for getting hitched.

One thinks the two should get married; the other thinks couples therapy is more apt. With nuptials perpetually in the air, conversations that
could be about honeymoon dreams or retirement havens dissolve into
shoulder-shrugging balks of indecision. Instead of a swept-off-the-feet
romantic declaration, talk of the altar feels like a boardroom meeting ("I've
checked with the shareholders, and they deem a merger with you unwise at
this time"). As for children, each partner assumes that wedding bells come
first, which feeds the loopholer's catch-22: we won't talk about kids until

the marriage issue is resolved, but we can't really talk of marriage until we know about kids. Offspring are one avenue to the big leagues, though it's inadvisable to throw the procreative dice and wager on an iffy future.

Is the slow train of habit too comfortable to jump from? Are you holding on because of great love or are you worried that there might not be anything better out there? Without a thorough diagnostic, a couple will languish in the limbo of lame cohabitation, hamstrung by a meek

---

THE PICASSO PREROGATIVE

Picasso wielded his genius (and genes) without shame and considered women "goddesses or doormats," yet thanks to peerless skills with paint and penis, he got away with it. For those loopholers who want not only a side door exit but an electric garage door relationship opener, this is it. The Picasso Prerogative is the belief that you were placed on the earth to share your charisma with every adoring muse. Creativity and sexuality are intertwined, as the same furnace that fires the artistic impulse powers the libido. Lovers are as collectible as Blue Period masterworks, dazzled and dropped according to bachelorhood imperative. The muse's unwavering devotion, however, is repaid with wily moods and procrastination, leaving her standing idly by. Against all reason, hopeful partners bank that a rough-cut prince, their own lovable artist manqué, will someday settle down. Of course, the boiler room keeps humming, as a man can become a husband or father at nearly any age, but the lady's clock ticks ever forward. Although some survive the turbulence, other maidens are strewn in the wake, wizened by neglect and frustration. The best solution for untamed artists is to live freely until either wisdom leads to commitment or a drug overdose in a Paris bathtub ends life on a high. After finally tidying up the debris of a globe-trotting past, reformed Picassos should throw back the drapes of their heart's studio and welcome a soulmate who shan't be traded hastily for another.

sense of purpose and fear of risk. After years in a holding pattern, don't gamble that love will magically sprout despite your bedmate's tragic flaws, especially if you're mouthing perfunctory "I love you"s at home while confiding doubts to pubmates. Stubbornness, erratic behaviors, vanilla sex, or half proposals (followed by returned jewelry boxes) are strong indicators that the relationship has run its course. To break the cycle of bickering and haggling, decide once and for all whether to break it off, ringlessly carouse without backtalk, or else get shopping for a ring.

Incidentally, for those loopholers struggling with the future but uncomfortable with a final goodbye, try a sabbatical. Like a bookish prof off to pen a treatise on Beowulf, take a scheduled break from the relationship to taste freedom and experience a change of surroundings. After nine months to a year, contemplate the relationship anew and either redouble efforts to commit or else continue as a free agent.

FINAL HURDLES

Dates, pickups, flings, and escorts pass by in the filmstrip of bachelorhood—often uninspired choices ignored by wise loved ones who knew they wouldn't last. With marriage contemplated, however, concerned friends are now quick to chime in when they sniff long-term promise, but perhaps reticent about identifying shortcomings in your fiancée. Other than intuition, your friends and family are the best outside auditors of your sweetheart's mettle. Regardless of public praise or criticism, perform your own sober scrutiny of your beloved's character and weaknesses before lobbing a proposal. Besides passion and financial health, there are societal black marks like past divorces to consider, as well as deal-breakers like conflicting views on children. Those who squander this last opportunity for calm reflection might find their next chance while pacing in the church vestibule, weighing sanity against deserting the bride, the smiling padre, and one hundred antsy guests. If only Willy Wonka's educated Eggdicator was available to determine whether your partner truly is a good or bad egg. Armed with poll results and a last look over the dossier, you'll conquer final hurdles more deftly than the leaping Edwin Moses running for victory in the 110m dash.

THE FAULT LINE

There is a great distinction between the sorts you screw and the gems you marry. Confusing love with ease of vice is an illusion that eventually bursts at the first sights of trouble, when one mate finds it difficult to publicly champion (not just lie under) the other. If the relationship started under dubious means of clawing fights and humiliating sex, it tarnishes the sacredness; watching her sleep with your friends was lust-driven party fun back at school, but do you really want a huddle of groomsmen snickering and hooting at the altar as you exchange vows? Rocky relationships forge experience, yet a louche past with a loose cohort portends a tumultuous marriage. You know you're in the wrong bed when easy lies and movie-of-the-week turmoil are the norm, especially if you abuse your partner's money and think monogamy is fine— for now—but that cheating wouldn't be terribly disrespectful.

WHEN YOUR FRIENDS DISAPPROVE

Do I need new pals or do I need a new fiancée? You've made a wise choice when friends voluntarily offer rave reviews of your sweetheart, but what if no compliments are forthcoming? If your inner circle shuns your partner, don't brush it off as one bad night. Even worse, if new acquaintances bristle at your mate's public persona after fifteen minutes of cocktail chatter, take stock. One or two bad reviews shouldn't be overly troubling, but beware the unanimous House calling for impeachment. Heed worthy advice instead of gripping tighter to a flawed lover out of pride. Friends are wary of meddling and even more gun-shy that their honest appraisal will be deemed a personal affront. So, over a pint, prod confidants for frankness without reproach. Listen for subdued affection ("She's nice, I guess . . .") or eye-opening indictments ("She's clingy and dependent," "You're being controlled," or "She has the class of a three-time felon, and the mouth to match"). Without an open forum for grievances, your friends' unspoken disdain for your partner may slowly expand into a critique of your character as well. Is a spate of bad press enough to pull the plug? Maybe not, but it warrants a moratorium on rings and joint property ownership, shifting the burden to you to prove why this relationship is worth fighting for. To gain a different perspective, invite a trusted couple to interact with your fiancée in the quiet setting of her home turf, away from the noisy mob unaccustomed to her subtler traits.

CREDIT RISK

Easier than explaining a short stint in San Quentin, both partners should disclose bankruptcy and tax liens before landlord credit checks and mortgage applications are categorically red-stamped "Denied." After heart-to-hearts about old flames and wild times, couples nearing nuptials should have a debt powwow to shed light on child support arrears and minimum monthly payments. When your mate's dating résumé includes trails of exes and court files, don't be surprised if her financial history is similarly blemished. If an engagement-bound relationship is on otherwise solid footing, follow the lead of a hurricane-ravaged township that qualifies for federal emergency funds and declare your spouse-to-be's major debts eligible for contributions from the joint account. Labeling select personal debts as "we" debts, not "me" debts, shares the responsibility and will settle outstanding balances more quickly. However, if the prospect of swallowing an affianced partner's mountain of high-interest loans inspires cold feet and fear of freeloading, extend the courtship until steady fiscal responsibility is demonstrated.

PRIOR RECORDS

Some flaws are spelled out on paper (divorce decrees, medical records) while others' lay genetically dormant (explosive temper, pathological lying). Both partners should disclose skeletons to ensure an honest path to lifelong intimacy. Hear the full testimony, as some prior records evince stubborn tendencies (depression) while others exemplify hard-learned lessons (teenage drug bust with military school stint). Like waiting a half-hour after consuming a peanut butter sandwich before splashing about the watering hole, consider an extra-long engagement to digest the problems and work out decades-old kinks. The role of savior requires additional sweat, but don't confuse happiness with a stouthearted crusade to play the knight in shining armor to a damsel in distress. Can you lug another's permanent record until your golden anniversary. Portraying the strongman leaves little time for marking personal progress, so step back if your own life is still shaky. In the end, two loners, former addicts, or crash survivors might make better therapy mates than roommates.

Besides the juicy stuff of rap sheets and medical files, prior records also include noteworthy romantic histories. Whether it be refused rings, splintered marriages, or unexpected loss, contemplate the following before inquiring on bended knee:

♥ **Broken Engagements/Annulled Marriages**: A distinct fear of commitment or keen eye of judgment? One false alarm may show courage; a drunken, impromptu Vegas nuptial ending with a honeymoon of puke evinces poor liquor management, but a string of returned diamonds suggests a mercurial heart. For some, engagement is the immediate step before marriage, but for others, like varsity-jacket-wearing cheerleaders who announce themselves "engaged to be engaged" to the star tight end, it's merely a small step closer.

♦ **Divorce**: The big D is a blemish, but whether it's a minor or major one is up to you. The length (ten years vs. ten weeks) and timing (shotgun wedding vs. puppy love) of prior marriage(s) is pertinent, but the paramount question to your paramour is why it failed. A rebellious, teenage elopement or impetuous coupling isn't a serious demerit, but a gold-digging prospector who trades in loaded hubbies like new model cars is a biohazard. Geography can also be a factor, as young marriages are more common in rural areas than suburbia. If a gala wedding is contemplated, make sure it isn't old hat for someone who's feted before. Zsa Zsa Gabor's great gams and peppery Hungarian accent aside, a partner's litany of exes becomes ludicrous at some point, leaving no good excuse why you should be number nine.

♥ **Widow**: Unlike trying to outdo an ex-boyfriend in the sack, you're not seeking to replace a memory but compassionately shepherd your mate on a new path. You may never be the first, best love, but hopefully at least a close second. Learn about the lost beau through anecdotes and letters so that a departed spirit isn't a ghost haunting the bedroom. Your spouse will have photos, teary dreams, and a deep connection with her late mate that you are better off embracing than resenting. If you're the green-eyed type, can you handle a lover subletting a room in her heart to a lasting memory?

SCHADENFREUDE

Schadenfreude is glee at another's fall from grace and may be brought about by deep-seated jealousy, personal dissatisfaction, or a dark streak of competitiveness. A little nudge from your darling's career success can be fuel for motivation; however, a healthy aggressiveness has turned cut-throat if spurred by passing thoughts of "I'm actually happy she didn't get that promotion. I should be the one making six figures." The durable, lifelong lover champions the other's goals, even during his or her own rough stretches. Silent bitterness is sinister and may only surface in middle age when weightier successes and promotions come to pass.

These can be nettlesome conversations. The specter of schaden-freude surfaces most poignantly with unconventional lifestyles, such as those of artists and musicians. Monetary success is often equated with

✦ WIDOW'S KISS ✦

♥ ✦ ♥ ✦ ♥ **Calvados** ♥ **Yellow Chartreuse** ♥ **Benedictine** ♥ ✦ ♥ ✦ ♥
♥ ✦ ♥ ✦ ♥ ✦ ♥ **Dash bitters** ♥ **Garnish with a strawberry** ♥ ✦ ♥ ✦ ♥ ✦ ♥

being better: her commercial memoir about dysfunction sells more copies than his university-press biography of Kandinsky, prompting him to secretly cheer a scathing *Times* book review that left her in tears. Before

IT'S JAHWEH OR THE HIGHWAY

Marriage is about more than just the two of you, and sometimes family, culture, and tradition will not budge. For example, in the early years of dating, your differing faiths may have rarely been an issue, and you gleefully munched matzoh at her Seder. As the relationship became more serious, however, pressure from the family led to agonizing over such potential deal-breaking questions as: How will we bring up children? Can we live happily after being ostracized from half the clan? Eventually, the strong-willed elders might throw down the *Arthur* ultimatum: leave your partner or be disowned.

To some, converting is not a big deal in the abstract; in practice, however, it can be hard to pledge allegiance to a new god, let alone any god (though, if financial security or romance is high on your list, sometimes trading your Talmud for the Gospel of Luke isn't so bad). The conversion process usually isn't rigorous, and most religions are surprisingly accommodating for a loving couple, though schisms can develop when there is a great disparity in piety. No matter the faith (or lack thereof), a Holy Roller and an agnostic will mash heads, beginning with premarital sex positions and ending with even stickier issues like babies and baptisms.

Recognizing spiritual impasses early on averts inevitable despair. Often, the pressures of family and faith unveil cracks in even the soundest relationships, ultimately toppling them. Survivors who've triumphed over fundamental gridlocks on fundamentalism demonstrate resolve and invaluable coping skills for conquering major snafus down the road.

deciding to permanently share an atelier with a fellow artist, recall writer couplings (Hellman and Hammett) that failed to blossom into a "How Do I Love Thee" sonnetfest à la poets Elizabeth and Robert Browning.

SETTLING FOR LESS

After attending the fourteenth wedding in five years, your inner imp begins to clamor, "When do I get to stand under the huppah in a rental tux and break the glass?" Throw in a few bouts of bad luck and biological clock-watching and you might overinflate a current squeeze to soulmate status. Woe to those who settle for a meaningless career and a second-string spouse. Marrying a partner who inspires you to say, "Hey, I could do a lot worse," is like purchasing a standard back-lot model without springing for such additional features as power steering or a working FM radio. Those who do can expect to spend many a sleepless early morning mentally flipping through the yellow pages under Attorney-Divorce.

Incidentally, Warren Beatty is the Hollywood king who wouldn't settle for less. If monogamy were a game of blackjack, he was dealt a 15, smiled, took a hit, and got a 3; then, he took another hit and paused at 20, until he pulled a final ace for a 5-card Charlie and a winning hand of 21. He played chicken with his biological clock, and at the tender age of fifty-five, he gunned the engine instead of swerving and won, marrying a knockout.

LAST FLING BEFORE PALOOKAVILLE

Stirrings of restlessness combined with missionary ennui spur hunger pangs for one last foreign teaser before settling down to the home-cooked meal of monogamy. As you approach the end of a successful stint of living in sin with your bride-to-be, you proudly recall that the nearest hint of infidelity was a spin-the-bottle smooch one forgotten Saturday night. But as the finality of marriage looms, survival instincts scramble, and your long-caged libido wants a work-release furlough. After a steady diet of restraint, the last fling is a "hot doughnuts now" Krispy Kreme binge, a reward for a spotless past and well-deserved sustenance for the long, faithful road ahead. You've been so good, what's wrong with one last fling before Palookaville?

FIDELITY CHURNING

Understandably, wedding and honeymoon logistics can crowd out needed time for extended reflection, churning up loneliness amidst the whirl of well-wishers and RSVPs. With no sympathetic ear to turn to, an addled gent might take solace in a stint of barroom me-time or a sit-down with an ex who won't fault you for lingering doubts and free-floating lust.

During these unsettled junctures, defenses are down and a last fling masquerades as a warm panacea for cold feet. The prospect of one final trick to round out your bachelorhood oeuvre is suddenly enticing. Like the legendary Ted Williams, who homered in his last at-bat, what young bull doesn't want to go out in style as the bucking maverick? As the sham of a last fling gains credence, you rationalize a racy encounter as an exertion of sexual freedom, reinforcing the idea that you're not a ball-and-chain supplicant. Impending life change and the maddening enormity of wedding plans are beyond personal control, but there is strange comfort in coordinating a final encounter that requires no deposits or approval by the in-law steering committee. Instead of drifting to sleep with thoughts of groomsmen gifts and honeymoon sex, your troubled mind ponders a final, glorious *Top Gun* buzzing of monogamy's tower, replete with sonic booms and motel rooms. You're not necessarily hoping to scuttle the wedding, but when life feels too smooth, an eleventh-hour affair can act as a self-inflicted stain on a sickly sweet Norman Rockwell scene.

THE IMPERFECT GAME

If you have a fidelity no-hitter going, why throw the game in the ninth? Getting off is no even trade for cheating on the eve of matrimony. The hush-hush high and frenzied orgasm is quickly deflated by a suppurating psyche and the unswallowable lump of regret that accompany grave errors of judgment. If you are looking to realize your dirtiest fantasies, one last liaison is a specious, vow-shattering act; better to channel your kinky desires into a spectacular, honor-preserving romp at home, even if it involves two furry sheep and a Little Bo Peep costume rental.

The engagement is a quasi marriage—the dress rehearsal—and if you plan to be faithful to your wife, why cheat on your wife-to-be? Thus, the closing bell for a last fling probably sounded when you started mixing laundry together. Likelier than quitting cold turkey, philandering should be phased out gradually like 25-cent peep shows in Times Square: in the beginning, even mild temptations are heartily considered, then the wandering eye recedes noticeably, and finally it stabilizes on ring-finger resolve. Tremors of doubt in the home stretch are not uncommon, but ceremony-stalling pangs lasting months, not days, mandate a timeout and professional counseling.

POST-OP

Those who face down temptation walk away with antibodies that beef up fideli-T-cells against future lipstick viruses. For those who succumb, a last fling is never right, but there are times when it's more wrong. A thoughtless hump the weekend before nuptials is far more mutinous than a misstep six months before the proposal. Nevertheless, a black mark before Palookaville will not automatically disqualify you as a good husband. Like a twenty-four-hour stint in juvee for joyriding, if you've been scared straight by this regretful lesson, a one-time dalliance will be expunged from your rap sheet after engagement, yet you remain on probation and a shorter leash until the next seven-year itch has passed without incident. Thereafter, recognize high-heeled weaknesses and remember the fleeting nature of tawdry trysts.

FRINGE BENEFITS

Besides the usual fuzzy issues of compatibility and love that dominate the marriage question, there are tangible returns on your jeweled down payment to consider. While a loaded dowry of gems and prodigious milk cows can't be expected in the Western world, sign up for the "till death do us part" special and get the following perks at no extra charge. Inconveniences that used to plague bachelorhood, like inquisitive landlords and illegitimate children, disappear in one ceremonious day at the altar. If you're not satisfied, call your lawyer and cancel any time:

♥ **Backstage Pass:** Like a lady's gay best friend, a respectable married man has off-limits status that affords him free reign around single ladies and occasional, blindfold-free access to dressing rooms. Upon this safe ground, flirtations with friends' flames can be bandied more openly, especially if you mention your wife and son in the next sentence.

- **Sexy Chatter**: Even among a group of hardened Calvinists, marital sex is a suitable topic for mixed company ("We're trying to have a baby . . ."). Try the same approach when dating ("We're banging every night, you know?") and expect odd stares. Before marriage, most parents assume you're having sex, but some hard-liners hold out a 1 percent hope that you're waiting for a special hymen honeymoon. Marriage eradicates all such doubts. As a corollary, wedded couples garner shared bed privileges even in the stuffiest homes (of course, this dashes the sublime pleasure of sneaking from the basement cot to her teddy bear–infested childhood twin bed).

- **Fresh Letterhead**: For ladies with too many consonants or an irksome celebrity-sounding surname, marriage is the easiest excuse for a change without offending parents or ancestors. Isn't that right, Ms. Glasscoch?

- **Authenticity**: After marriage, you are taken more seriously as an adult, or at minimum, you now have something in common with all the squares over forty. It's like your romantic life has achieved legitimacy by getting its own website or B-level celebrity spokesman. Marital couples are simply given more shrift than nonmarrieds. Take a page from politicians who tote their spouses along for photo ops and bask in the bonded image of a finished adult who is implicitly trusted by at least one person.

♥ **Rite of Passage:** The ordeal of wedding planning aside, the seriousness of the entire venture infuses a man with lionheartedness. Akin to graduation (*cum laude*), it's a sense of accomplishment worthy of tossed mortarboards and rice.

♦ **Coattails:** Your partner boosts your credentials: her achievements become your successes ("Your wife is a pastry chef, how interesting . . ."), and you're invited into the same circles. Pooled intellectual resources form one powerhouse unit. For a modest gent, his darling becomes PR Director and can spout testimonials about him to new friends, sparing him the label of crowing braggart.

♥ **Accountability:** Demanding landlords, co-op boards, and insurance agents presume couples are responsible, an image that is ideal for landing hard-to-get apartments and lower monthly premiums. Even better, ringed twosomes are green-lighted for smirk-free check-in at seedy motels.

♦ **Safety Net:** Marriage means joint health insurance, commingled finances, and family gym memberships, not to mention the sweetest career plum, increased opportunities for nepotism at her daddy's steel empire.

♥ **Valet:** Eagle-eyed partners spot crooked neckties, spinached teeth, and lint colonies before a man's evening affair. In return, an observant hubby zips up her strapless dress, makes sure the hanging ribbons are stowed, spots out-turned tags, and doublechecks the well-adorned lady. Kind, watchful eyes espy back-of-the-knee stocking runs and unsightly bra and panty lines on her, or neck, nose, and ear hair on him to avoid embarrassment.

PREPARATION M

The ointment of matrimony won't explicitly cure individual hang-ups or character flaws such as limp creativity, urban neuroses, or a mean streak of infidelity. Nevertheless, marriage can be an over-the-counter salve for those unsightly blemishes on a persona that need a mild remedy. Progressive duos either learn from each other's good example or face the electric shocks of daily reproofs. In short, upgrade your skills the easy way or get treatment the HARD WAY.

H ONESTY: A boyfriend might get by with half-baked white lies, but a husband lives by his word or is fitted with the choke collar and a short leash.

A CCOUNTABILITY: Favor staying out late without calling? You'll change after three no-shows and two all-nighters land you on the couch with neither a blanket nor a smooch good night.

R ESPONSIBILITY: Your sweetheart wants to go on sabbatical and earn her master's, and you want to blow the marital pot playing poker and smoking Dutch Masters. At some point, you'll want extra time to tinker with vintage hot rods in the garage, so fold this hand and provide encouragement . . . next time, it's your deal.

D OMESTICITY: After upgrading your living space, shoddy furniture and a free-rider attitude are cured by a spouse who places the dirty dishes on your side of the bed until you take up the sponge.

WANDERLUST: If you're trying to save for a down payment, forget about joining the Peace Corps or skipping town to sell glow sticks and hash brownies at Phish shows. With a standup spouse cementing your respectability and focusing you on local challenges, there's no need to change zip codes yearly or sate unrealized dreams hitchhiking the on-ramps of I-80.

AFFECTION: Coy and wordless regard won't do anymore. A lifelong sweetie requires steadfast reminders to keep the box spring from sagging with neglect. Download some romance to replace your usual monosyllabic grunts of "Luv ya" with surprises, compliments, and hot words of woo.

YAMMERING: Formerly a powder keg set off by a six-pack? Single friends put up with your volubility and protean temper, yet a strong-willed mate locks you out of the house after a night of loose profanity and Friday fisticuffs.

- **Patsy & Confederate**: Marriage grants easy exit strategies from uncomfortable situations. When workplace tardiness or unsightly sweater vests demand explanation, you can guiltlessly pin it on your patsy spouse. Though, choose wisely those times when you cowardly deflect blame; overuse this out card, and your friends will unfairly label your wife an irresponsible dimwit with no fashion sense. More-over, two half-truths nearly make a whole truth: embroil a spouse to back up a white lie when your keister is on the line.

▼ **Legal:** The law protects spousal conversations, and husbands and wives can't be compelled to testify about such communications in court. In addition, most states give spouses certain probate rights to the deceased's estate. For criminal molls and those living outside the law, you always have a wheelman.

◆ **Matchmaking:** Happily married couples long to maneuver others into the same bliss (or, if that fails, they savor the vicarious pleasure of mining both subjects for the juicy details of a salacious breakup). As missionaries of monogamy, enjoy the pleasures of marketing single friends to the masses and pushing stalled relationships to the next level, if only to have other parallel twosomes for weekly sushi outings.

RING BEARER

◆ ♥ ◆ ♥ ◆ ♥ ◆ ♥

ALTAR EGO

[groom-to-be]   [bride-to-be]

[ring]

By the time you're fastening shirt studs and cinching your cummerbund, hopefully you'll have logged sufficient training hours to earn that government-issue marriage license. Unless the jeweler is doling out instructions on love along with velvet boxes, however, you'll be left to negotiate all on your own the tender questions of proposals, parental permission, and the pitfalls of shiny rocks. In *The Modern Gentleman* we explored the lesser-known points of rings and vows, and below we've spotlighted our most useful policies for avoiding engagement snafus. In lieu of bullying past hordes of brides-to-be corralled in the "wedding etiquette" section at the bookstore, squeeze a fresh limeade and take a poolside flip through our "Altar Ego" suggestions.

MR. & MISCELLANY

GEM STRATAGEM

If mention of "the Rock" conjures only WCW wrestling and the belly-to-back suplex, visit a sophisticated dealer to learn about the four Cs: color, clarity, carat, and cut. Find something vintage and steer clear of strip-mall dealers hawking dime-a-dozen trinkets. Adventurous sorts might consider commissioning a signature piece from a local artisan. No bring-home-to-mom girl wants a husband in serious hock for a rock, so for young couples with staggering postgraduate debt, wouldn't $5,000 be better spent on a down payment? For eclectic moderns, the diamond rule is no rule at all: mine the jewel district for other crown-worthy gems that leave her breathless and sparkly. Nonetheless, distaste for the diamond cartel doesn't forgive the gent for utterly ignoring her ring-finger fantasies and lazily substituting a Champagne-colored pebble for imagination and romance. When the bankroll is slim, seek counsel from a familial matriarch. Heirlooms abound around an old-growth family tree, and great-grandma's vaulted jewels may be available for an encore on your bride's finger. Antiques aren't for everyone; inquire about freshening ye olde stone in a more contemporary setting.

PILGRIMAGE TO PAPA

Elementary schools require signed field-trip permission slips before yellow-bussing the tots to Turtleback Zoo. Shouldn't you secure the parental thumbs-up too before taking the lady aside for a heart-to-heart with the ring box? Make a pilgrimage to her homestead and don't leave daddy with chest pains at a surprise engagement that rouses him to squash scurrilous suitors. When a face-to-face is impractical, a letter in longhand is a more personal alternative than email, postcard, or balloon-a-gram. Ease into negotiations by presenting a bouquet to mom and a bottle of Old Granddad to dear old dad. Then, in exchange for blessings, prepare for a mini Senate-confirmation hearing. Barring a scot-free endorsement, future in-laws may press tough questions about your long hair, flat feet, family history, or career outlook.

After receiving resounding support, look for clues as to what they'd like to be called in the postengagement future. Do they prefer Christian names, neighborhood stickball monikers, or the more formal Mr. & Mrs.? Are they hinting at "Mom and Dad"? Note the difference between: "Dee-Dee and I are tickled for you two lovebirds, *son*," and "Mrs. Weber and I are pleased that Gillington will be affianced to a fine young man."

BENDED KNEE

Likened to Oscar-winning films, some proposals are sweeping best-picture epics with archetypal romance and beautiful cinematography à la *Out of Africa*. Others, like *Total Recall*, are action and adventure blockbusters content to win for visual effects over true substance. Whether your proposal is impromptu or rehearsed, on home turf or away, be creative without being kitschy and strive for a torrent of true affection, not just a shower of artifice. Prepare a few cogent phrases beforehand, but skip crib notes scribbled on sweaty palms; for those in broadcasting, a teleprompter is permitted. Kneeling is optional—former offensive linemen with surgically repaired menisci and those with thinning hair may want to strike a more flattering pose.

Planned or Surprise. Engagements hashed out on yellow legal pads three months prior to a preset proposal date feel more like a business deal than a wedding plan. Lingering over gemstones and wedding cake as you stroll by jewelry counters and French bakeries helps gauge tastes, but teleconferencing on the exact when and how of a proposal short-circuits momentous surprise. An adroit sense of timing involves more than catching your lover off guard; rather, it's about seizing the perfect instant. As when asking your boss for a raise, wait to proffer the proposal until your stock is on the upswing and the partnership has restabilized after any recent turbulence.

Nice touch: Outright spontaneity takes a little forethought. Keep the proposal handy during a holiday getaway when the outlook is favorable for sunny skies and an emphatic "Yes!" With a ring pinned inside your swimming trunks, you won't have to run back to the hotel when your spunky mood intersects a sweetie's loving disposition on the shoreline.

Foreign or Domestic. There's undeniable cachet in an engagement story that begins, "When he first took my hand over an aquavit in Minsk . . . ." Those who pose engagement on the Sicilian summit of Etna, however, must contend with airfare, lava flows, and the prospect of having their special little spot blasted to kingdom come. Pop the question locally and you can later revisit the romantic site for a redramatization of the original proposal. Yet, too close to home—your pigsty bedroom, for instance—dilutes the otherwise extraordinary occasion with an unsightly dose of everydayness.

White Tablecloth. Long-standing eateries with high Zagat scores are equipped to handle the any-given-Saturday stream of ring-bearing suitors who forget to order flowers or request a corner table. If a wining-and-dining courtship has made you bona fide regulars, by all means, enlist a trusty maître d' to plan a four-course proposal. On the other hand, why risk a grand moment to the perils of overcooked entrées, changeable moods, and stoned waiters who interrupt your loving proposal with a sample dessert tray.

Novelties. Billboards, JumboTrons, and skywriters are effective for beer ads, batting averages, and beach blowouts, but when rented to deliver a heartfelt message, proposals come across as cheeky and impersonal. The proposal ought to be remembered more for its uncommon sincerity than its gimmicky coverage on the eleven o'clock news. Novelty works only when paired with a kind of supersized sentiment that isn't upstaged by a galloping white horse or the Boston Pops delivering a symphonic "Marry Me" medley.

Incidentally, engagement-ready relationships, like missions to space, have a launch window during which there had better be a proposal or else the whole venture might be scrapped. Every serious suitor wants to get his life together before shopping for rings, but foot-dragging on wedding plans saps relationship vitality. Don't let urgency expire—this isn't rocket science. Overdue proposals lose the element of surprise and leave you scrambling upon bended knee for a retort to, "It's about friggin' time!"

RINGLESS PROPOSALS

Al Green might chime, "Let's get married today," but if you lack the hardware, the ringless proposal is a bold proposition. Should suitors put their mouth where their money isn't while love is on layaway? Most men advise to wait for the ring, whereas many women urge that a bent knee and open heart trump diamonds every time. Waiting until the optimal moment of financial security sounds mature, but that solvent state might not come until her ring finger has long since atrophied into an arthritic claw. Set a deadline: even a deadbeat can pawn his old baseball cards and muster a decent trinket within sixty days of a ringless proposal. When you do land the jewels, expect a second celebration, like cheering for a touchdown and again for the extra point.

Ringless proposals unfortunately carry a sense of informality, akin to the difference between oral and written agreements. Therefore, when you can't produce actual gemstones, back up your pledge with some other significant collateral. A down payment submitted in cash or bearer bond is generally considered poor taste, although family heirlooms, personal treasures, and ring pops serve as sturdy proxy until the promised jewels are delivered.

Not for traditionalists or tenuous relationships that hang in the balance of carat weight, ringless proposals are for contemporary couples who care more for undeniable sentiment than flaunted rocks to loupe-bearing friends. Reserve this proposal for long-pondered true-love confessions, not post orgasm blurts during a week of sin in Bangkok. The ring is hard evidence of your love, and time spent selecting a perfect four-prong setting acknowledges that you've thought through your intentions. A successful ringless proposal demonstrates foresight so that your obvious sincerity isn't misperceived as a rash, flimsy oath concocted under the influence of too little cash and too much nerve-stiffening sildenafil citrate. Afterwards, consider keeping the sexy secret to yourselves until the ring makes its debut. Just as a postponed wedding ceremony calls commitment and enthusiasm into question, a proposal without an undisputed token causes smirks if leaked to an unenlightened public.

AFFIANCED

The engagement period transitions the ringed duo from garden-variety monogamy to the early stages of matrimony. Even though you're a lame-duck bachelor, frivolities with single friends that won't jibe with marriage are grandfathered into the engagement: take Air Force One out for a spin, sign pork-barrel legislation, and carve out time for lost weekends of skydiving at Camp David. Put your black book to rest and pay close attention to how your farewell tour is received by the bride-to-be. If you didn't know before how long a leash to expect as a married man, you'll know by the time a last-hurrah ski trip to Vail is filibustered.

THE LONG ENGAGEMENT

Just as the proposal has a launch window, so too does the wedding. Traditionally, an extended engagement tempered itchy jeans and those extra months of sober reflection prevented scores of impetuous teens from stumbling half-assedly into unwise legal matrimony. Couples routinely went sexless until the honeymoon, and much like today's three-day waiting period to buy firearms, the reasoning went that only august motives could withstand the cooldown of a lust-killing lull. Now, more than just a measure of patience, lengthy engagements ensure sufficient time to squeeze in prenuptial labors and shed five more pounds for the pictures. Lollygag too long, however, and you risk overcooking the relationship soufflé until it collapses in a deflated heap.

In sales parlance, getting engaged exhibits "buying signs," and you're never hotter to buy, or get hitched, than soon after the ring slides on her finger. Dawdling corrodes excitement and fuels public doubt as your shaky psyche forces a lover to play defense and make excuses. Note the quizzical looks generated by your wishy-washy response to, "Congratulations. Have you set a date?" As a feckless procrastinator, count on fielding flak if the bridal shower pictures are yellowing with age while the ring is rusting over her knuckle. The gravity of forever may chill your feet, but the prospect of never may ice her heart indefinitely.

At the very least, narrow it down to a year or season, if not the actual day. Health troubles, incarceration, and imminent job relocation are legitimate reasons for an open time line or postponement, but mere wedding-hall and swing-band unavailability shouldn't sidetrack plans. The engagement provides ample time to hammer out the fine print of prenups and catering contracts, but it shouldn't be proffered to appease a partner who pines for matrimony, nor should it be used as a cram session to finally determine whether you really want to get married. If you're still unmarried after twenty-five months, something is fishy and it's not the smoked salmon canapés.

CONTEMPORARY NUPTIALS

The long-standing wedding strictures have eased in the last thirty years and unorthodox ceremonies are no longer a breach of social etiquette. Miles away from church, bride and groom can tie the knot beachfront in Rainbow sandals, officiated by an Internet-ordained surfer guru before the backdrop of a longboard altar and unity candle fashioned from Sex Wax. Of course, the traditional wedding playbook is a helpful template and certain commonsense traditions endure: flowers, the procession, formal photographs. In the event that an inflexible financial backer demands the conventional, enlist a married mentor and fight for distinctive touches that personalize the program.

Since the shelves are sagging with heavy tomes on wedding protocol, we reserve our comments for those areas ripest for individuality.

PURSE STRINGS

Whoever foots the bill holds ultimate editing power for the script. Expect friction recalling adolescent rebellion when parents push white-wedding visions that don't match your modernist views. With someone else holding the purse strings, be prepared to relinquish control over important aspects like the guest list or presence of the Almighty.

They Pay. If you've endured a long eighteen years of tightfisted parenting or recently joined Greenpeace against their law-school wishes, don't expect a glorious shift in values for your sake. This is parents' last major opportunity to stamp your lives with their indomitable brand of aesthetic, religion, and celebration. The more disapproving both sets of parents are of you and your mate's current lifestyle, the sharper the contrast between your fanciful ideas and the final result. On the other hand, the puppy-love set with recent teenaged memories should submit to the whim of knowing parents or risk consummating cheap vows beneath a drive-thru window. You'll thank the folks and in-laws later when you realize that drinking Champagne in suits and ties was more refined than your youthful master plan of plastic cups and kegs, with a rave DJ for your tatterdemalion, blue jean–clad school chums.

You Pay. If a singular affair is more important than avoiding debt, pay your own fare. Young professionals with style can scavenge under couch cushions for loose change and drink domestic beer for a year in order to fund-raise a small wedding budget. If your credit rating is worse than your mediocre GPA, consider an "intimate" experience where the number of guests barely outnumbers the statutory number of witnesses; there's always the option of a future "Hey-We're-Married" barbecue fête under a rented tent. After months of successful solo planning and unbounced checks, anticipate family offerings of 401(k)-style matching contributions to help meet the final estimates. With the power over a streamlined guest list, the couple can fashion a deluxe experience for inner circles as opposed to an address-book cattle call when a herd is fed from a trough off paper plates.

Incidentally, to attain home field advantage, don't go home. With your parents a short drive from the hometown wedding chapel, your out-of-state status relegates your authority to that of a rubber stamp, as you concede to the convenience of Mom and Dad negotiating flowers and bands with but a local call.

THE AGE OF WISDOM

One hopes the bride and groom are old enough to throw a charming reception, and the guests sensitive enough to appreciate the sanctity of the event. The most sophisticated weddings typically occur when the couple is age twenty-seven and above. This is not a statement on the strength of the marital bond itself or a hard-line minimum age requirement, merely an empirical observation about how sense of ceremony is enhanced with the extra seasoning of age. Older couples rely more upon stylistic graces and less on assembly-line McWeddings held in banquet halls sourced from the yellow pages. Before age twenty-five, a cookie-cutter wedding is likely since you haven't yet developed a vocabulary of refined entertaining and lack a posse of time-tested friends who prefer decanted Porto to Dixie-cupped Jell-O shots.

SCENE OF THE CHIME

For the sake of momentum, the optimal scheme is the same venue for both ceremony and reception. An inordinate delay between vows and the punch bowl chills the wedding high; tuxes start to feel like straitjackets when the dance floor is one hour and twenty-five country miles in the future. For those long-distance guests, consolidation alleviates the annoyance and expense of mandatory car rentals or taxicab headaches (especially for guests with small children). Better than vapid, big-box venues with drop ceilings and one way in and out, secure a beautiful space that accommodates weddings rather than a reception mill that churns out five gigs per June weekend. An ideal facility is more than one cold square and allows lovers to canoodle in the study, smokers to stroll on the veranda, and merry minglers to powwow in the lounge with brandy snifters and a verdant view.

The wedding doesn't end when the mocha-cream-smeared dessert plates hit the industrial dishwasher. As midnight approaches, tighten the circle. When a block of hotel rooms is reserved, snatch an extra and christen it the hospitality suite, open to all as a central meeting place, crash pad, and mini bar, not to mention an after-hours gathering place for close-knit guests to puff robustos and sip Tuaca.

CHURCH & STATE

If faith is immaterial, orchestrate your own ceremony and appoint a nondenominational officiant. The novelty and import of a culturally diverse and symbolic wedding can be a crowd-pleasing, memorable event as well. Though, the very devout might spare most guests an ass-numbing afternoon in pews by holding the interminable orthodox ritual among your closest circle the evening prior, followed by a lighter ceremony and full reception the next day.

Incidentally, don't foist radical values onto guests: all-vegan or all-meat menu, death metal band after dessert, extreme venue (mountain-top, underwater) or worse, a dry reception.

PREGAME SHOW

Prewedding events are like foreplay; instead of plunging right from the airport to the ceremony, prime everyone for the wedding-day climax. Budgeting for one sharp pregame activity (even if it's just a nightspot gathering after the rehearsal dinner) ensures that introductions at the wedding reception aren't the first icy contact. Instant name recognition and familiar shouts about last night lead to an easy transition into vibrant dancing and clique breaking. Besides, don't you want to see friends who traveled a light-year for more than a brief squeeze after the cake cutting?

Nice touch: During the engagement period, sock away $20 to $25 per month in a groomsmen slush fund. It's a warm feeling to pick up the bar tab for long-traveled buddies, pay greens fees, tip generously all weekend, or kick around loose scratch for last-minute trips to the store. The money will be spent. If not, you'll have extra cabbage for the honeymoon or your return, so ramen noodles won't necessarily be your de facto dinner selection until the next pay period.

VOWS

Look to favorite poets, writers, and song lyrics for inspiration. The traditional template is nice, but why recite the same ole thing umpteen others have uttered (sometimes more than once)? Fashioning vows is not a master's thesis and needn't require iambic pentameter perfection or rock 'n' roll pyrotechnics to wow the crowd. Impromptu sentiments from the bride and groom are compelling; instead of just passively reciting your lines like a good boy, assign each spouse an open-ended moment for unscripted declarations. To help the audience keep track, print excerpts of vows, readings, and highlighted quotations in the program.

Incidentally, do not completely neglect the classic stencil—the exchange is not an avant-garde production, performance-art piece, or excessive tearjerker. At the altar, answer with an unblinking "I do," not the corny "I will" (which suggests compliance in the indeterminate future, not necessarily anytime soon). To seal the blessing, plant a soulful-but-tasteful kiss . . . marriages consummated with a prudish, cold peck are doomed from the start.

STILL LIFE

It's sad when the first magical hour is needlessly squandered on flash-bulbs, rather than celebrated with friends still flushed with rice-throwing glee. Formal photos are quite necessary, but think about snapping the majority beforehand to quell jitters and provide for a seamless transition into revelry following "I do's." The mood-killing mire of posing beside the hall's ornate fireplace often clips the postceremony momentum. As soon as you're married, you should be sipping Champagne and carousing instead of forcing smiles as every possible permutation of gender, family, and bridal position is staged and restaged to absurdity. To blazes with the taboo of seeing the bride before the ceremony . . . she'll still take your breath away.

SOUNDTRACK

Even the flimsiest budget can influence the melody of the wedding with a collection of mixed CDs. Though, for the ceremony and procession, better to tap your circle of guitar-strumming friends and sonorous sirens. Remember, "Here Comes the Bride," taken from Wagner's opera *Lohengrin,* is not a joyful tune. This minor-keyed march forebodes tragedy whereby the bride, Elsa, heeds evil advice and betrays her groom's knightly honor, culminating in the lugubrious loss of her husband and life. With fat pockets, this is a good place for lavishness: perhaps something classic for cocktail hour (string quartet, jazz trio, mambo ensemble), and then an energetic band for party time.

FEASTING

Put aside visions of a Shoney's all-you-can-eat salad and fixin's bar—buffet-style receptions remain an elegant and user-friendly way to feed the congregation. The sit-down dinner encourages torpor and interrupts inter-table interactions, chilling hot chat and compelling guests back to their seats just because the salad course has arrived. Most important, a buffet quiets niggling fussbudgets who carp about serving sizes, dressing on the side, meat temps, and miserly slivers of cake. Nevertheless, don't blow the whole dowry on the menu. Booze enthusiasts can stock a serviceable bar and still value-shop for palatable table wines vastly superior to jug-handled plonk.

RECEPTION TRIPE

Certain outmoded wedding fillers are force-fed onto hapless couples signing up for a package deal. Decide for yourself which traditions are worth preserving and which are best left for the junior prom. In place of creativity and cool, try these:

♥ **By-the-Book Frilly Invitations**: Spare the invitees ostentatious doilies, illegible Old English fonts, and stationery bells and whistles. Funds are better spent on jazz and bubbly at the reception or a suite upgrade during your honeymoon. Ornamentation aside, put crinkly tissue paper inserts to work by imprinting a meaningful poem or lyric that sets the wedding's sentimental tone.

♦ **Receiving Lines & DJ Introductions**: Like waiting in line to pay respects at an open casket, this traffic jam promotes antiseptic hand-shaking, not spirited carousing. These dinosaurs become obsolete when guests have already interacted at pregame events.

♥ **Bar Mitzvah Touches**: Is the chicken dance, the Macarena, or the electric slide the only way to get your over-thirteen-year-old friends gyrating together? Are you relegating your guests' enjoyment to a seventeen-year-old "professional"? Slick-haired DJs should spin and never speak (though, they aren't forbidden from landing a bridesmaid backstage atop a sturdy crate of LPs).

♦ **Bouquet & Garter Toss:** This special day is not a two-part episode of "The Facts of Life," and the single dames in attendance won't turn into spinsters without a toss of the wedding-predicting nosegay. Secondly, do you really want to objectify your bride's thigh and encourage some unknown stag to slip his hands up the bouquet-catcher's unstockinged leg?

♥ **Cake Crumbs:** Year-old wedding cake in the back of the icebox is a needless artifact—why not also double-wrap a moldy king crab leg from the night you proposed at the Lobster Shack? If the mother of the bride insists on stashing a piece in your freezer, chow it down when a nasty sweet tooth hits following the honeymoon before the leftovers are rendered inedible.

FOOTLOOSE

Dancing is one tangible barometer of the reception's style and success, but must the dance floor lay barren until the bride and groom take their first steps on cue? Everyone can still clear the parquet for the marrieds' waltzing debut, yet after the second refrain, the groom should invite guests to join in. As the night wears on, is the dancing demarked by four lonely circles that never mix, one packed with close friends linked by group hugs, or has it devolved into a shirts-off, crowd-surfing mosh pit? A fanciful, romantic vibe develops out of sheer celebration and fellowship, not forced by laughable emcees or artificial party facilitators. Party-promoting groomsmen and the most fleet of foot should fill the floor when they hear the crickets chirping.

Nice touches: Handcrafted invitations replete with a menu of suggested activities for out-of-towners; reception martini bar (with proper glassware); deluxe coffee/espresso area with milk at the froth; a side table of cigars and dessert cordials; a local band in place of a wedding singer for hire; mic and toast time offered to bridesmaids or other honored guests; and for the truly opulent, an elaborate ice sculpture. If you can't muster the postage for a reserve-the-date card sent six months in advance, at least leak word to avoid calendar snags caused by last-second invitations.

THE GUEST LIST

[writing utensil]

[obligatory invites]

Like the grotesque meritocracy of Studio 54's door policy, not everyone makes the list. Why be stuck schmoozing with strangers and playing polite during the culmination of your romantic life? With a well-pruned guest list, you'll gaze knowingly upon a room of familiars instead of wrinkling your brow, "Who's that bald guy with that Gorbachev-like red splotch on his pate?"

Big, garish weddings reek of '80s excess and feel more like an impersonal stadium concert than an intimate club show. Yesterday's hoary etiquette empowered the mothers of the bride and groom with sole control over the invitees; of course, this was also the time of social secretaries and Model Ts. Even if Mummy is shelling out for filet mignon, why are you going along with an overblown, ego-serving head count? Today, an invitation should be a tough ticket and each guest should feel part of a privileged group, not a faceless label on a mail merge. If you have one hundred guests, each one is a measurable percent of the dynamic. As numbers multiply, conga lines get unwieldy, and individual personality is dispersed across the room rather than focused into a spotlight of energy around the bride and groom. Often, a big party devolves into a string of little parties happening in the same room. A small guest list minimizes anonymity since no one is hidden behind the centerpiece, stuck at their table-26 fiefdom with little chance of mingling.

OBLIGATORY INVITES

With an outside sponsor, expect a slew of obligatory invitations (Dad's boss, Mom's bridge partners). Even if you pay, expect constant needling regarding comped tickets to the sold-out affair. You have three options: (1) grant both sets of parents carte blanche; (2) cap the number of unquestioned invitations; or (3) whittle down the guest list with a faraway wedding. A distant affair is an effective guest list editor since tagalongs will undoubtedly scoff at the airfare and visa requirements. Only the most dedicated will attend a foreign ceremony, and you'll likely lose 85 percent of small-timers and only 10 to 15 percent of cherished guests, depending on whether it's land or sea they'll have to cross.

WANING PALS

How many of your friends' addresses are written in faded ink? Who are they dating? When are they eligible for parole? Close friends with independent regard for your beloved are shoo-ins, but the sticky part comes when budget forces a sorting out of semiclose buddies. When relations have withered—it's been years since you and Sergio went on all-night casino junkets—a noninvite resigns the friendship to stagnancy. On the other hand, if you're willing to lay out the cash for the extra canapes and chicken satay, upgrading a small batch of idling friendships from the wait list to the finals can restore rapport to glorious heights. For recent party pals with whom you've never broken bread (just the law), your judgment should be similarly swift. If you must scroll through your Palm Pilot to score someone's P.O. box number and the spelling of their last name, perhaps the rapscallion is best left off the list. Nonetheless, don't discount important transcontinental friends who are unable to grace your guest room but once per year.

Nice touch: Should a wait list slot open up, fill the place setting with a wild card or new friend on the bubble. Perhaps their RSVP will generate lasting bonds; at worst, years from now over glances in the wedding album, you might strain to remember the names of the wacky couple with berets and checkered shirts.

LIST CREEP

Be merciless: trim the guest list like city social programs under a Republican mayor. Without vigilance, "list creep"—sly additions of two acquaintances here and four clients there—pollutes the once-potent wedding cast. Fight parental strains of ancient patronage; with resolve, the meaningless cycle can be broken. Your wedding is not the forum to appease second cousins thrice removed with the tit-for-tat, "Great Aunt Martha invited us to her son's Bar Mitzvah twenty years ago—it's only right to include them." Strangely, the underlying rationale is that a shutout means you won't be asked to their daughter's wedding or their grandson's bris in the future—a cruel punishment or unexpected bonus? It's no honor to be a guest without a connection to the scene, cemented to your plate, with no real diversion other than chitchat with the restroom attendant.

Incidentally, wedding invitations aren't college admission letters, when the selection committee sends out more acceptances than slots, rightfully assuming a certain percentage will enroll in other schools. If a fair number of fringe invitees can't attend, all the better. Gift fishing—purposely inviting probable no-shows to extract something off the registry—is despicable. May such underhanded newlyweds drown in a sea of defective blenders, leaky saucepans, and bounced gift checks.

After the master list is set, trim the fat by cutting these nonessential personnel:

♥ **Distant Relations**: This poorly dressed grab bag haunts the outer tables. Let us introduce: cousins you met once at your grandfather's funeral when you were six, alligator-skinned great aunts from Florida, and the odd lot of unknown matrons from Poughkeepsie stuffing their purses full of dinner rolls. Every peripheral figure left behind equals another flower arrangement and band upgrade, and the difference between personal groomsman gifts and dollar store–bought crap. If you're craving a gathering of the splintered family clan, invite *en masse* based on a coherent plan. Instead of relatives receiving mysterious invitations bearing odd names, send out explanatory letters and call up heads of family to gauge interest in staging a reunion of sorts at your wedding.

♦ **Co-workers**: Classical etiquette suggests inviting at least your supervisor, if not the members of your department. Modern manners differ. Unless you're an associate on the cusp of making partner or a tenured company man with a twenty-year pin, office invitations are always optional. Though, for tiny LLCs or over-the-garage tech start-ups, invite the entire software division of three. Should you decide to expand the guest list, beware the slippery slope—asking the work group means including everyone, not just hunting and pecking four favorites among six cubicle mates. If certain co-workers are bona fide friends, send invitations to their home address; those left out will probably be relieved that you've spared them a wasted June weekend

TIGHTENING THE CIRCLE

When genetics and hormones play havoc with sensitive follicles, a once bushy coif dwindles and frizzy gents either closely crop what's left or sport a friar's tonsure cut and become a bread baker at the local monastery. Similarly, upon engagement and thereafter, there is a great Rolodex thinning as some friends fall out of favor. Tightening the circle is natural: some chums drop out of sight when you move in with a serious love, and a few more fade as you graduate from faithful attendance at nickel-beer night to a leisurely microbrew-of-the-month personality.

Sadly, part of tightening the gentleman's circle also includes distancing himself from wild fillies, the ones more likely to be invited to the bachelor party than the wedding. Sociability is no longer defined by the byte size of your address book, and at this point, it's best to either deprogram these phone numbers or downgrade relations to daylight hours. If the two of you shared more than just platonic coffeehouse chat about Rimbaud, presume that this second-string fling will never be lover-approved. Sigh longingly and acknowledge that there was nothing holding up such booty-call relationships but the sturdy kickstand of your cock.

and a debit card drain at the gift registry. Ultimately, there's no reason to ruin career aspirations over an extra place setting, so if a snub to your boss is dicey, invite the chief out of politeness.

♥ **Worthless Dates:** When penning the invitations, you should invite spouses, fiancées, and long-term lovers by name, not the impersonal "+ 1." For friends of questionable status, inquire if they are dating someone serious. Those who are loosely connected or single altogether need only be issued one ticket so that they aren't encouraged to bring a disposable to a reception full of fellow comrades. Assure any singles that you've stocked a bi-gender pond in order to avoid a mob of bachelors eyeballing the one pair of unaccompanied ladies justifiably afraid of being pawed by a pack of wilding drunks.

♦ **Exes:** Invite an old flame and prepare for either a sullen sad sack moping at the reception or a reprise from *The Graduate,* with a ceremony-stopping confession of love and a mad dash for the local bus. No one wants the joy muddied by some ex's disconcerting ramblings of regret ("That could'a been me up there [sob]. I really should'a gotten off the stuff.") If the ex is a long-standing friend with more hours logged since the breakup than before, add her to the B-list, as long as she has developed an independent rapport with your wife-to-be. All others— bad breakups, ex-wives, unstable souls, recent flings, or the best screw of your life—are mandatory noninvites.

SABER THE DAY

During Napoleon's early-1800s heyday, the Hussars (French cavalry) celebrated victory with *sabrage,* the art of beheading a Champagne bottle with a saber. Rumors abound that the tradition began with the grand widow of bubbly, Madame Clicquot, who gave handsome mounted officers bottles of Veuve Clicquot. Inspired by thirst and the recent Reign of Terror, horseback soldiers drew sabers and decapitated their bottles like so many antirevolutionary traitors.

The guillotine is long since retired, yet *sabrage* lives on with the bottle-chopping *sabreurs* of the *Confrérie du Sabre d'Or* (Brotherhood of the Golden Sabre). Champagne sabering is now reserved for special occasions too festive for extracting corks with a mere twist of the hand. Bastille Day is never an inappropriate time to behead a bottle, and personal holidays worthy of the spectacle include anniversaries, birthdays, and weddings. Don't fret if you can't spare the airfare for a trip to saber school at the *Grand Chapitre;* we've spelled out the practical swordsmanship necessary to saber the day:

1. Make sure the Champagne or sparkling wine is well chilled. A warm bottle has higher pressure and risks the foaming loss of much wine, not to mention a loved one's eyeball. Remove the foil and cage; if the bottle is cold enough, the cork won't shoot off prematurely like a horny teen still fumbling with the wrapper.

2. Examine the bottle and find one of the two vertical seams running up the sides. The spot on the bottleneck where this seam meets the lower lip is the weak point, for which you'll aim. Until you've logged

angle 30°

NOTE: *Be sure bottle is well chilled*
before removing foil and cage

[annulus]

[strike here]

[seam]

[aim away from yourself
and cherished others]

[punt]

some saber successes, remove any remaining foil from the neck to spot your target more easily at the base of the ring-shaped lip, known as the *annulus*. (Should you muff the beheading and maim a bridesmaid, note that this word is conveniently located on the same dictionary page as *annulment*.)

3. Place your left thumb (unless you're a southpaw) inside the *punt* (bottom indentation) or simply grip the bottle firmly around the base. Angle the bubbly around 30 degrees above horizontal, pointed

away from nearby persons, chandeliers, or stained glass windows. Use a serviette or napkin to dry off a sweating, slippery bottle.

4. Take the saber in your other hand (handle perpendicular to the seam) and lay the blade flat just below the lip of the bottle. With the blade aimed at the annulus, take a couple of slow-motion practice swings to get a feel for the coup de grâce to come.

5. Swing with full force away from your body, upward along the neck, and into the bottom of the lip, making sure to follow through. To minimize spillage, immediately turn the bottle upright. The impact, combined with the bottle's internal pressure, spectacularly separates the head from the neck and thrusts the cork, annulus still intact, several feet into the air.

When the bottle is struck perfectly, anticipate a breathless pause before the saber clang against glass gives way to a dramatic gush of fizz. You ought to lose no more than an ounce of wine, fair trade for the gallons of accolades poured upon the *sabreur* who masters this feat.

Laguiole, king of handmade French cutlery and corkscrews, produces a rose handle saber just for beheading Champagne. Priced as a generous wedding gift, it's the ideal present for a bride and groom to open at the reception, right before it's put to use on the bubbly for the best man's toast. If no one ponies up a gift-wrapped saber, don't reach for great-grandpa's WWI rapier or a faux samurai sword bought at a county fair swap meet. Simply ask the caterer for a heavy blade or any massive knife you'd use to carve a turkey. For the sake of the chef's good manner, turn the honed end around and strike with the back side.

Nice touch: Position two groomsmen: one plays centerfield with a top hat as the other bides with a Champagne flute. The outfielder catches the cork on the fly while the other spares precious drops of bubbly with a glass at the ready.

WEDDING TABLE
PECKING ORDER

Consider your wedding reception the trendiest trattoria in town; you're the maître d', and this Saturday night, all the regulars clamor for the best table. Classic etiquette texts only provide guidance on seating the bride's and parents' tables, leaving the other 80 percent of guests still standing. It's easy to manage the heavy hitters, but secondary and tertiary guests should be plotted according to our Wedding Table Pecking Order. With a spot at the Power Table, for instance, an exalted guest relishes the finest cuts of meat, generous Viognier refills, and deferential stares from the proletariat. Among the crew at the Set-Up Table, entrée flirtation might lead to B & B keys offered discreetly after dessert, while across the room, forgotten ragtags at the Pluto Outpost founder in conversation and are mired in slow service and lukewarm coffee.

For modern nuptials, we suggest assigning guests to the following categories:

1. **Power Table**: The ultimate "in" invite, this table boasts the bride and groom, plus or minus the bridal party. With an invisible velvet rope surrounding the A-list, those without a boutonnière require a family sponsor to enter hallowed ground.

2. **Avis Table**: It's not the ring of power, but being number two isn't shabby. You'll likely place wayward groomsmen or unmarried bridesmaids here, along with nominees who didn't win a seat in the wedding party. Despite the mixed blood, this table is a close-knit, motleyed clan of the newlywed's confidants, forming the backbone of the wedding's oligarchy of cool.

3. **Insular Bunch**: With the full spread and an open bar, this crew of libertines and unattached college chums is the hub of wine-guzzling boisterousness and dirty candid photos. After cake and single malts, off they go to reminisce on the patio and catch up on gossip. These are the last friends to leave, but the first to shed jackets, bowties, and reasonable sobriety.

4. **Distant Family Enclave**: The out-of-the-way island nation of far-flung family invitees—you'll need a whispered reminder before politely addressing Uncle What's-His-Name with a semi-sincere "Thanks for coming."

5. **The Melting Pot**: Where the elder relatives from both sides of the aisle meet for the first time and exchange tales of the Old Country. Worried about two warring factions? Interpose extra seats between feuding kinfolk whose strained relations might upset the day.

6. **The Floating Crap Game**: This collective consists of one missing person from six different tables. A few of the refugees have escaped from their incompatible seating assignments, the rest have been expelled. They have fortuitously found each other and formed their

own tableless union around the bar. This is the smoking/drinking castaway clique who regularly miss group toasting and slow dancing. You'll find them on the smoking porches or back parlors trading cigs with the bartender and trying to pick up the white-hatted carving girl with bad puns about rare meat.

7. **Lucky Seven**: Because of proximity to the headliners, these coach-class guests enjoy first class service by the catering staff who mistake them for adjuncts of the Power Table. Perks include early pouring of

---

HOW TO LOSE A FRIEND
IN THREE EASY PAYMENTS

Sandor, the part-time photographer, is snapping photos; Pargol, the alternate bridesmaid, is preparing the prime rib; and cackling cousin Cypress is arranging the cala lilies. In an effort to cut costs, you've hired pals to do the wedding. The couple is happy for the bargain, but friends are fed up because they worked twice as hard for half as much and have never endured such full-time bitching from even full-paying clients. Even worse, when a deposit check bounces or deadlines are flaunted, the trusted friend feels like a hired lackey, cursing the day when she joyously agreed to cater the affair at cost. Dreams of serving Norwegian salmon with basil beurre blanc sauce quickly sour as the pressure to be perfect is maddening, and it's not until dessert that the frazzled friend gulps a well-deserved double bourbon on the rocks.

Photographers, caterers, and florists in your social circle make for diverse dinner parties, but hiring your intimates instead of strangers for your wedding can turn out terribly, especially for a $5,000 band gig, as opposed to a $100 favor to strum guitar during the procession. Soliciting a close friend to

Champagne, an especially sprightly centerpiece, and apparent influence to ask for seconds on the delicious wedding cake.

8. **Set-Up Table:** The scheming bride and groom have slyly seated these eligible singles next to each other. As flirtations heat up, the bride playfully stokes these sparks with extra attention, sugary asides, and little winks.

9. **Pluto Outpost:** Divide 117 guests by eight and you will get a remainder—welcome to the Outpost. No matter how fastidious your method,

snap photos at the ceremony is truly fraught with negatives: ask for a nice price and you get a resentful, polite smirk; get handed an exorbitant estimate, and you become huffy. Worse, haggle posthoneymoon over unforeseen costs or user rights, and you have cashed out a friendship for the going rate of several hundred dollars. The smarter move is asking friends for outside referrals and arranging a favorable deal. In the end, you garner a slight discount yet still engage in an arm's-length business transaction—and the friend remains a carefree guest tramping on the dance floor instead of keeping an eye on the beer-smuggling kitchen staff.

Despite the perilous terrain, some couples apparently have friends to burn and choose to hire from within. If this is your path, step lightly, and (1) speak honestly about your vision; (2) agree on time lines and ground rules for status reports to avoid having to make irksome business calls masquerading as friendly check-ins; (3) settle beforehand on price, travel expenses, plus future rights and uses (e.g. photographic reprints); and (4) draft a sales contract incorporating the above, along with a promise that you'll never ask for anything again.

misfits are regretfully dropped into this stewpot. At this table adjacent to the noisy corner where the bus tubs are emptied, the ratio of guests to empty chairs is nearly 1:1. The miscellany consists of last year's neighbors, late write-ins, dateless former co-workers, and obligatory invites. The newlyweds will make an orbit to this cold, distant colony once every 269.4 years, leaving this mishmash to decay in its own boredom.

THE DYNAMIC GROOM

A groom's deep confidence begins with a massage and a hot shave and continues with a sly, vivacious vibe during the ceremony, punctuated by a prevailing bliss that lasts well past the honeymoon. Donning a shimmering polish of manners, he embraces the spotlight of favored friends and family, all tied up in the poignancy of romantic union and rite of passage. Of course, this effulgent force isn't automatically produced by showing up on time but begins with knockout attire, a dedicated supporting cast, and a newfound intimacy with the bride.

HEAD TO TOE

The sharpness of dress underlies the groom's role as supreme escort to the starring bride. With the ultimate home-court advantage of a brimming closet and phonebook full of haberdasheries, this is no time to recycle office clothes. For those allergic to the formality of formal wear, skip the black tie and with it, the incessant fumbling with uneven cravats and meandering cummerbunds that allow white shirttails to peek over your belt. Moreover, you'll save yourself the embarrassment of loose straps or tags hanging below your vest, allowing nosy guests to read your rented tux VIN number. Even the most respectable lout can still wear a suit and manage sophistication by capitalizing on seasonal creativity in color, style, and texture. As for the small things, swaddle yourself in luxury from the inside out and don't befoul an otherwise singular ensemble with holey socks, a digital watch, or a wash-worn undershirt.

If the groomsmen aren't black-tie guys, don't force their square peg into your round buttonhole of tuxedoed perfection. Be extra conscientious concerning ragamuffin student/artist friends with thick portfolios, thin wallets, and barer closets. Even if you're dressed in a dinner jacket, your attendants might wear sport coats and open shirts. Unless Phil Spector is running the soundboard, dressing up the groomsmen as a matching, be-tuxed Motown group, with you as an extra-sequined front man, isn't pretty. In any event, since groomsman pay is low (a scant but tasty rehearsal dinner), don't enforce mandatory uniforms that set the chaps back two Franklins while failing to express their individual style.

To stave off wedding-day fiascos, pack a spare outfit and accessories to guard against reception killjoys such as cake frosting calamities soiling your slacks or red-wine tsunamis dousing your white-ruffled breast. Advanced planning downgrades a vexing crisis into a minor inconvenience, when split seams and lost buttons (or a jump in the pool) call for

WEDDING BELLE

♥ ◆ ♥ **Gin** ♥ **Dubonnet** ♥ **Splash cherry brandy** ♥ **Splash orange juice** ♥ ◆ ♥

a costume change. Though, the groom shouldn't be the first gent to strip his jacket and tie, or roll up his sleeves. This blasphemy smacks of the dreaded "I don't-want-to-feel-like-an-adult-yet" syndrome that highlights the stark reality that the entire ceremony was force-fed to you, right down to your skivvies.

Nice touch: In the final week, amidst the scramble for tailored alterations and airport pickups, prevent dark-ringed bleary eyes by carving time for stress-reducing workouts, stolen naps, and solitary sessions of flasking and journal writing in the park.

HONEYMOONSHINE

In antiquity, the honeymoon was a thirty-day period following nuptials whence the couple drank a honeyed wine (mead or hydromel) to ward off evil spirits and confer fertility upon the union. Attila the Hun was a legendary victim of honeymoonshine and purportedly keeled over dead after overdosing on the sweet hooch.

Today's marriage-consummating getaways are vacations deluxe, unforgettable fortnights of romance whiled away in Parisian cafés, Venetian canals, or the Disneyworld Best Western. Take advantage; not since lazy college summers have you been given such freedom of movement. Even killer work schedules and choleric bosses soften to the primacy of a planned honeymoon. Soak in the special treatment afforded hooneymooners—free cake, adoring smiles, first-class upgrades, Champagne on the house—but don't overplay the newlywed card by panhandling for comped amenities with every tab. Besides, never was a few hundred dollars of credit card debt worth more: honeymooning is about luxury and decadence, so don't skimp on a few bucks' worth of finer vintages and double desserts.

BRIDEGROOMING

Unmired in the minutiae, a dynamic groom overlooks modest gaffes and shortcomings of guests, the service staff, or himself. Be light and playful on your feet, and when the shady bartender offers to sell tabs to your sister-in-law or dips too heavily into the Jack, delegate a groomsman to put a cork in him. Mind your tongue and booze and be remembered as the groom who cha-cha-cha-ed with all the matrons, not the louse shooting chilled vodka and doing knee slides in an ill-fitting tux. The happy couple receives ultimate behavioral leeway, yet the groom doesn't exploit this

---

If you are coming off six months of hellish timetables and wedding logistics, play it unstructured. To avoid a cotton-mouthed kickoff to the rest of your life, reserve the postwedding day for sleeping, packing, and decompressing before a long flight. Around-the-world trips requiring ten connections and shots for dengue fever perpetuate the hectic cycle, and after being told where to stand and how to promenade by some pipsqueak wedding consultant, do you really want to be on the rigid itinerary of a cruise ship?

While recharging in the islands, create an impenetrable bubble. The honeymoon allows the glue of loving vows to properly set far from prying eyes and worldly responsibility. Making new friends over dinner at the inn is nice but shouldn't trump the importance of being together. You'll go on holiday in the future, but you'll never again be on your honeymoon.

Incidentally, following an off-white wedding, sex isn't a deflowering virgin diversion, yet remains a major attraction for newlyweds formerly living in sin. Diversify. Sacred tender unions ought to outnumber twelve-hour romp-a-thons, but don't neglect adventures into connubial kink with the unwrapping of privately exchanged toys that never graced the gift table.

amnesty. The crowd might forgive a soused husband who slurs an untoward comment at a distant cousin, but why ever plummet to that wretched
point? Ideally, joyful mingling and attentions to the bride should leave
little time for gross reception excess. If immoderation is your demon,
groomsmen should work in shifts to shadow your movements, monitor-
ing intake and loose tongue until the seniors and right-wing kin are
shuttled out the banquet hall. When the band finally breaks down the
drum kit after-hours, open-collar decorum begins without pause.

FINAL EMBRACES

So much schmoozing, so little time. Glide as smoothly as if on casters
and flee mundane chitchat ("The food's great—again, congratulations").
The clock is ticking for you and the bride, and thoughtful guests know
not to monopolize your time. To multitask, carry a gaggle of guests along
on the rounds to catalyze inter-table introductions and then deposit
them in your wake as you move on. In between extended meet-and-
greets with your loyal subjects, steal a moment of solace in the bathroom
or quiet corner with an overview of the reception. Take it all in and consider snatching the lovely bride for furtive whispers and kisses that aren't
prompted by spoon raps on wine glasses.

   Besides saying hello to peripheral guests, connect again with each
bridesmaid and close friend. Swathe them in poetry, saying heartfelt
things you used to write to them in jest on birthday cards or exclaim with
the artificial abandon of alcohol, now with more import. While riding
high, invest needed capital with in-laws through memorable asides and
sincere appreciation, deeds that will offset a future marital gaffe involving
a co-worker's going-away party and a hooker named Cookie.

The
STALWART
HUSBAND

LOVE'S
LABOUR

♦ ♥ ♦ ♥ ♦ ♥ ♦ ♥

WE-CYCLE

Delicious moods and temporary broods are the extremes of a long-term relationship, none of which are everlasting (thankfully, for the blues; unfortunately, for the sweet, sweet highs). The we-cycle plots such household biorhythms, measuring passion and possibility, as well as the doldrums of disconnect. Unexpected joys (surprise promotion) or bad news (burst pipe over the new Steinway) ensure that the peaks and slides are sometimes beyond a couple's control, but the we-cycle brings a measure of science to bear on the subject of a couple's happiness.

Like a campaign manager minding approval ratings, a married gentleman monitors the we-cycle to anticipate trouble spots and forecast likely upswings. While relationships aren't predictable sine waves, where a positive mood is thereafter offset by a negative period, one can assess we-cycle wellness by relating the current direction of your relationship to one of the four active states: Morning After, Horse Latitudes, Upswing, and Turbo Boost.

After stalling in or revving up to one of the four zones, most we-cycles resettle into the Lane of Contentment, a middle ground where a good day at work on the one hand and unfilled birdfeeders on the other neither warrant a party nor necessitate a counseling session. Even a souring relationship, with its slow drain to disdain, lingers at times in the Lane of Contentment before the final, inevitable plunge ("We had some times, didn't we? Well, more bad than good"). If a couple is tired of sitting on the comfy median, they must actively nudge relations upward. When alert mates sense rising momentum, they capitalize on strong tailwinds and push the relationship to new levels. Upon catching whiff of foul skies, flagging relations are stanched with affections and adventure, preventing a further nosedive into the pit of ennui.

PHASES OF THE WE-CYCLE

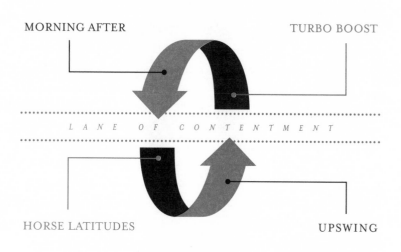

MORNING AFTER

TURBO BOOST

LANE OF CONTENTMENT

HORSE LATITUDES

UPSWING

Turbo Boost. All ecstasy, all the time. Mistaken for glowing newly-weds, your relations soar on a hot streak. This is the optimal time to renew vows, burn frequent flier miles, and squander laundry quarters on vibrating motel beds. Within this cloak of invincibility, a brightened pair boosts the kink factor and digs deeper into personal confessions that bond two lovers more tightly.

Morning After. As last month's heights of celebration fade, bitter-sweet reminiscence provides the pillowed landing for vacationed-out, city-hopping couples returning to routine. After building speed, you're now contentedly coasting on leftover kinetic energy. Though, after a high, there's no mathematical axiom that dictates a couple must then sink into a sustained low. If the settling mood is artfully managed, the twosome glides into the haven of the everyday (already planning the next escapade) instead of crash-landing into a deficit below the Lane of Contentment.

Horse Latitudes. Just as pesky rhinovirus germs can sideline a Saturday night, cubicle stresses and a stack of overdue bills can waylay a couple. During these doleful times, the pair's listless love weighs down the household ship, as smiles, spontaneity, and rousing invitations are jettisoned over the side in the name of bad luck and crabby mood. Left untended, a home dynamic headed toward the Horse Latitudes will sputter into irritability times two and lovemaking minus ten.

Upswing. You emerge from the clutter with a spring-cleaning of the house and psyche that reinvigorates the we-cycle. This recovery mode is like a shot of B-12 and a stomach pump following a twenty-four-hour whiskeyed fugue. With the relationship dynamic under new management, a romantic evening of dinner and dancing is joyously planned, and instead of running off to the links alone, you remove the dustcover from the two-seater for a Sunday picnic and roll in the bushes.

NOSEDIVING

The mercury dips on occasion, either because there is a widening disparity between two partners' states or because the twosome is slumping. In the former case, one spouse sags while the peppy supporter attempts to uplift spirits. Unlike your Eastern European grandmother, don't be a stoic. A steadfast partner patiently shoulders the weight when the other stumbles over career woes, family issues, or final exams; for clarification, each mate might check the "for better or worse" clause under the marital contract. However, disparate energy output can't last. Eventually, the

Pollyanna, smothered by a needy mate, succumbs to exhaustion and the couple veers into an extended nosedive.

In the slumping scenario, both parties flounder and neither leads a charge out of the Horse Latitudes. Bedtime can't come early enough, and usually chatty suppers degrade into silent, caloric exercises under a dim chandelier. Decay mirrors the disheveled home, as relations and tidiness decline from mere dustiness to condemned disorder. Moreover, major ills compromise monogamy's immune system. Look out for fast-food bingeing and substance excess that can trigger a spate of spouseless carousing and lead to a feverish smashing open of a piggybank of affairs.

Beware these three common causes of the Horse Latitudes:

♥ **Lack of Together Time**: Frequent business travel or family obligations short-circuit one-on-one activities. Eating cold cereal and dry toast for a 10 P.M. dinner with attention glued to reruns doesn't pass for meaningful interaction.

♦ **Sexual Dry Spell**: Even mediocre or selfish sex marginally contributes to the carnal connection or at least breaks the inertia. However, when sex is supplanted by solitary hobbies and sidetracked by right-hand worship, both parties are tapping their libidos without sharing personal porn stashes and amorous moods.

♥ **Space Squeeze**: An out-of-the-blue flu waylaid a spouse last weekend, dreary weather spoiled outdoor antics the week before that, and an overburdened calendar just wiped out Friday night's gambol. Broken plans and an unwelcome spattering of compulsory events (visiting in-laws, dog-sitting a yappy mutt) exacerbate cabin fever. For a night, unhitch the guest room Murphy bed for yourself; when the couple needs space to breathe, a small dose of me-time is a refreshing tonic.

INDEX OF WHIMSIES

Spent a few days in the doghouse or a month in the doldrums? For a weak-pulsed we-cycle, pull a remedy from the Upswing dispensary and introduce a fresh transfusion of romantic vigor. A simple cure-all, like sweet-scented bouquets and wrapped surprises, stirs smiles after a downturn. Even without spending a dime, unexpected affections, kind notes, and thoughtful favors awaken a dormant dynamic. Similarly, attentive gestures reaffirm a soaring we-cycle. Instead of breaking out the whimsy during emergencies only, practice the pleasant side work of advancing harmony even at the top. Whenever you pass in the hallway, the urge to stop for a peck or playful spank is unquenchable. These subtler affections are the healthy snack between table-clothed meals of intercourse.

- **Modest & Meaningful**: Gather the gang for an impromptu clam bake; order a simple corsage for an evening on the town; whip up homemade desserts and puddings; mail-order a regional delicacy, microbrew, or hard-to-get kettle chips; complete a home-improvement project while she's away for the week; pick up the dry cleaning, service her Honda, and otherwise pamper your mate with five-star service; rent flicks and stock the fridge with finger food goodies before a weekend blizzard empties the store shelves of everything but cans of frank 'n' beans and potted meat. Dust off little-used racquets for three sets of mixed doubles or knock the caked mud off hiking boots for a trek amongst the conifers.

♥ **Lavish & Lovely:** Showcase doting panache by renting a luxury road-ster for a daytrip to the country; importing an interstate friend; arranging for a shopping spree, with livery driver service; plotting a last-minute Canadian getaway, with plant waterer and dog-sitter pre-arranged; enrolling in joint lessons (ballroom dance, sushi prepara-tion, foreign language, home brewing); securing sold-out concert or sporting tickets; and preparing a sexy feast with immaculate setting and under-the-table intermezzo. See what happens when you go for a drive with a picnic basket, a bottle of bubbly, and a $100 bill.

FALSE ALARM

Sometimes, a we-cycle landslide clouds your head with disquieting doubts. Prompting a brood in the basement, a lengthy stretch of lousiness conjures panicky what-ifs about past romantic crossroads ("I married this overbearing shrew? What if I'd stayed with my wild Michela?"). Dips in the we-cycle inflate minor hurts as you romanticize bachelorhood and obsess over your spouse's imperfections. The passage of time scat-ters this temporary fog; after a sunny afternoon together or moonlit night between the sheets, you're quickly reminded of your beloved's allure. In the aftermath, a sober mind identifies these episodes as man-ageable marital potholes, not craters of divorce, and the wise mate

=== **THUNDER & LIGHTNING** ===

◆ ♥ **Brandy** ♥ **Powdered sugar** ♥ **Egg yolk** ♥ **Dash cayenne pepper on top** ♥ ◆

moves on without imperiling the romance with transient urges better left unspoken.

Incidentally, to permanently cripple the we-cycle, face the false alarm by shacking up with an ex, putting an attorney on retainer, launching into an interstate bender, or orchestrating a ritualistic love-letter inferno on the back lawn.

LIGHTS & DARKS & DISHES

[dutiful hubby]
[spin cycle]

Even with a leggy mademoiselle stopping in for weekly French maid service, modern lovers still need to lift a helpful finger, especially if the we-cycle has hit a bear market downturn that only a garage junk purge can cure. Mind the mess: splattered counters and crumpled tissue wads abandoned beside the wastebasket are domestic no-no's. Wouldn't you rather fight about whom to invite to your threesome instead of who's going to scour soap scum? Unlike shaky finances or nosy in-laws, house chores are finite headaches—there are only so many square feet of flooring to mop.

House parties used to mean passing out on a humanity-filled, beer-soaked carpet with a dirty dishrag as pillow. Nowadays, the ethic of a clean home is a testament to an orderly, flowing routine. Stockpiles of old newspapers, brimming hampers, and under-the-bed quagmires invite apathy. Apart from summer beach rentals strewn with towels and sandals, it's hard to picture life moving forward with great momentum when a couple must slalom around a trashed apartment. With minimal effort, a daily fifteen-minute regimen keeps you ahead of the entropy curve. At the very least, spackle unsightly picture holes and scuffs, dust-bust hard-to-reach corners, and spare your partner the displeasure of a week's worth of white-crusted spittle on the bathroom mirror.

Are you orderly or clean? A "clean" house denotes houseguest readiness and healthy spic 'n' span sparkle that costs nothing but time and elbow grease, while an "orderly" one connotes an everything-in-its-place tidiness that might not pass a fusty mom's surprise inspection, yet it shines under the dimmed light of cocktail company. Excepting the Addams family, cobwebs and hibernating dust creatures are not kooky house pets, though actual pets will treble your dust trouble and at times raise your dander. Furniture-straightening worrywarts make for annoying housemates, so don't hector over stray magazines or a cookie jar knocked askew when big-ticket cleaning chores and general sanitation are under control. In fact, some studies suggest that antibacterial fanatics armed with Lysol are killing beneficial microbes and spawning powerful superstrains in a futile genocidal campaign against household germs. Rather than spending all your leisure time disinfecting, trust your immune system and save the white-glove treatment for well-deserved spanks in the boudoir.

SHARING THE LOAD

The notion that house chores are woman's work is laughable, yet the lady is still regarded as the Heimdall-like guardian of the inner space, responsible for the final call on flatware, furniture, and dish-soap brand. Gents should still flip through mod catalogues like *DWR (Design*

Within Reach) and offer two cents about decor to avoid waking up emasculated in a four-poster, suffocating under a Laura Ashley floral bedclothes overdose. Despite gender equality, the good husband spares his consort the noisome task of garbage and silently tends to its removal and curbing. Likewise, a cautious lady with a closetful of delicates might assume the laundry, if only to prevent a bleach-infested hot water calamity that leaves her wardrobe brittle, shrunk, and bled of color. In return for crisp shirts, the man of the house ought to scrub the W.C. and tend to all things leaking, rusting, or broken. Offering unsolicited compliments for your mate's completed chores eliminates the silent animosity that builds when one party diligently performs to a silent audience. Like the beautiful emulsion of a freshly whisked vinaigrette, most newlyweds eventually attain synchrony: Mr. Neat and Ms. Sloppy compromise, whereby the neatnik's lofty goals are lowered and the slob is finally taught to push a broom.

THE SPIN CYCLE

At the corner launderette, the ever-bachelor empties his hamper, overstuffs the machine, feeds the quarters, and blindly mashes the button for Permanent Press, praying that his white croquet shorts, black sweats, and red knit shirt will all play nicely together. Before babies and terriers are bred, you should seek mastery of colorfast cottons, silky delicates, and strappy unmentionables. If you're lucky enough to have a Maytag heiress sweetheart, turn the page. However, for hapless others who've fallen into the lint trap, here is a five-minute laundry primer to help you avoid bickering over stain sticks and spray starch:

Duds Diligence. To reduce fading, turn jeans, pants, and decorated shirts inside out. As it says on the care tag, don't wash synthetics with natural fibers (for example, polyester with cotton); this blasphemous coupling erodes fabrics, which might be ideal for breaking in concert T-shirts but not for preserving your swank evening wear or her sexy top. Purchase well-known suds for your duds, as cut-rate detergent not only stays undissolved in the machine but also emits a cloying scent akin to mixing cheap cologne with sweetened hog sweat.

Dishes are washed in scalding hot water, nonwhite clothing is not. Warmer waters, while ideal to dewrinkle shirts and launder heavily soiled articles, cause colors to fade. Sturdier items can survive a warm wash (with a cold rinse), but as a default for nicer things, the cold water cycle prevents premature wear and running of dark/bright colors. As a rule, newly purchased communist reds invariably bleed and mate with whites to spawn socialist pink undies. To avoid these spin-cycle hybrids, launder strong colored pieces separately several times before designating them for group washes. Don't neglect trampled bathmats and throw rugs, especially during the busy winter season, when a warm wash and dry before company arrives is never untoward.

Fluff Air. Overdrying garments in the machine promotes pilling and ingrains wrinkles even Oil of Olay can't remedy. Dial up the high heat for sheets and towels but remove more fragile clothes from the dryer while slightly damp and hang to dry: your sleeker wardrobe will gain years in life, and a brief stint of air-drying eliminates the need to plug in the iron. Master the fluff air setting for drying delicates or freshening smoky party clothes that beg a short spin with a scented dryer sheet. To avoid a blizzard of fuzz on black shirts, separately dry lint producers (towels, flannels, quilts) and lint absorbers (darks, corduroys). Lastly, on temperate afternoons, break out the clothespins and use the venerable clothesline, sunny porch railing, or vacant volleyball net to capture the country scent.

Incidentally, overused, diseased bath towels that still have a telltale odor of unwashed feet after a full wash and dry cycle must be euthanized. Instead of leaving an old favorite on the shower rod for months, rotate in fresh towels more regularly to avoid premature death and putrescence.

Segregation. In 1963, when Dixiecrat George Wallace stood before the schoolhouse door to block racial integration at the University of Alabama, who knew the only thing he was right about was the wash? In laundry, "Never mix lights and darks" is just as important as the mantra "Don't play with matches" is in childhood. Sort laundry into three groups: whites, darks, and delicates. Those in South Beach can also separate brights (yellows, chartreuses, neons) and maintain flowing color with a dash of leftover margarita salt in the cold water wash. New Yorkers have it easy, as they need only sort into blacks and dark grays and toss in the cold cycle. While undershirts and handkerchiefs can survive a dioxin spill, greenhorns should stick with the basics and never bleach anything of value. As for disco sequins and hippie fringe, place these and other delicates in a mesh washing bag (in a pinch, a knotted pillowcase) to prevent damage. For more fragile items, fill a vintage washbasin or unscummed sink with cold water and gently knead clothes into a foamy meringue of Woolite or mild dishwashing soap.

Dainties. Be the good laundress and hand wash or dry-clean: wool, silk, cashmere, lace, and certain synthetics like rayon or nylon stockings. Cheaper bras and cotton panties can be washed and dried cool. Underthings worth sniffing that contain Lycra should be hand washed and line dried, and as a rule, anything that gets you hot—nighties, teddies, camisoles—should receive the same treatment, but laid flat to dry.

Splotch & Stain. Consult the big detergent manufacturers' websites for tips on how to fight more serious stains or else surrender your spills

Promises made to clean by dinnertime are often trumped by the splendor of afternoon naps and ballgames. With your sweetie's return pending or guests soon to knock, don't get caught with a pile of breakfast pans on the stove and pillows and blankets heaped like a burial mound. Ten minutes isn't enough time to shampoo the shag, but it's ample for a sponge-toting sprint through the major traffic areas. Whether you're seeking to avoid a tongue-lashing or simply need a cardio boost, follow our minimalist maintenance plan when you've only got ten to tidy.

BATHROOM SWEEP (2.5 minutes)	Pull the shower curtain into place, neaten the towel rack, swipe the counter, stash the floss and dentifrice, whisk away whiskers, and hit the chrome and glass for a cheap shine. Reload a meager toilet paper roll, flip the lid into position, and realign the bath mats toward the homeland. Stow embarrassing unguents and pilfered hotel toiletries, and proudly display $40 moisturizers and overpriced shave tonics.
KITCHEN PRIMP (3 minutes)	Transfer countertop clutter to the dishwasher. No time for that? Shroud a sinkful of dirties with a clean dishtowel that mysteriously conceals the backlog. Run a sponge over the range to gather loose crumbs. Empty the trashcan, check the paper towel supply, and put out fresh kitchen linens on the oven door. If ahead of schedule or woefully behind, recheck the liquor cabinet and consider a snort of bourbon or two fingers of tequila while poised at the halfway turn.
LIVING ROOM SHUFFLE (2.5 minutes)	Fluff the pillows, neaten the coffee table, then tidy the periodicals and miscellany (keys, mail, loose change, unanswered subpoenas). Open the curtains and raise the blinds to even heights, turn on soft lights and mellow tunes, slide the ottoman into place, and stow the remote controls (not in the sofa cushions).

BEDROOM SCAMPER **(2 minutes)**	With the more important hot spots tamed, use the remaining time to redirect sheets toward the headboard and breeze covers into place as though stretching a picnic blanket out on grassland. Shut the dresser drawers and use the closet bottoms and the far side of the bed, if necessary, to hide eyesores such as laundry piles and spent pyjamas. Lubes, creams, and plastic machines might find their way into an innocuous-looking shopping bag by the bed.
EVERYWHERE ELSE	As you pass from room to room, closet loose shoes and banish stray garments from the common space. In a single basket, collect uncategorized clutter that litters the side tables, arms of furniture, and seat tops. This method is much faster than stashing individual documents, but you must swear to your maker that you will return to this central pile forthwith, lest the overdue auto insurance invoice end up with the take-out menus.

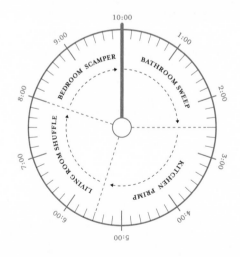

to the dry cleaner. Most important, if a stain hasn't come out in the wash, never place the item in the dryer.

Following are a few fun stain tips beyond the use of the ubiquitous club soda:

♥ **Blood**: Night-marauding lycanthropic friends of Lestat might flush fresh wounds in cool water, brush with ordinary soap, and rinse in cold water. For dried bloodstains, pretreat with a splash of peroxide.

♦ **Red Wine**: For oenophiles who overzealously swirl Malbec onto their cuffs, liberally dose with salt until the grains draw out the stain (salting also works for oil stains). Then, treat with a dollop of domestic white wine, rinse with club soda, and wash as usual.

♥ **Deodorant Buildup**: When things get flaky, soak the stained area with white vinegar (Champagne vinegar for the gourmand). After a half hour, wash shirts in the warmest temperature recommended by the care label.

♦ **Lipstick Traces**: After an indiscretion, philanderers ought to scrape off a paramour's rouge residue with a butter knife, then rub *(the clothing)* with petroleum jelly or vegetable shortening and throw in the wash.

♥ **Candle Wax**: When errant drips miss the aureole and hit the satin sheets, don't panic. Scratch off as much as possible and then place a brown bag or paper towel on top of the waxy stain. Run a warm iron (no steam) over the area until the paper absorbs the wax. Pretreat and toss in the wash.

THE GENTLEMAN'S CELLAR

[drinking vessel]

[merrymaking libation]

The era of creaky armchairs, third-hand coffee tables, and rattrap apartments ends when your love life settles. As a twosome refurbishes their surroundings, the quality of lovers' vice undoubtedly rises as well, diverting disposable income to that rewarding adjunct to the healthy kitchen: the gentleman's wine cellar. After years of traipsing to your neighborhood liquor shop for single-bottle purchases and cursing the blue laws when caught empty-handed for a Sunday picnic, it's time to take the plunge into volume. You don't buy tuna and tomato soup one can at a time, so train yourself to stock the cellar as resplendently as your pantry. Such an undertaking doesn't require traveling around the south of France in a seersucker suit with a walking stick to bid at wine auctions—a cellar is easy to start, though its infectiousness makes collecting all but impossible to stop.

GRAND INVESTMENT

Get into the game without taking a second mortgage. For a cool grand, you can amass a deep enough collection to supply romantic interludes, yacht christenings, and everyday drinking alike. Like the ghosts of Christmas that haunted Scrooge, a proper cellar represents the past, present, and future.

1 Case (12) of everyday/party tippling wine ($100): A quantity of under-$10 bottles means that you'll never run dry midway through the merrymaking.

6 Mixed winners for minor company ($90): When the neighbors drop by, open something with a little pizzazz that won't make you cry if they leave half a glass unfinished.

3 Rip Van Winkles ($150): Forget these babies for forty years or until you can afford to replace them with older ones. Cellarable prospects and bona fide investments include these killer Bs: Bordeaux, Burgundy, Barolo, Barbaresco, and botrytised whites (e.g., Sauternes).

3 Oddities ($75): Surprise even the savviest connoisseur passerby with a trio of obscure grapes, defunct producers, or underrated regions discovered on distant travels. When the label is unfamiliar, keep an eye out for intrepid importers who sniff out boutique beauties: Eric Solomon (France, Spain, Portugal), Kermit Lynch (France), Leonardo LoCascio (Italy), and Broadbent Selections (worldwide).

3 Bubblies ($65): A bottle each for modest, fine, and vintage thirsts keeps you sparkling whether you need a last-minute hostess gift or an elegant aperitif.

2 Treasured gems ($300): What would you serve if Robert Parker showed for meatloaf night? When a moment calls for something extraordinary, dust off a classic that's ready now.

 2 Magnums ($125): Supersize an exceptional evening when one bottle is hardly enough.

 2 Locals ($25): During domestic travel on county roads, tote home a regional wine along with the local corn or microbrew. With wineries in all fifty states, there's no excuse not to explore American viniculture from Virginia to Missouri to New Mexico.

 1 Porto ($30): Pensive letter writing or wintry decanter pouring deserves something substantial.

 1 Sherry or Madeira ($25): Go old school and learn what fortified the founding fathers. These wines are nearly indestructible; hence they'll last until you're mature enough to relish them.

 1 Sticky ($15): All you need is a 375-ml bottle if the wine itself is dessert or when a lover's sweet tooth ought to be sated.

TOTAL | **36 bottles = $1,000**

A three-case rack fits snugly in most any room, and divvied up in this fashion, half your wines will be under $25, with the remainder averaging about twice that amount. With five to six glasses per bottle, you're spending around $5/glass, far less than at a trendy downtown bistro. Should ten Franklins prove to be beyond your means, build the collection over several months, not just a one-stop shopping trip at the corner package store. For shameless winos, spread the word to friends and secret Santas that all you want in your stocking is a pretty bottle.

STOCKING UP

If you love a young wine and can swing the simoleons, buy a case and get the discount. Open a bottle immediately to gauge its maturity. Is it ready to drink now for next week's affair or begging for time to mellow? Uncork another bottle next year and keep track of the wine's progression in your cellar journal, the most joyous of paperwork. Most commercial wines are produced to be drunk the year of release, but the noblest vines of the world yield nectar that takes years to evolve. Heavy tannic reds, oaked whites, and sweet/fortified wines mature more slowly than a class clown. Worse than drinking wine too young, however, is letting a magnificent bottle expire in your cellar until it is unpotable, broken juice. Large collections warrant regular inventorying and spreadsheet software to prevent such disasters.

Most of the grand wines of the world are in no greater supply now than they were during the Official Bordeaux Classification of 1855. Thus, increased demand from winos with big bucks has pushed up prices while relegating superlimited lots to auction blocks and back room sales. Even important retailers earn but minute allocations of collectible gems, and savvy proprietors offer these bottles first to heavy-hitting regulars. Don't be a "cherry-picker," who flips through the phone book randomly calling liquor stores to inquire after cases of the rarely seen Romanée-Conti, Cloudy Bay, and Screaming Eagle. Frowned upon by industry insiders, these sorts seldom score a rarity. Rather, the best way to land on the A-list is to make friends behind the counter and spend often.

PINOT PAMPERING

Bag-in-box wines require no more care than a pet rock, but finer wines merit real TLC. Ever since you learned to swirl and sniff your chocolate milk at age twelve, you've known to store wine bottles horizontally (Champagne and Porto excepted) so that corks stay moist as sediment is collected. Temperatures between 50°F and 60°F with 60 to 70 percent humidity are ideal cellaring conditions. This environment should remain consistent, as fluctuations in temperature and humidity will unduly age your vino. Even short exposure to heat above 77°F cooks the wine, permanently damaging it, and UV rays from direct sunlight are also harmful. Lastly, since vibrations and blaring punk rock disturb the sediment, peace and quiet are as good for *grands crus* as they are for grandparents.

Despite your vision of a handsome, alphabetized-label arrangement in full view, storing your collection in a sunny kitchen or dining room is rarely smart—blacked out bay windows and a chilly clime simply aren't hospitable for guests. Barring a noble bloodline that lands you the family castle, you probably won't inherit the perfect underground cellar. Instead, clear out that odd closet beneath the stairs or put your handyman skills to work in the basement to build a cellar with polyurethane foam insulated walls, hardwood racking system, and computer-controlled cooling units.

Incidentally, care less about appearances than your wines' health? When you can't swing the three-thousand-bottle showpiece, pick up a handsome refrigerated wine cabinet for under the counter or bargain hunt for a secondhand fridge to do the job in your garage (the crisper alone holds cold cuts and nearly a dozen bottles).

HOUSE POLICY

To avoid stumbling upon your choicest bottle sitting empty in the recycling bin, set a vino policy that separates wines into three classes: Call Your Friends, Call Me, and Call Your Attorney. The first category is for patio quaffs and replaceable wines; the second group applies to wines meant for sharing, as long as you're present to enjoy them; the third class is reserved for one-of-a-kind treasures—you're the executor, and you'll rightly specify the terms of company and conditions for the ceremonial opening. In this fashion, grape-loving sweethearts can entertain in the other's absence with full blessings and a key to the cellar. Akin to department stores that budget for yearly pilferage, those with curious teens in the house should plan to chalk up a percentage of loss to basement experimentation.

Keep a wine journal with labels, tasting notes, and vinous memories. More important than the notations of "hints of cassis" or "nose of truffles" is the increasingly scribblier script logged over the course of an enchanting dinner with intimates. To remove a wine label for journaling, don't muss your manicure. Instead, fill a teapot; when it whistles, fill the bottle with hot water, cork it, and let it sit for a minute to loosen the glue. Then, drizzle water on the label, starting with the edge, and slowly peel it away as you continue to pour. Otherwise, to avoid poaching your fingers, look for label-removal sheets sold in wine shops. If you have a cellar, paper the door with wine labels and tile the walls with the winery-stamped slats from wooden case boxes.

Nice touch: At home, say a few words about a remarkable bottle. Without being pompous, shed light into the glass about region, vintage, or tale of its purchase so that guests can join in the wine appreciation before they've heedlessly washed down a half-chewed breadstick with a once-in-a-lifetime treat.

VESSELS

Coffee mugs and juice glasses are ideal for train-hopping hobos used to swilling dreck from brown-bagged pints, but for those with a job or nearby Crate & Barrel, decent glassware is a fine-wine mandate. Unless wedding guests gift wrapped Riedel service for eight, an eclectic table dressed with unique finds bought at thrift shops turn even ordinary wines into conversation pieces. For cleanup, hand wash an infantry of red-stained empties under hot water with minimal soap to remove greasy fingerprints and lipstick. There are three ways to damage glasses: (1) loading delicate dirties in a powerful, abrasive dishwasher, (2) flooding the insides of the glasses with scented dish soap that lingers into next week's dinner party, or (3) the Twist: wringing the base and the bowl in opposite directions while you aggressively shove the sponge into the mouth of the glass until it snaps in two.

Decorative square-sided scotch decanters provide instant class to plain-labeled rotgut and upgrade a late-night highball to a sexy nightcap. Similarly, wide-bottomed and duck-shaped decanters open up younger wines, aid in pouring an unwieldy twelve-liter Balthazar, and separate sediment from older wines and Porto.

GRANDI BOTTIGLI

Bottle size was originally determined by the amount of air in the glass-blower's lungs. Eventually, a standard bottle was agreed upon, and Champagne merchants added the poetic flourish of naming the large-format bottles after famous kings of the ancient Middle East (Salmanazar = 9L, or 12 btls, Nebuchadnezzar = 15 L, or 20 btls). Aside from the dramatic impression of presenting special-occasion bottles the size of a hobbit, these vessels serve the practical purpose of ageing wines more gracefully. The ullage, or pocket of air between cork and wine, is nearly the same whether in a half bottle or magnum (= 1.5 L, or 2 btls). Thus, smaller bottles' wine oxidizes more quickly, while magnums, with their minimal air-to-volume ratio, are the ideal vessels for laying down premium wines for a number of years.

Recalling the courtly days of amphorae, it is good luck to toast an entire room of chums from the same vessel. Unlike the coin-saving twenty-four pack of diapers, however, a double magnum is typically pricier than buying four standard bottles because the larger bottle itself is more expensive and bottling lines aren't tooled for them. Also, producers know that the wine is better and they want to discourage suburban bargain hunters from fashioning decorative parlor accents out of pristine Jeroboams (= 3 L, or 4 btls sparkling/4.5 L, or 6 btls still).

Incidentally, a hundred years hence, oenophiles will chuckle, "Remember when people shoved cork-tree bark down bottle necks to stopper the wine?" Screw-tops and synthetic corks are inevitable and, indeed, good, as they inhibit the cork taint that afflicts 3 to 5 percent of all bottles. Everyday wine aside, though, there is poetry in the cork presentation tradition, and a soaked-through vintage cork makes a better keepsake than a polyurethane plug.

GREEN THUMB

Once you have the bedroom blooming, take your craft into the solarium. Gardening gladioli in perfect rows is an art that requires sandy loam, agile knees, and a sturdy trowel. If you still think horticulture and swan neck hoe are pimp lingo, stick to houseplants, the ultimate latchkey hobby necessitating only a slim-spouted watering can and meager quantities of common sense and Miracle-Gro. Besides being one of the sharpest and least expensive forms of home design, houseplants beautify and detoxify the atmosphere. Spider plants, for example, purportedly excel at eliminating airborne formaldehyde. Though, unfortunately for the yellow-toothed set, plants are mostly ineffective against cigarette smoke, even the low-tar variety.

Get in touch with tender tendrils and impress a sweetheart with leafy know-how. Most plants need regular light but not oppressive, direct summer rays, which harm and yellow exposed outer foliage. Plant tags that advise "low light" do not mean "no light." Thus, a nonwindowed bathroom is better off with silk plants, which are now remarkably realistic, especially on upper shelves away from 20-20 scrutiny. "Bright light" plants should be near the room's brightest natural light source, not on the opposite side of the room or stuck in a shadowy corner behind the armoir. During temperate days, open windows offer fresh air and humidity to stuffy rooms, although constant drafts can cause leaves to droop or fall. Leaves also appreciate the foliage equivalent of a massage: an occasional wipe down to eliminate grime and maximize photosynthesis.

Plants wilt and die with too much agua and shrivel up with too little. A weekly regimen of watering is well meaning, but plants, like booze hounds, need to be watered whenever parched. Bedroom Lotharios and floraphiles alike can rely on the handy index-finger test for dryness: insert your digit into the soil past the first knuckle, and if it feels damp, the plant is content. If dry, add enough tepid water to reach the bottom of the pot; whatever isn't absorbed into the soil within thirty minutes should be poured off. Overwatering refers to watering too often, not how much water you tip into the soil all at once; without time to dry and aerate around the roots, the plant actually drowns.

Incidentally, fake ficus trees are the toupees of horticulture yet work nicely as background for junior prom photos or dolled up with Christmas lights for a cheap den-of-love arboretum.

Since your abode will never have the same lush light and double-walled polycarbonate glazing as the nursery, expect some thinning and a six-week adjustment period for new specimens. Despite the best care, leaves may brown, yellow, or mottle due to conditions beyond your control, such as higher branches overshadowing others. Most of the time, browned leaf tips are due to an overabundance of direct sunlight, and wilting means a dearth of humidity. Browned tips can be trimmed with scissors before the problem spreads, requiring radical whole-leaf amputation. Growth can also be squelched when plants outgrow their original containers. To check if repotting is necessary, turn the plant upside down and tap its derriere to pop out the plant for closer inspection. If the roots are visibly bunched like brain tissue, time to buy a bigger pot.

Nice touch: Knowing a quartet of distinguished botanists will boost your popularity at the American Fern Society annual: Theophrastus (Aristotle's pupil and the father of botany), Carl Linnaeus (father of modern plant classification), Liberty Hyde Bailey Jr. (father of American horticulture), and E.T. (distinguished alien botanist and purported father of Drew "Gertie" Barrymore's outer-space love child).

BEGINNER SELECTIONS

WARM, SUNNY ROOMS	Aloe, Cacti, Mother-in-Law's Tongue, Snake Plant
HANGING BY THE WINDOW	Coleus, Wandering Jew, Virginia Creeper
MODERATE SUN	Cat Palm, Basil, Weeping Fig, Moses-in-the-Cradle, Ferns, Ivy
SHADED GOTH SURROUNDINGS	Aspidistra, Rubber Plant, Chinese Evergreen (Aglaonema Silver Queen)
HEARTY, FORGIVING PLANTS	Wheatgrass, Philodendron, Corn Plant, Spider Plant, Epipremnum (aka Money Plant, Pothos)
FLOWERING PLANTS	African Violet, Busy Lizzie, Peace Lily, Geranium; Poinsettia and Amaryllis (for winter holidays)
EXOTIC BUT EASY	Traveler's Palm, Ficus Asahi, Grape Ivy, Iron Plant
OUTDOOR FLOWER BOXES	Unless you live in the temperate climes, stick to flowering annuals from the garden center, which you can replace each year. Houseplants will not survive outdoor frost.
CACTI	Practice the subtle art of neglect and watch your cacti thrive. Succulents need only slightly more water than Gremlins; though unlike Gizmo, cacti may be fed at night. Flat-leaved cacti can stand more water than spherical or columnar types, but when in doubt about watering, either consult the Scottsdale precipitation forecast or refrain altogether, especially during their dormant phase from late November until March.

Hanging plants dry out faster than their floor-bound brethren and therefore require additional watering. Avoid the local Italian/Mexican restaurant tactic of letting vining plants wander like Rapunzel's golden tresses, spreading miles of leaves around the room. The plant eventually devotes its energy solely to the farthest ends, resulting in yards of brown, leafless vegetation nearest the soil. To escape this fate, clip the ends when they reach desired length, thereby encouraging lush, full growth closest to the pot.

STASH

For those with a hankering for a homegrown Humboldt high, there's always the organic hobby of indoor marijuana plants harvested in a makeshift closet grow room. Before embarking on this unlawful path, inhale, hold, and read the available literature to bone up on lighting and soil composition. After cramming for midterms, can you recite the pros and cons of HID lighting systems and the germination periods of narrow-leafed *sativa* and wide-leafed *indica* varietals? Having a feminist bent is helpful, since male plants aren't desirable product and are usually up-rooted. Be smart: hanging garbage bags over the windows and splicing into the city power grid are dead giveaways of your budding operation. Regardless of your setup, you'll have to reckon with the problems of excess heat and humidity and the telltale sinsemilla odor emanating into the hallway.

THE BITCHIN' KITCHEN

[gourmet range top]— [oven]

—[warming tray]

Transitioning from the sparse bachelor fridge populated with half-opened tonic water and wilted celery stalks, the young, single professional upgrades to a kitchen stocked with hardware and appointed with a tony spice rack. However, a peek behind the new German-made coffee grinder reveals a distinct lack of substance—a paltry pantry of convenience rather than an abundant icebox. Take-out menus crowd out peaches from the fruit bowl, meals-in-a-box and taco-making kits hog shelf space, as toaster pastries and toy-in-the-box cereals monopolize the breakfast menu.

Some married couples aren't much better. For shame, All-Clad saucepans, an armory of Henckels knives, and Le Creuset enameled roasters from the registry still in boxes, trophies from a bloated wedding reception. Moreover, pity the life of mutual at-the-dinner-table newspaper readers, where the mate on "cooking duty" only breaks away from their favorite section to tend to the ding of the microwave. If the butter dish houses a glaucous blob and the milk is two weeks past due, your household dynamic is truly dispirited.

The evolved couple hearkens back to the hearth, when the kitchen was the bustling depot that heated the entire living space. Indeed, the best relationships are as hot in the kitchen as they are in the bedroom. A warm, cozy space with whisks drying in the dish rack is a sanctuary that soothes workday nerves and serves as a staging area for late-night, Dagwood-style refrigerator raids. To break the monotonous prime-time ritual, turn cooking into a dual event; with two aprons working prep, the oxtail will be braising in the oven in no time, leaving you free to deck the table with dinner linens. On occasion, think stockpot. When the temperamental rains of spring foil weekend plans, restore morale with an Old Country ragu or bubbling five-alarm chili, guaranteed to fortify the household's stomach for days to come.

THE LARDER

A stroll through the local farmers' market provides valuable lessons in odd salad greens and attunes your shopping list to seasonal availability. Get biblical: fruits referenced in the Holy Scripture—grapes, pomegranates, dates, olives, figs—make the perfect light snack. Hearty utility vegetables that can stand a spell in the fridge (squash, carrots, peppers) are the versatile black pants that can accompany many dishes. Get used to munching on things other than potato chips and vittles made by trans fat—flinging elves and save the boxed saltines for those radical dieters who consider them a square meal.

There are unavoidable expenses like electricity or bedroom lube, and there are places to trim spending. However, food is both a necessity and entertainment expense and a great place to indulge. Shelling out a few extra dollars for artisanal cheeses and rustic breads provides the makings for three evenings' worth of appetizers over a bottle of rosé. Whereas a living room extravagance might be a $5,000 leather loveseat, a kitchen splurge is $19.95 of jumbo back fin crabmeat from the fishmonger. Similar to a stocked home bar obviating side trips to the all-night liquor store, a full cupboard gives the couple flexibility for last-minute additions to recipes and the wherewithal to whip up three courses on short notice. The booze enthusiast's handy assortment of liqueurs and bitters finds its culinary equivalent in a colorful gourmet array of herb and spice staples; quality oils, vinegars, and extracts; dried foodstuffs; and favorite sauces and condiments. When the cupboards are full of possibilities, last-minute guests can be accommodated with but a few chops at the cutting board.

THE BIBLIOGRAPHY OF TASTE

Rather than stealing your Nana's file card box of meatloaf surprise and sour cream cake recipes, outfit the cabinet tops with cookbooks that match your culinary zeal. You needn't master the awe-inspiring skills outlined in the CIA's *New Professional Chef* cookbook to develop a lifelong rapport with your cookware and sweetheart. For those intermediate epicures unafraid to prepare a demi-glace but too short-staffed for the über-artistry of *The French Laundry Cookbook,* clear a galley shelf for our Bibliography of Taste:

♥ *Essentials of Classic Italian Cooking,* Marcella Hazan: Widely acknowledged as one of the great cookbooks of all time, and with good reason. Hazan is an incredible teacher, managing passion and eloquence without wasting a word. Like the Dead Sea Scrolls, the amount of knowledge imparted in these few hundred pages is staggering.

♦ *French Provincial Cooking,* Elizabeth David: Every collection needs an old-school powerhouse, and this timeless volume, originally published in 1960, deserves a permanent place setting at the table of modern classics. The prose is redolent of the scents of a country kitchen in France, and David's regional recipes inspire readers to improvise.

♥ *Classic Indian Cooking,* Julie Sahni: Sahni stands over your shoulder, explaining not just what to do, but what to smell, hear, see, feel: all without a single photograph. Like in Hazan's book, the recipes don't come until she's thoroughly covered the essentials of the cuisine's pantry, guiding traditions, and a detailed ethic of Indian cooking.

♦ *Think Like a Chef,* Tom Colicchio: One of the best chef cookbooks of the past decade, it lives up to its title by conveying the whats and hows of intuitive cooking. His concept of three-ingredient "Trilogies" is more enlightening than a month of droning sermons.

♥ *Catalan Cuisine,* Colman Andrews: Andrews is the current editor of *Saveur,* and his passion for Catalonia and its food is legendary. This is something of an offbeat choice and thanks to its fascinating baroque touches, the familiar Mediterranean themes never lapse into cliché. The superb prose guides the reader diligently without pretty pictures.

♦ *Essentials of Asian Cuisine,* Corinne Trang: This recent book does for Asian cooking what Hazan and Sahni pulled off for their respective cuisines. A true gem, it is perhaps the best one-volume treatment of this massive subject, backed with excellent information on pantry staples and food traditions.

♥ *How to Cook Everything,* Mark Bittman: An astoundingly reliable book, which belongs in every kitchen. This 944-page, poppy yellow–colored tome is your "Sunday in the Park" of cookbooks—expansive, enchanting, yet depicting the everyday basics of food. With a useful mix of staples and advanced fare, Bittman boasts exact instructions without *herbes de provence* pretense.

◆ *Gift of Southern Cooking,* Edna Lewis and Scott Peacock: Break out the buttermilk and bacon grease: Edna Lewis, the doyenne of Southern cooking, pairs up with her much younger protégé to champion traditional techniques and dishes. To anyone stuck up north with a hankering for Dixie, get out the cast-iron skillet and open these pages.

♥ *The French Menu Cookbook,* Richard Olney: Iowa-born and Provence-inspired, Olney is a true grand master and as much a certified gentleman as the culinary world has ever seen. Olney's seasonal approach to cooking, presented in this, his first book, inspired such food luminaries as Alice Waters and Jeremiah Tower during the formative years of California cuisine. As food writer John Thorne expressed it, "I almost believe you could put this book under your pillow at night and wake up a better cook."

◆ *The Thrill of the Grill,* Chris Schlesinger and John Willoughby: Hailed as a cookbook worth reading outside the kitchen, this tome is not for charcoal debutantes, rather for experienced grill folk who are learned in the ways of smoke, hot peppers, and the Scoville-unit heat scale. The book features exotic beverages for washing down spicy dishes and sophisticated but hands-on techniques for motivated cooks who know that grilling is more than patties on the barbecue.

♥ *Local Flavors: Cooking and Eating from America's Farmers' Markets,* Deborah Madison: Nothing tastes like produce from the yard, and Madison paints a portrait of America's local food landscape that embraces sustainable farming and regional, seasonal recipes. Before slipping into your chef clogs, you'll first learn how to shop for market oddities like lemon verbena, blood oranges, palm sugar, and orange flower water.

- *Cucina Fresca* and *Cucina Rustica*, Viana La Place and Evan Kleiman: These volumes make an irresistible gastronomic duo, encouraging you to read the recipe, close the book, and before lifting a wooden spoon, visualize the uncluttered beauty of a finished plate. *Fresca* lays out simple dishes served at room temperature, which when prepared ahead of time allow ample opportunity to carouse with guests instead of sweating under the broiler. *Rustica* presents the country genius of combining fresh, unfussy ingredients to perfection. Relish the beautiful Italian names that spring off the tongue . . . ah, *Melanzane con Cipolla.*

- *Maida Heatter's Book of Great Desserts*, Maida Heatter: Compiled by one of the monumental figures in baking, this sweet text is in the James Beard Foundation Cookbook Hall of Fame for a reason. In this 1974 classic, savor ladyfingers, puddings, rum cakes, and kumquat cream, without the pomp of overdone pâtisserie flourishes. As a side dish, pick up the diminutive *Pancakes A to Z,* by Marie Simmons, for weekend brunches and breakfast-in-bed flapjack favorites. Keep a mate forever by mastering the splendor of iron-skilleting a Dutch Baby and flipping Thai-style Zucchini-Ginger pancakes.

- *The Bread Baker's Apprentice*, Peter Reinhart: From the essentials of equipment, fermentation, and kneading to precision recipes for rustic loaves, holiday breads, and flatbreads, this classic book covers it all for those who want to bake like a *boulanger.*

BREAKFAST IN BED

Since monogamy dictates blueberry pancakes instead of strawberry blonde tarts, dust off the ornamental tray and spoil your mate with the can't-miss A.M. favorite: breakfast in bed. This indulgence requires a plan, even if the idea only occurred that very morning, prompting a sly slip out for white-boxed treats. The idea may be to surprise, but a five-minute warning creates anticipation so that a lover can greet a fresh croissant without groggy eyes and morning breath. When you don't have time for the multicourse feast, a simple continental perk-up with a Danish and the daily rag is a quick treat on a Wednesday morning that needs more than a caffeinated jump start. Whatever your breakfast stratagem, make the whole affair your gift, including cleanup and dish duty as your lover ponders the funny pages.

GRASSE MATINÉE. For these extra-lazy weekends in bed, indulge in a lavish indoor picnic featuring exotic fruits, creamy pastries, and signature brunch fare presented with culinary and aesthetic flair. Either begin or end (or begin and end) with sex and fade out on tousled bed sheets into a tummy-filled nap that lasts into the P.M.

WINNING AMENITIES. Fresh berries and seasonal melon; warmed carafe of maple syrup; a linen-lined tray to prevent items from sliding (or, lay a tablecloth on the bed and use plates to steady beverages); diminutive set of salt and pepper shakers; mimosas or Moscato, along with coffee or tea setup; softened butter (no frozen pats or unsightly tub of margarine); pen for the crossword; a small bowl for discards (tea bags, fruit rinds, spent roaches); jam served in a cordial glass with a demitasse spoon; edible flowers garnishing the tea tray; and background jazz à la Duke Ellington, Oscar Peterson, or Phineas Newborn Jr.

NICE TOUCH: Wheel in the entire buffet on a stolen hotel-style service cart. Breakfast in bed is also an ideal time for small gifting—imported candy, beaded necklace, spirited undies, framed photo, or recited poem (memorization optional).

REHEATING

Sometimes, a stubborn drop in bedroom frequency is tough to jump-start with lingerie and foreplay alone. Remedy a sexless workweek of drudgery with home-baked cuisine. Besides, if you're in the doghouse, the kitchen is a more conducive place to initiate a ceasefire than the bedroom. Oft overlooked, the galley allows for easy neck nuzzling while your partner is chopping vegetables or beating the egg whites stiff. The interplay of food and touch makes the kitchen the grassy baseball diamond of home play, with plenty of counter space for extra-base hits. For inspiration, emulate the livid sink-top passion of *Fatal Attraction* and the gastronomic fore-play of *Like Water for Chocolate* or even re-rent the otherwise forgettable *Miami Blues* to find fading star Alec Baldwin mount a saucy, prostrate Jennifer Jason Leigh two short yards from the range. Get each other's hands dirty with batters and icing, share nibbles, gesture suggestively with the rolling pin, and thwack derrieres with dish towels.

♦ ♥ ♦ ♥ THE HOMESKILLET ♦ ♥ ♦ ♥

♦ ♥ ♦ ♥ **Canadian whiskey** ♥ **Sweet vermouth** ♥ **Maraschino** ♥ ♦ ♥ ♦
♦ ♥ ♦ ♥ ♦ ♥ ♦ ♥ **Dash bitters** ♥ **Garnish with a cherry** ♥ ♦ ♥ ♦ ♥ ♦ ♥ ♦

FINANCES & COMMON CENTS

[moolah]   [piggy bank]

Ordinary working couples without shady stock options or Tyco-esque $6,000 shower curtains need to set ground rules for living within the means of two honest paychecks. Without firm financial compatibility, his gambling, her shopping, or a mismanaged joint account can undermine love faster than the bank can stamp "Insufficient Funds."

The pillars of household liquidity are reliability and adaptability. Reliability is spending and behaving in a manner consistent with your financial means. For example, a trustworthy spouse refrains from $2,000-credit-busting e-commerce sprees when paychecks only tally $800 per week. Adaptability means being able to adjust consumption to a marriage's shifting bank balance, a skill especially useful before salaried career paths are solidified and discotheque cover charges are replaced with bassinette expenses. Learn to turn on a nickel and dime—like down-shifting from Pellegrino to tap water—when transmission overhauls drain savings and derail vacation plans. On the other hand, with a healthy bonus or Fantasy 5 windfall, practice the art of temporary extravagance. For freelancers with undulating take-home pay, adaptability is a survival skill ensuring there's not too much month left at the end of the paycheck.

When rocky times require spending cuts, prioritize expenditures using our three-point scale, highlighting areas for reduction. Editing your lifestyle is painful, but God willin' and the creeks don't rise, a little thriftiness now means you'll be able to rejoice when a promotion or financial surge warrant the triumphant return of lost B- and C-class luxuries.

♥ **A**: *Mandatory, fixed expenses:* rent/mortgage, insurance, transportation, mistress's hush money. These are the nondiscretionary Medicare and Social Security of your household budget, set expenses that won't change unless wholesale reform and lower-rent digs are considered.

◆ **B**: *Things you could live without, but really shouldn't:* organic groceries, smart work clothes, salon coif instead of mall hairdo, rechargeable sex toys. "B" includes slightly dear luxuries that often get trimmed of fat but never fully eliminated until financial catastrophe strikes or credit maxes out, forcing a scale back of usual quality and comfort.

♥ **C**: *Things you could live without:* premium movie channels, personal trainers, weekly four-star dining experiences, his and her Cessnas. These opulent treats fluctuate with the times. In a fat economy, you might be drinking Super Tuscans and Penfolds Grange, but if saving for a down payment has become a priority, then it's $15-and-under value bottles until purse strings are loosened.

As financial changes trip your budgetary thermostat, convene a family conference to cool down spending below showroom temperature. Plot your ABCs and employ flexibility when tighter times call for a redrawing of priorities. In the end, synchronize wallets to avoid the rancor of one party saving pennies for the newborn while the other is still blowing thousands on 500-watt car speaker cabinets.

WAYS & MEANS COMMITTEE

Spending first and lobbying later does not curry favor with the appropriations committee. To avoid a budgetary crackdown over expensive fur coats or hefty Water Buffalo club dues, obtain partner preapproval on big-ticket items or risk pleading afterward to prevent returns. Wise couples set a maximum dollar amount for unilateral purchases: anything under this limit will not be questioned during times of stability. Once the ceiling is set, complaints are grumbled at your peril; for instance, if it's under the magic number, must you bellyache about $40 Kiehl's eye cream after you've loaded up on martini lunches and new DVDs? By the first grays on your head, you'll learn the consequences of frivolous spending since every selfish dollar you fritter away on another video game system saps the household's net worth. In the end, you realize that money isn't just a personal stash but the vehicle for future family holidays and children's college funds—events far more substantial than your single-handed attempt to stimulate the market economy.

Nice touch: Stave off debt-spiking mail-order spending binges by slyly intercepting and recycling incoming catalogues that hawk tempting ornamental schlock on glossy pages with promises of free shipping and no money down. If later discovered by a trash-rummaging mate, proffer a white lie: "Oh, that Pottery Barn catalogue? I smashed a palmetto bug with it this morning."

LOVE THY ACCOUNT HOLDER

After living in sin and acclimating to dual lifestyle expectations, the transition to commingled finances ought to be smooth. Spending trends shouldn't change much after marriage merges two salaries, though old jalopies and bedroom sets might be upgraded as more income funnels from individual paychecks into the newly opened joint account. The ideal system promotes stability and independence: the lion's share of each spouse's salary is earmarked for the joint account, covering shared expenses, with the remainder placed into savings and slush fund accounts for individual petty cash. Percentages are determined by the total household income level. As a starting figure for two wage earners, expect only 10 to 20 percent of each paycheck to trickle down into the separate accounts. However modest, individual checking accounts should be maintained lest partners lose face and financial freedom when even a pack of chewing gum must be charged on the joint debit card. Furthermore, this arrangement preserves the surprise of in-house gift giving while preventing the faux pas of purchasing a sweetheart's birthday present with her own money.

Incidentally, if you both partake, joint money is indeed joint money.

BREADWINNER'S CAVEAT

Flamboyant costumery and handlebar moustaches aside, the breadwinner is not the feudal lord of the estate. A shortcut to subordination and divorce is razzing your spouse over pay stubs, equating higher salary with a higher rank in the marriage. Since bringing home bank does not necessarily equal working harder, the breadwinner should be crowned anew each week according to labor, not FICA deductions. Invaluable perks such as a prime parking spot in the breezeway and avoided bureaucratic headaches at the DMV or tax assessor's office ought to be offered to the dog-tired mate, not the slacker with an overpaying sinecure. Regardless of income disparity, make sure you're both enjoying a comparable lifestyle: only a major income-earning ass regally pays the bills and then hoards kingly luxuries for himself. A new leather briefcase is fine, but no stalwart husband is seen tooling around in a Jaguar XJ series while his wife burns oil and leaks antifreeze in an old Buick Skyhawk.

WALLOWING

Sometimes a couple decides that one partner will stay at home to pen the next best seller or care for diapered children. In other instances, an unexpected downturn or herniated disk strikes at the household's financial and emotional stability. For example, the man is stuck in a workless rut, so the lady of the house plays the gray-suited moneymaker, or the career woman's social science degree doesn't play in a recession job market, so the gent gamely stretches his paycheck for two. The joint account is for the marital commonweal, and today's modern couples should care not a whit if one partner is the sole contributor for a spell. Society may unduly brand a dependent man more pathetic than an out-of-work missus, but either scenario requires the same consideration at home.

Even among otherwise-patient lovers, a strained vibe can develop after the unemployed partner enters month three of miserable skulking over cold coffee and a warm laptop, fruitlessly surfing the online class-ifieds. Lacking the credibility of a business card, the wallower feels most like a domestic parasite during these key moments: (1) when the working stiff goes to bed, leaving the idle mate reclined on the couch rapt by a late night feature; (2) early morning, when the homebody snores through the employed partner's alarm; and (3) later, when the 9-to-5er comes home tired and stressed as compared to the free agent who's just finished reading another detective novel before stretching for a refreshing jog in the park.

Similarly, a sole paycheck can feel like a scepter of power, but during unnerving times, domineering and patronizing comments should not be hurled at the wallower ("I see you've worked on your tan . . . how about working on the house for a change?"). No one, man or woman, likes to be undercut like an ungrateful juvenile accused of sponging off his parents. With a loss of respect, communication breaks down and the unemployed begins to walk on eggshells, ever fearful of speaking out lest the "j-o-b" word is uttered. Instead of striving to improve, the broken mate is reduced to stubborn and defensive beggary, especially when panhandling extra spending money for a night with friends. Left unchecked, self-esteem flags, sex appeal withers, and limpness seeps from bankbook to bedroom.

The starving artist genius, the bespectacled academic, and the skilled craftsman get a pass—for a while—but for everyone else, rapid changes must be made to prevent a financial rough spot from scarring relations. Enact a new budget and take a respectful tone toward the downtrodden to prevent his or her total ego collapse. Include the out-of-work mate in financial affairs and bill paying, so that the domestic piggy bank isn't a guarded secret. A weekly allowance on a joint debit card discourages the wallower from ringing up additional debt on high-interest plastic and eliminates the ignominious Monday ritual of handing out a weekly cash dole. In return, the idler shoulders the brunt of housework, chores hopefully lauded by the working mate, not assumed as part of financial servitude. Regular monthly reviews ensure that the foot of resentment

MILLIONAIRE

♥ ◆ ♥ **Dark rum** ♥ **Apricot brandy** ♥ **Sloe gin** ♥ **Juice of one lime** ♥ ◆ ♥
♥ ◆ ♥ ◆ ♥ ◆ ♥ ◆ ♥ ◆ ♥ **Dash grenadine** ♥ ◆ ♥ ◆ ♥ ◆ ♥ ◆ ♥ ◆ ♥

doesn't snub out sexual crackle. Lastly, homebodies need to demonstrate a committed plan to reenter employment; waiting for the world to magically discover your half-finished canvases as you lounge in a haze of dope smoke and midafternoon naps will eventually land you poor and single.

IN-LAWS & OUTLAWS

"Hold on, I'll get her." These words define the classic in-law relationship: cordial but not chummy, and like your mother-in-law's cooking, satisfactory but rarely yummy. Then again, perhaps you got lucky and inherited a sane family with a tradition of culinary expertise, wine appreciation, and healthy dowries. Early on you'll both know whose roots are knottier, especially during holidays. If your own family gatherings are punctuated by malfeasants bearing gift-wrapped twelve-packs, thank the heavens that her parents' Thanksgiving debates are only about marshmallows in the sweet potatoes.

When Daddy still presumed that you were a foul-minded suitor looking to tarnish his little girl's sterling maidenhood, the savvy modern lover tolerated his future in-laws, if only for the sake of propriety. Now, as a newly minted member of the family, you are wise to embrace the clan and play anthropologist, observing dinner table dynamics and sibling quirks to gain greater hereditary insights into what to expect from your mate down the road. Moreover, coax tales about the family crest and Ellis Island adventures to endear yourself to an overly suspicious, if genial, caste of elders. Once scribed into the cover of the family Bible, you are free to explore the possible fringe benefits and anguishes of your second family. Does the Memorial Day barbecue roster boast an investment banker, publisher, or airline pilot with an amazing stash of diminutive liquor bottles, or is her uncle Marvin an insider trader and cousin Josiah a bail jumper, prompting fears of 4 A.M. calls from a holding cell? Shake a family tree hard enough and some fruit will fall out.

Jams for the tea tray, stogies to Papa, and chocolates for sis are never amiss. Sow the seeds of good relations with bestowed flowers and high-profile compliments, not just toward your darling but also her ravishing mother. Like when you grinned your way through pre-prom parental meet-and-greets in the sitting room, play the polite provider to spare you harder questions about your grandfather's background with the Teamsters.

NAGGING DISTANCE

As you navigate the roaring rapids of another's kin, there are two ways to avoid obstacles: (1) remove in-law intrusions from the equation by putting a down payment on a faraway address, forming a buffer of at least four smaller eastern states or two boxier western territories; or (2) settle at a reasonable call-ahead distance.

Option 1 is tempting, but option 2 is more viable for most couples, particularly when children are in the mix. Nearby in-laws can be first-aid kits to newlyweds and shaky veterans alike. One hour provides a minimum driving time that affords enough warning to fluff sofa pillows and recycle the empties. While anything closer is convenient for babysitting, living in the same voting district fails to provide a physical and emotional buffer zone. There's peace of mind for a pair who can handle things in-house before choosing to go public with ills; by stretching the highway miles, you control the news ticker feed of money troubles and forgettable spats.

Should your spouse fail to ratify even a short move, fret not. Staying in town spares you packing headaches and unneeded hernias, and avails you of an extended network that can be counted on for support (as well as running commentary on your foibles). Jump into the family fracas eagerly and, if you're feeling bold (or underemployed), join the family business. Assuming that you're not living in a neovegan commune where families reside no more than an organic beet toss apart, you and your honey can create distance by setting a weekly quota for phone calls and discouraging unannounced stopovers.

Regardless of parental proximity, it is the nature of in-laws to sniff out trouble. Concerned parents ought to reach out during stormy weather, but no one needs a barrage of emails for every drizzle ("Honey,

---

YOUR MOTHER

Mom is typically counted upon for the "you can do no wrong" routine. With the rose-colored hue of maternal specs, she might seem like the ideal person to voice gripes to when you're in the doghouse. Nevertheless, it is vital to establish your wife as the most important woman in your life. Early on, your mother sized up your mate over dinner with twenty questions about educational background, family pedigree, and homemaking skills. Even though the *nothing's-too-good-for-sonny* scrutiny abates posthoneymoon, a good husband understands the slight uneasiness his wife feels when talking to his mother alone. You can't control your mother-in-law, but exert some control over your own mom's meddling by stemming the outflow of information and the influx of disparagement. Modern love is hard enough without a pull of the reins from a backseat driver. Instead of offering an indictment of your wife's shortcomings to a biased judge, extol your marital harmony with a showcase of good news ("You wouldn't believe Arianne's broccoli rabe casserole, and her new backside tattoo is a vision!").

is he out playing Texas Hold 'Em with the mortgage again?"). With more relatives to answer to, cultivate a poker face and play coy, particularly when referencing your spouse's gaffes in front of her parents. To ward off boresome invitations, be a little private with your affairs and date book; a tactfully vague "That's not a good weekend for us" should suffice. Newlyweds can always play the "We really just want to be alone" excuse, which triggers mother-in-law's swoon: "Oh, grandchildren soon?"

Incidentally, if the two of you are facing real financial troubles, remember that marriage is like bipartisan legislation: with the ring, the newly united appropriations committee may offer monetary support from both sides of the aisle.

THE EXTENDED VISIT

When Mom and Pop pull up a wagonload of valises for a long stay, you'd better do more than edit the contents of the medicine cabinet. Horny couples might schedule an all-nighter earlier in the week to avoid cooled passions from Dad's snoring in the adjacent guest room. On long weekends, in-laws get favored guest treatment. However, in exchange for a fortnight foray, delegate light kitchen and laundry duties. When it's your parents, expect to man the tour bus and guide the walks to town; when it's hers, sit down at dinner together but ignore any finger-wagging over a skipped weekday luncheon as you stick to previous commitments. Orchestrate festive opening- and closing-night ceremonies but worry not if two consecutive evenings land the family on the front porch with no more entertainment than gin rickeys and easy chat.

HOLIDAY ROTATION

Her parents want the couple there for Christmas, but your mom is quick to recall that you've spent two of the last three away from her side. To avoid playing favorites, run the holidays on rotation. When this apolitical method fails, declare home field advantage and tell everyone to bugger off ("No can do—we're spending Arbor Day at our place"). Since most families can handle the holiday trade, practice the shrewd negotiation tactics of a seasoned, deal-making general manager ("You can have Easter, Columbus Day, and New Year's this year, but my mom wants Groundhog Day, Washington's Birthday, and a federal holiday to be named later").

Nice touch: When visiting the in-laws at the ancestral home in the sticks, join in local customs. Tag along for 4 A.M. ice-fishing on the pond or skeet-shooting on the range. If strange marmalades and group toasts with Swedish glog are family traditions, shrug and sip as if the finest nectar. Creepy rituals, such as joining relatives to kiss great-grandmother's headstone behind the tool shed, are optional.

THE RAP

Avoid taking the heat for your partner's unpopular choices. Has your wife decided to opt for the powdery paradise of Taos in lieu of her mom's Christmas ham or freeze her kid sister out of intimate New Year's party plans? If the situation is left unexplained, you will be considered an accessory to, if not the instigator of, her breaches of family loyalty because it's easier to point the finger at the presumed interloper than their doting, perfect daughter. These black marks are stored in the incorruptible memory banks to be brought out during your next misstep. Accordingly, a conscientious partner shields you by admitting that the decision to be the dissident was hers alone, not the result of your insidious lobbying.

OUTLAWS

With the rise of half-siblings, stepparents, friendly exes, and live-in kin, you might wonder, Just how deep does the in-law roster go? It's okay if peripheral family, such as your wife's mother's sister's first husband, don't make the holiday card cut. Outside of the immediate circle, you get first right of refusal for gifting and sifting through the issues. The rehab-rebounding second cousin who never returns an RSVP . . . screen his call. The first natural dividing line is the receiving line—especially for small weddings, whosoever attended the ceremony warrants continued regards. Though, like gerrymandered legislative districts during election years, relationship boundaries get redrawn from time to time.

DOUBLE AGENT

Play show-and-tell with your brother-in-law but don't be wooed into a false sense of brotherhood. Just because you two traded tales of exploits at the bachelor party, recall that he's wired for sound to report back to sis. If you have a wealth of harmless secrets to confide, dish those out rather than disclosing major improprieties that would taint your standing with the in-laws.

Establishing brotherly relations is easier when you're both married. A silent understanding akin to the mutually assured destruction (MAD) Cold War doctrine develops: you sink me with tabloid retelling to the family, and I'll bury you in triplicate all the way to divorce court. Each party's nuclear arsenal is clear to behold and a pleasant détente develops. When positively leveraged, the more dirt you have on each other, the deeper your bond can go, up to the rank of a trustworthy first cousin. On the other hand, an unmarried brother-in-law is a wild card. Beware the tempting bachelor with stay-out-all-night tendencies, a steady connection, and a penchant for luring you into seedy downtown massage parlors.

SISTERS-IN-LAW

The tight-lipped precautions taken with brothers-in-law are multiplied for sisters-in-law, the rat finks of the family. While they are a prime source for dirt on your spouse's old flames, beware ill-advised disclosure of your own secrets, guaranteed to reach the entire family faster than the spread of plague through fourteenth-century England. Younger sisters-in-law often admire older sibs and view you, the dashing groom, in a princely light. With a gaggle of sisters, however, befriend the eldest first since the opinions of low-ranking, unmarried allies carry less weight.

Take note of the strength of bond between sisters. Is there a predictable nightly call after 10 P.M. or just cordial contact around birthdays? Whereas brothers with sixty-hour workweeks may only keep current with major developments, sisters are more likely to hunt down the daily scoop. Expect a married-with-children sister to serve as a sounding board for minutiae that never reaches your ears. Although this intimacy might bring home racy gossip about your sister-in-law's acrobatic sex life, realize that it is bartered for near 100 percent replay from your wife's side of the bed. This two-way information highway explains the knowing nods you notice over family dinners following an especially kinky weekend.

MONTHLY REVIEW

Former three-term New York mayor Ed Koch famously barked, "How'm I doin'?" Mimic this rallying cry and setup the monthly review with your partner to acknowledge what's working, what's off-kilter, and what new patterns are exciting or excruciating. Regular fireside chats complimenting last Sunday's pot roast or panning last Saturday's temper tantrum are the ultimate Gallup poll of relationship approval ratings. Practiced often, they are a great show of active listening, verbal affections, and respectful debate. Expect a new and improved marriage, with 33 percent less nagging and 25 percent more constructive criticism.

A regular monthly powwow stems current troubles, but most of the time, it's merely an abbreviated java jive or pleasant date to affirm continued satisfaction on both sides. This scheduled day is the couple's monthly open office hour for directly voicing kudos and criticism. Warm up with plusses that soften a partner's receptiveness to reproof. Aired grievances begin with a close look at household basics like chores and finances before moving into the pleasant logistics of holiday calendars and social obligations. Then, zoom out for a big picture view of more pressing matters like shaky fidelity, long-term plans, and sexual requests (which are ideally granted upon adjournment).

While rave reviews are great, a year of straight A+s feels like an eerie wonderland of blissful deceit. Sugarcoating upsets used to make sense to preserve the status quo of fuss-free, steady action. Now, shying away from frank disclosure and touchy subjects stunts marital growth and bottles up minor anxieties until they explode. Only so much trouble can happen in a month, even the thirty-one-day variety. Regular honest appraisals let you know if it's bad (and getting worse) before a year of discontent erupts, seemingly out of nowhere. If you've both done your homework, that last bite of creamy tiramisu during your anniversary fête won't be choked down with the bitter lump of "I haven't been happy since last April." With small course corrections, you'll avoid running too far in an unwise direction, like Wrong-Way Riegels who picked up a fumble and ambled sixty-six yards toward the incorrect end zone, costing the Cal Bears the 1929 Rose Bowl championship.

Incidentally, if things go dreadfully wrong for too long, it's best to have your attorney present at subsequent monthly meetings—these are usually expensive affairs called *depositions* and will determine whether you will be sleeping in your own bed or a Motel 6 until the next court date.

Chapter Seven

MOMENTUM

♦ ♥ ♦ ♥ ♦ ♥ ♦ ♥

HIS & HERS

[fluffy pink] — Hers — {nappy taupe}

Couples who don't preserve their identities, musical tastes, and ideology merge into one-word appellations like "Kim&Ken," and outsiders can't tell where one spouse ends and the other begins. Worse yet is a relationship plagued by trust issues and frequent squabbles; one partner's suspicion leads to a crackdown on the other's individual pursuits, rendering him into a homogenized skim version of his old farm-fresh buttermilk self. Contrast these sorry situations with a fulfilled twosome whose household stability is so well established that his and her hobbies are not only tolerated but encouraged. Personal goals and causes célèbres, whether artistic, political, or herbivorous, aren't always shared: she's off to renounce urban sprawl at the town meeting, and he's seeking enlightenment at two-for-one draughts and poetry night.

SANCTUARY

While separate pastimes are essential to a healthy relationship, big problems arise when diversions become a sanctuary from the marriage itself. You may not be a secretary-mounting infidel, but you're time-cheating. Repairing to the sweaty haven of triathlon training is unimpeachable as long as you put in your quality time at home too. The alternative is doubly poisonous, whereby a partner not only stews over neglect but also curses your racing bike, wet suit, and running shoes.

Remedy the "bad hobby, bad hubby" rant with an invitation to your studio. Unless you're a temperamental genius or work with isotopes, your work area should not be off-limits to your spouse. It's heartening to have a blithe muse nearby providing inspiration and a refreshing lemonade. Some creative hobbies, like painting, are obviously a solo gig, but a partner in the same room can be hard at work at her own passion and might even learn to adore your craft. How can a chess master command respect on the international circuit if his wife still thinks that "white castling" means ordering a crinkly bag of mini-hamburgers?

#1 FAN

Each partner's primary pursuits are sacrosanct, not free-time resources to be poached. Pick up extra slack and forgive domestic errands while she attends her weekly gallop at the stables. Couples work around one another's activities and refrain from tainting leisure with guilt ("Have fun at theatre rehearsal. I'll be home tarring the roof all by myself"). Practice is one thing, but tourneys and invitationals dictate your willing attendance—even if her annual découpage exhibition makes you want to cut and paste yourself in front of a firing squad. However, frivolous pleasures like sci-fi fixations aren't always prominent enough to require joint appearances. Excuse your partner from duty and pursue your own cult worship of *Battlestar Galactica* without dragging a mate to the cinema dressed like a Cylon.

Incidentally, family and holidays trump the hobby bug. The New Year's Eve Central Park run is delightful for a jogging twosome but loathsome for the family of antsy partygoers shivering in tuxedos like idiots, with Champagne flutes in one hand and Gatorade in the other.

SPOUSELESS CAROUSING

[footloose and fancy-free]

Eng and Chang, the illustrious conjoined twins of Siam, were forever connected at the chest. Despite this, the brothers married two American sisters and, with a flair for ménage à trois, fathered twenty-two children. Every three days, one brother would surrender his will to the other, and thus the two commanded separate farms and families. After years of doing everything together, with zero time allotted for solo outings, modern marrieds become similarly attached at the hip. True, marriage needs two drivers to navigate, but each must nevertheless exclude the other now and again for an independent night of spouseless carousing.

Extroverts revert to shydom without enough at-bats on the social scene. Torpid homebodies become short-syllabled at cocktail parties, quietly morphing into pathetic twitches who forget how to mingle without the security blanket of a nearby spouse. In addition to polishing your charm, circulating among strangers casts your sweetheart in fresh light, as a lover's winning traits are magnified after window-shopping the unremarkable masses. The peek back into single life's less glamorous aspects also brings the more general benefits of a solid home life into relief. With an espresso-laden bloodstream, linger on the town for a panoramic dose of the "last call" world of lonely souls looking for "the one" in between tequila snorts and slurred come-ons. Mind your manners on these jaunts since spouseless carousing works on the demerit system: expect home-front friction if you accrue too many black marks from regurgitative boozing, rash spending, stained clothes, or body damage.

Other times, your lover wins the coin toss and elects to receive. When her chums appear at the door in fresh lipstick ready for Ladies' Night, slip into the background and wordlessly volunteer to sit this one out. Ideally, both spouses carouse separately with their own roving bands only to meet up and exchange tales. However, if your darling bows out altogether due to a drippy nose or whooping cough, at least stick around long enough to provide homespun TLC before jumping into your party pants. With an assortment of meds, tissues, and bedtime stories, the well-attended recuperating mate can peacefully convalesce in a quiet home while you battle disco fever with provocative friends.

Incidentally, designate a few activities—tapas, trainspotting, Tarrantino films—"for couples only." A gentleman holds these favorites aside and indulges only with his lover. Then again, yikes to those codependents who call dibs on everything ("But cupcake, *I* wanted to watch the *Sex and the City* finale with you").

TAKEN

During most interactions, marital status is tangential; nonetheless, it is your responsibility to manage perceptions of your availability without erecting unnecessary boundaries. Aside from your-place-or-mine propositions, must opposite-sex encounters warrant a ring-finger salute and quick-draw of the wedding license? Integrity ultimately determines the glass ceiling of flirtatious encounters, and it's okay to hold off about your status as long as you speak up before you appear the conniving two-timer looking for a willing accomplice. Still, can't a bit of sassy persiflage and winsome eye contact simmer a while before your gold badge of commitment is prominently flashed along with a yard-long wallet reel of family photos?

Incidentally, leave the wedding band behind during yard work, dips in the ocean, or messy lube jobs, but a ringed finger is mandatory for spouseless outings. When your groin attempts a nightclub coup d'état of your better judgment, the ring is a palpable nudge of temperance. Lame excuses, such as "Sweetheart, I just can't grip the pool cue properly," won't wash, even for lobotomized spouses.

LONE SWEET HOME

With your dearest on the town for a night, an empty house is invitation to indulge. Turn up the tunes and steal a smoke on the porch, but don't feel like a zero if you just curl up with a novel or a rental flick for a little extended DIY. But don't jolt your high-heeled, mini-skirted fox back to flawed reality by letting her find you snoring an off-tune concerto on the couch amidst a ghetto of crumpled beer cans and leaky take-out containers. Worse, a towering landfill of neglected dishes or a shoes-strewn foyer suggests passive aggression toward your lover's exciting eve without you. Welcome her home instead with a tidied main room and kind ear, not an interrogation of whereabouts, consumed drinks, and busy lips. Indeed, this is no time to reawaken trust issues or lay down far-flung

ONE EXCITING NIGHT

♥ **Gin** ♥ **Dry & sweet vermouth** ♥ **Orange juice** ♥ **Frost glass with sugar** ♥

edicts, like Khrushchev's repressive Soviet fist clamping down on freedom in the Balkans.

Nice touch: Next time it's your turn to head out for an extended
spouseless getaway, leave a breathy voice mail, then stuff love notes in her
dresser drawer, daily planner, compact, and car visor, not to mention
suspended in the ice tray, inked on the next rolling-paper sheet, or
folded inside her preferred antianxiety prescription bottle.

ON-TIME DEPARTURES

[timepiece]

[twenty minutes late]

Hearken back to family vacations when you were wedged in the back of a
station wagon next to a drooling border collie, awaiting the final push-
off from the driveway. One twitchy parent always held up the show with
one last loo visit, oven check, curtains look, patio door–latch test, and
druidlike ministrations over the already twice-watered houseplants. The
engine would then start, but before the parking brake snapped back,
"Wait! What if the kids scrape their knees water-skiing? I'll get the peroxide." Fast-forward to adulthood when the stopwatch is ticking down to
an 8 P.M. dinner reservation, and your partner is . . . almost ready.

WHEN YOU'RE THE TARDY PARTY

The Battle of Waterloo ended Napoleon's One Hundred Days, as the
Duke of Wellington's beefy allied troops prevailed over French forces that

squandered precious minutes waiting for marching orders (and fresh baguettes). Unless you also seek exile to St. Helena—or the living room couch—learn from this famous skirmish and quit dillydallying. While timeliness is a laudable goal, it shouldn't come at the expense of appearance. It's not as easy as throwing jeans and sneakers on anymore to meet the boys in the cul-de-sac for a game of capture the flag. To keep from holding up the caravan, avoid these last-minute clock-eaters:

♥ **Unprepped Auto**: No gas, beverages, decent music, or confirmed highway directions needlessly waylay the departure. In extreme climes, while your spouse is powdering her nose, scrape the windshield, de-ice the locks, shovel a path, and blast the interior heat. An under-the-seat umbrella covers unexpected downpours, and an ashtray full of coins eliminates the mind-numbing twelve-minute waste to break a fifty at the full-service toll lane or hunt quarters for a meter.

TESTY TIMETABLE

TIME	FLIGHT	STATUS
7:30	Call from In-laws	ON TIME
9:30	Dinner with Friends	DELAYED
12:30	Love in the Bedroom after Evening Squabble	CANCELLED

• **Appearance & Inventory**: Showering after packing spares you sweaty patches and wrinkled duds on a July day. Chic moments call for a newly paired ensemble, but when minutes are precious, select from proven shirt-and-slacks combos ever ready to grab and go without sacrificing style. For frequent overnighters, invest five whole dollars in a shadow set of travel-only toiletries to avoid ransacking the medicine cabinet for floss and cotton swabs as your ride rides the horn at the curb.

LATE LOVER

When your spouse is thirty minutes behind (as opposed to thirty days late), the goal is to exit the house expediently with minimal antagonism. Barring critical appointments when seconds count, a gentleman moderates his tone when coaxing punctuality. The ten ticks saved through watch-tapping harangues, needless name-calling, and key-jingling huffs aren't worth the residual bitterness that sullies the start of an otherwise joyous evening. Moreover, "Let's go!" shouting matches compound over time into a nagging issue, all for the sake of not missing previews at the cinema.

Early arrival is ideal, but don't naysay a trailing yet elegant partner who embodies the multitiered process of sophisticated femininity in action. Instead, seek out your lover face-to-face with a low-volume request for her Estimated Departure Time (EDT) in minutes. With this number in hand, calculate the Actual Departure Time (ADT):

$$ADT = 2 (EDT) + 5$$

Thus, double the EDT ("I'll be ready in 15") and add 5 minutes.

$(2 \times 15) + 5 = 35$ minutes until Actual Departure Time

This sum is the grace period given to your spouse. Disputatious hollers from down the hall are counterproductive, as such loss of cool results in a mandatory five-minute spite penalty. For the perpetually tardy, use ADT as a countdown to offer a gentle nudge of urgency: "Darling, the car is packed. As Johnny Cash crooned, you've got twenty-five minutes to go." If necessary, invoke the NASA launch protocol and count down in ten-minute intervals until the final ignition sequence. Though, before bellowing, ensure you are 100-percent ready and not the colorblind frump in need of a costume change or the thoughtless chump who squandered ample time watching the telly instead of walking the pup.

Incidentally, leave it behind. After badgering a mate out the door with a torrent of clock-minding shoos, never mind retrieving forgotten trifles. A dash back inside at this juncture earns you an automatic demerit.

LINT PICKING

When running late, the threat of overlooked clothing tags and toothpaste splotches looms. On the way out, each partner should perform final quality control on the other: look for razor nics and shaving cream evidence; lipstick smudges; stocking runs and mismatched belts; zippers at half mast; and renegade nose hairs, which may provide an immune system bulwark against invading contaminants but are still gauche in most circles under age seventy-five. If you think leaving for the concert on time is bad enough now, double your displeasure when kids and their bagged needs are inserted into the equation.

RHYTHM METHOD

Steady and married couples swear off promiscuity and in return should bask in a steady fount of earnest, loin-quenching sex. In the younger days of woo, few responsibilities meant limitless time for rattling the bedpost. Presently, as 9-to-5ers with a booked nightlife, healthy duos settle into a rhythm that is less voluminous yet still satisfying. Left unchecked, however, sexual frequency slips far below the recommended weekly allowance, with such concurrent side effects as weight gain, bedside channel flipping, underworked prostate, bushy privates, desiccated wit, and skyrocketing porn budget. Despite the ease of climbing into comfy sheets and nodding off with but a peck on the cheek, steer clear of this PG-rated love rut whence workaholism and lassitude render hot sex a once-per—Halley's comet conjugal treat.

Sexual regularity, like it's colonic cousin, is tied to diet: going malnourished for a week won't kill you, but over time, haphazard intake will befoul a once vibrant pelvis. An otherwise solid couple can fall back on the friendship bond during a drought, but a bevy of bedless months ultimately undermines closeness. Lovemaking is a salve to most abrasions: when sincere apologies and constructive talk are exhausted, tender tumbles smooth over minor hurts and major wounds alike. For couples in a low-frequency state, sexual healing isn't an available treatment. Indeed, a miserly sex quotient can exacerbate brewing discontent, escalating civil chats into the twelve-round main event of nightly dinner-table sparring.

For better or for worse, live-ins and marrieds sign an enduring contract that ensures security even as regularity temporarily dips or gradually decreases over forty wonderful years. Yet, this isn't an excuse to settle for sexless companionship or so-so love. When a season of slumping turns passion from plump fruit to shriveled raisin, the couple should redouble efforts to flood the bedroom with frequency.

QUARTERLY PROJECTIONS

While a gent isn't stocked with a finite supply of hard-ons, he shouldn't let too many slink away unheeded. A meteoric rise in prophylactic expenses is offset by the satisfaction provided by regular action. There is no magic number appropriate for every relationship, though one to two times per month is the bare-assed minimum. Either write down an attainable goal (not necessarily an actual integer) or set an innate alarm to sound when lingerie has gathered too much dust. The daily paper is tough to beat, but a couple should at least come more frequently than quarterly periodicals. Indeed, the occasional double shot of Sunday morning love defrags the couple's hard drive and soothes a week's worth of backaches that even health club whirlpools can't unkink.

Incidentally, a vigorous sex life is the first and best jetty against a rising tide of infidelity. Satiety wards off distractions and corrals a lad's wandering eye. Undersexed, fidgety partners are reduced to erotic mouse clicks, twenty dollar lap dances, or worse, desperate flirtation with the lithe teenage Good Humor girl, prompting the driver to quip, "Go home to your wife."

CALENDARING

When business meetings and arbitrage emergencies conspire to stifle valuable sack time, make a plan for sex ("Tuesday? I can squeeze you in at 6:30"). It sounds businesslike, but a date assures a night of potency on the docket: silky threads, long candles, favored props, deactivated phones, and a chance to pull down (or up) the shades, whatever your fancy. A whole day's foment of fantasy preheats the bed, priming eyes for the first bare gaze upon your partner. With time to spare, shake up the lackluster "thrust, roll, and snooze" with a dual gym workout to warm the blood. Then, pop in a sexy Andrew Blake rental, stretch out for sensual massage, or draw a lingering bath. For a bout of wild, vocal sex, book an overnight stay—perfect for live-ins with roommates or couples with but inches of drywall between their bed and mom's ear.

REQUIRED ROLLICKING

Don't be the partner whose sexuality lies barren like a once vibrant wetland drained for a strip mall. Even the most sex-challenged bedfellows should never miss these mandatory opportunities, when any excuse less than a fractured limb or communicable disease won't exempt you from duty.

♥ **Landmarked Days**: Consecrate on birthdays, anniversaries, and holidays. If it's worth cutting cake, popping corks, or suspending alternate side of the street parking, it's worth spreading out the satin sheets.

♦ **Jet-Setting**: Relations are compulsory the night before and the day after any solo trip that requires checked baggage. To save run-ins with airport security or hard choices with faraway convention floozies, don't leave the house loaded.

♥ **Room Service**: Unfamiliar environs and worry-free surroundings are an automatic aphrodisiac, so turn it up with turndown service. Don't worry if you leave handprints on either side of the full-length mirror or track tub suds from bathroom floor to bed.

♦ **Black Tie:** Strapless cocktail dresses and feathered boas—feast on your
honey's finery after the masquerade ball. Spur a listless we-cycle back
on the upswing with a frenzied stripping of cuff links and stockings.

♥ **Last Call:** Heed the two-minute warning when a lover throws down the
imminent-sex gauntlet ("Either we hit the sheets by sundown or I'm

---

BAD REVIEWS

The corrosive cousin of sporadic sex is bad sex. A stubborn spell of sexual
malaise is a string of four or more lifeless sessions that feature climaxes no
higher than a C+ (with the class curve). When this week's sex feels like a
predictable rerun of last week's ho-hummers, postcoital prattling begins and
ends with, "What's on Bravo tonight?" A few botched encounters inevitably
lead to thoughts of diet, exercise, and a plate of oysters, but after an unin-
spiring month of dull humping, a lasting silence chills the headboard.

If a partner's hang-ups routinely shortchange pleasure, bring it up without fanfare over a glass of warm milk in bed rather than questioning the inner
workings of your hardware. As for your own sluggishness, barring a medical
condition that leaves you limper than a mink stole, a slump can happen now
and again without sounding the alarm. Desires change with the seasons:
expect winter days of asexuality, spring periods of insatiability, autumn afternoons of increased masturbation, and summer eves of a quietly surging libido
brought on by pounding surf, sand, and substances.

No one expects a showstopper every time, and a conscientious lover
grants clemency for occasional stumbles. Retreat to the less complicated
pleasures of the oral arts and work your way back to quality intercourse. If
all else fails, a prodigious amount of tequila clears worried minds, perhaps
breaking the spell and replacing bed aches with headaches.

gonna do it myself"). Moreover, keep tabs on your lover's cycle and synchronize to her peak of arousal before the monthly intermission.

• **Coattails:** Satisfaction radiates zeal: a frigid pair might do well to bask in the rays of a sparkling couple's sizzling demeanor. Carousing with an infectious naughty twosome? It's natural to find your own vibe inspired upon the return home.

LIP SERVICE

If a spate of quickies and half-baked *schtups* shortchange affections, revisit a classic: there is no better foreplay than a sultry make-out session. Lip-lock that stirs old-fashioned hot-and-botheredness is as potent as a *Kama Sutra*—inspired night of suspended congress. Long-term couples unfortunately relegate kissing to second-class steerage, a hasty act I before the denouement of intercourse. Recall the time when every exploratory touch was novel by traversing the semipublic erogenous zones of wrists, digits, and shoulders. Vary technique with more than a spelunking tongue. Try the vacuum kiss (sharing breath), electric kiss (shuffling feet on a shag rug before a smooch), butterfly kiss (eyelash fluttering), or upside-down kiss. Meanwhile, tousle hair, caress arms, sigh, and don't rush into more—like an otolaryngologist, you still have the ears, nose, and throat to tend to.

GOING TO POT

[disinterested]

[dissatisfied]

During full-press courtship, you were up on contemporary authors, indie labels, and off-the-avenue eateries, and as an adventure-seeker, you boasted a taste for moguls on the ski slopes. As the dating life gave rise to long-term amour, the drive for metropolitan savvy gradually mellowed in the face of monogamy. Face-plants, formerly into Killington snowbanks, are now onto the living room sofa in perfect Andy Capp—apathy position. In the golden days of exquisite evening plans, you slyly preheated a handful of enticements—little gifts, sexy whispers, after-hours jaunts—that have long since gone the way of your hairline. Instead of seeking to impress a steady femme at every waking moment, you cruise on wooing autopilot. After a fifth consecutive listless weekend, your restless partner bewails your lazy overgrowth and caterwauls about this ghost town of a social life. Unheeded, this haranguing becomes nagging, which begets sulking.

In dating days, you were a credit risk, and wise companions didn't float you a long-term love loan without a decent return on investment. Once married, a gentleman fights the urge to lean on past efforts while barely paying the monthly minimum. A series of small declines left unchecked refuels

a chugging train of old bachelor habits: unkempt hygiene, disheveled clothing, homebody inertia, and free-floating flab. Robust relationships are
strong enough to survive temporary dips, yet without vigilance, even a
little household slouching can turn into a paralysis of nonchalance.

THE EVIL NIELSEN ROUTINE

Arrive home from work pushing your briefcase like Sisyphus's stone,
microwave dinner, stare at the TV, brush your teeth, and go to bed.
Rinse and repeat Monday through Thursday for a dull life. It's important to have solo transitional time after work, and for many people, premium cable and video games are the decompression chamber that never
disappoints. Partners are wont to understand and even encourage time
apart for woodworking in the toolshed or full-court hoops, but try to
explain the saddle sores and joystick callouses caused by countless hours
of swashbuckling simulation while your real damsel distresses. When
your ESP breaks through during ESPN, auguring discontent, tune out
Chris Berman and tune into your personal development.

In lieu of latching on to the electronic teat, break the routine. There
are books to read, languages to learn, and love to make. The same tired
souls who say they haven't time to reply to a letter have a surfeit of hours
for prime time. Hitting the gym is doubly productive, and even a one-
dish meal can be prepared and enjoyed with a mate at the dinner table
instead of on vintage Holly Hobbie TV trays.

GOING SUBURBAN

After saving money to buy the dream house outside city limits, you've
childproofed everything, even though you don't have kids. Insidious
suburban blandness is marked by the distinct lack of any dirt or objec-

tionable content in your house and life. Your routine is so sanitized, it has all the character of a strip mall: catalogs pass as reading material, trips to shoppers' clubs outnumber bedroom sessions, and on any given Sunday, workweek malaise lands you too tired for more than a rented snoozer. Life has been reduced to a consumerist adventure of direct deposit from work to department stores to the couch. When's the last time you alighted to a gallery, chilled with an international crowd, or stayed out until breakfast time rolled around? In the end, 401(k) stability shouldn't be at the expense of a modern gentleman's savoir faire.

Incidentally, a couple that goes nowhere . . . goes nowhere. Trips and framed mementos serve as tangible evidence of your love. Besides producing sleeves of pictures to pore over during rainy Sunday nights, a foreign trek jump-starts a polyglot gent gone to pot. Promises of faraway sex in an Italian *pensione* are a surefire kerosene kick to the loins.

STAVING OFF RECLUSIVENESS

Leaving the house used to require no more suggestion than a friendly invitation or warm westerly breeze. Of late, all the king's horses and all the king's men can't drag you out for a pint now and then. If spontaneity left along with your trusty jump shot, declare mandatory date nights or impel activity by booking your calendar with planned subscriptions to the philharmonic or six-packs of tickets to the ball game. In-home entertaining is hands down the best excuse to shake the dust off your home bar and vacuum the house. An at-home soirée reinvigorates local friendships, sparks new acquaintances, and imports outside cool to your door, exposing you to the Three Mile Island fallout of popular culture that failed to radiate into your shut-in life. All in all, remove the social slipcovers and soak in new tunes, lest a hip guest wryly comment over the din of your Eagles and Wings mix tape (affectionately titled "Band on the Long Run"), "Don't get out much, do you?"

Besides hosted affairs, take cues from seasonal change to freshen a lagging spirit hopelessly chafed by the upholstery. December begs a tour of the holiday party circuit, so grab your velvet-clad lovely, bake gingerbread cookies, and ho-ho all over town. In hormonal June, dine al fresco and sip Pastis under an umbrella at a sidewalk café. If the living room feels lifeless without a glowing tube, invoke some parlor fun with bouts of gaming or card playing. Cheap, enriching entertainment options include: postprandial strolls, free lectures or readings, unfussy book and wine clubs, one-thousand-piece puzzles, and whimsical midnight food shopping (squeeze the Charmin and if the mart is devoid of customers, roll a few frames of turkey bowling in the frozen-food aisles).

DETANGLING

Going to pot starts with a moribund social calendar and eventually migrates to appearance, especially for freelancers without an office dress code. In younger days, scraggly hair and dressing down were rock 'n' roll rebellion from the square, parental wishes of a tasseled-shoe and frilly corduroy lifestyle. Once the dress-to-impress wooing motive falls away, a forsworn sense of unstyle can re-emerge. Limp ponytails and hobo attire won't capture hearts for most gents; to stand out in the growing postgrunge renaissance of refinement, you're more chic with a shaved head and smart duds. Just because you work under a hood doesn't mean you have to look like one. Indeed, the versatile lover can quick change from paint-splattered aprons to a sport coat in under a half hour. Though powerless against the aging process, maintain panache until you're an octogenarian retiree boasting daily ascots and pocket-squared pyjamas.

PART FOUR

The
POLISHED
SPOUSE

Chapter Eight

TENURED

♦ ♥ ♦ ♥ ♦ ♥ ♦ ♥

MODERN ANNIVERSARIES

[apple of her eye]

[lady of the hour]

Grandma and grandpa's golden jubilee is priceless, but to newlyweds, those first five years are accomplishments in their own right. Assuming a couple marries young and reaches a decent life span, they will mark eleven major anniversaries (one through five, ten, twenty, twenty-five, thirty, forty, fifty) and scores of minor ones. Classic etiquette texts list time-honored anniversary traditions—iron for year six, for instance— but modern lovers prefer contemporary celebration and gift-giving, not blind adherence to last century's rules.

The overly prudent hoard fine china for special occasions that never seem to come (perhaps the dusty settings will be unveiled for a lonely seventy-fifth birthday party in a dark, empty house). Party poopers who don't fuss over their own birthday might ask, "Why run up the credit cards for anniversary hullabaloo?" Besides an excuse to make international hotel reservations, anniversary celebrations break up the daily duties of love and provide a vista as you both gaze upon the previous twelve months. What's changed? Are the years running together or does this one stand out? Anniversaries are worthy of ceremony, even for ringless carousers who might observe the date of their first kiss or the day they closed on a house.

Many of the same rules for February 14th apply here: six months of high notes practically negate the need for an engraved tennis bracelet, but expect a rough spell to look especially dismal through the lens of a lackluster anniversary. Rejoice in a manner that reinvigorates home life and adds solid-state goods to the house. One, five, and ten are the first milestones; six through nine might be observed more modestly, as you earmark pennies and vacation days for building out the attic or launching a small business venture. Ten and the rest of the 0s are especially worth preparing for ahead of time, with trips to the tropics and 100,000-mile urology checkups. When the big day falls near Friday, devote a full weekend to merriment or skip town together.

Incidentally, while there shouldn't ever be pressure to perform a perfect marathon of prodigious passion, anniversary sex is compulsory. Demonstrate your desire, even if you have to mainline Spanish Fly through a hidden bathroom IV and apply stay-hard cream as if it's aftershave.

Make your anniversary a safe haven from the harsh realities of finances and in-law squabbles. Forget last week's spat in the orange juice aisle over pulp content and declare a day or week of amnesty if blustery upset threatens the fun. A cease-fire in observance of anniversary week is welcome relief; even the Brits and Germans laid down their rifles and played a friendly game of soccer on the battlefields of Flanders during a World War I Christmas truce. Whereas monthly reviews are for airing grievances over morning croissants, an anniversary is the yearly awards show for counting blessings. Even in the gloom, there's always something to toast ("You know, the dry cleaning has been particularly fresh and crisp of late").

Below, we outline our Modern Anniversary Hit List, expanding the usual gifting array from traditional to modern and quirky, outlandish and kinky. Congratulations.

1 **PAPER**	TRADITIONAL: Monogrammed stationery MODERN: Floral origami; watercolor or charcoal; weekend getaway to Elmwood Park, New Jersey, home of Marcal Paper Mills KINKY: Snap naughty digital pics and print them at home
2 **CALICO/** **COTTON**	TRADITIONAL: High-thread-count sheets MODERN: Plantation inn stay; nineteenth-century tapestry; calico kitten KINKY: Rubber sheets
3 **LEATHER**	TRADITIONAL: Monogrammed attaché/satchel MODERN: Chaps and equestrian lessons KINKY: Matching BD/SM–fetish wear (with or without leash)
4 **SILK**	TRADITIONAL: Pyjamas/kimono MODERN: Persian silk carpet; lepidopterist starter kit (net, round spectacles, loopy hat) KINKY: Blindfold
5 **WOOD**	TRADITIONAL: Lap desk MODERN: Chess, backgammon, billiards table KINKY: Paddle
6 **IRON**	TRADITIONAL: Wrought-iron bed frame MODERN: Antebellum tour of Richmond, Virginia's Tredegar Iron Works; tickets to Extreme Ironing Championship KINKY: Ball and chain

7 **WOOL/** **COPPER**	TRADITIONAL: Lineup of cookware and lessons MODERN: Welsh sweater; outdoor sculpture KINKY: Threesome with Welsh porn star Kelle Marie
8 **BRONZE**	TRADITIONAL: Bronze bust of lover MODERN: Bronzed lover's bust KINKY: Lover's bust bronzed
9 **POTTERY**	TRADITIONAL: Bake your own clay pot; raku vase MODERN: Moroccan tagine (with hearty stew inside) KINKY: Reproduction Grecian urns depicting orgiastic scenes
10 **TIN OR** **ALUMINUM**	TRADITIONAL: High performance luxury sedan; pressed tin ceiling MODERN: Trip to Tinseltown; Grand Canyon tour via ultralight KINKY: Handcuffs and Miranda-reading role-play
11 **STEEL**	TRADITIONAL: Stainless steel watch MODERN: Steelers tickets; steel drum night in the Caribbean; tickets to a steel cage match KINKY: Chokers, pokers, and medical props
12 **LINEN**	TRADITIONAL: Table linens; summer linen suit MODERN: An odalisque in charcoal on heavy linen paper KINKY: Hire a topless laundress to wash and fold
13 **LACE**	TRADITIONAL: Crocheted bedspread; vintage negligee MODERN: England excursion, with a daytrip to Nottingham, the Victorian lace capital KINKY: Thongs and G-strings

14 **IVORY**	TRADITIONAL: Antique pianoforte MODERN: Pre-embargo hippo or nut palm ivory scrimshaw; bar of soap and candlelit bubble bath KINKY: Marilyn Chambers box set
15 **CRYSTAL**	TRADITIONAL: Crystal decanter; chandelier MODERN: Baccarat Louis XIII Rémy Martin cognac KINKY: Nipple jewelry in a glass of chilled Cristal
20 **CHINA/** **PLATINUM**	TRADITIONAL: Matching platinum bands MODERN: Trek the Great Wall KINKY: Matching platinum blondes
25 **SILVER**	TRADITIONAL: Engraved or monogrammed flatware MODERN: Private silver screening of her favorite old film; party with the good silver and your twenty-five closest friends KINKY: Long dong silver
30 **PEARL**	TRADITIONAL: Stunning necklace MODERN: Trip to Pearl Harbor; oysters and caviar feast KINKY: Beaded belly chain
40 **RUBY**	TRADITIONAL: Custom jewelry MODERN: Voyage for rubies in India or Sri Lanka KINKY: Naked fly-fishing in Ruby River, Montana
50 **GOLD**	TRADITIONAL: Gift wrap a fistful of Krugerrands MODERN: Book a suite at the Golden Nugget and laugh at the memories KINKY: Golden shower

PEARL NECKLACE

[elegant strand]

[lovely bustier]

Despite its association with the salacious XXX money shot, the pearl necklace remains the classic romantic gift, treasured by ancient Romans, Victorian blue bloods, and corn-fed neighborhood girls alike. Before pearls were made available to anyone with a Service Merchandise catalog, "angel's tears" used to command staggering prices worth the GDP of kingdoms. In fact, eons ahead of the fraternity goldfish-swallowing fad, Cleopatra impressed Mark Antony when she consumed the riches of a nation by dissolving a marvelous pear-shaped pearl into a glass of wine and then gulping it down. Later, in a blockbuster trade not seen since the 1626 trinkets-for-Manahatta swap with the American Indians, renowned jeweler Jacques Cartier traded two pearl necklaces for the lot that still holds the company's landmark Fifth Avenue store. Whereas Mardi Gras beads must be earned through suggestive wiles of the skin, a strand of pearls is often bestowed on a lady via a graduation gift, grandma's bequest, or a suitor's overture of love.

Natural pearls—now extremely rare and priced only for Trump mistresses—are formed when an irritant enters the oyster shell, stimulating production of nacre. Layers of translucent calcium carbonate (same material as the shell) build up around the nuisance, eventually forming a pearl. To keep up with demand, however, cultured pearls dominate today's market. Farmed in saltwater, they are indeed real pearls, coaxed from nature by artificially implanting a mother-of-pearl nucleus into the mollusk to stimulate nacre growth. Missing the usual raw bar destiny on the end of a cocktail fork, pearl-bearing oysters take years to produce, and in the end, only a small percentage of the yield is gem quality. Of the cultured sorts, Japan's Akoya pearls are the most plentiful, while the incredibly lustrous South Sea pearls are pricier; beyond silvery white, black pearls are especially admired in Asia, where they vary in luminous shades of grey from dark to light. As for the rest, freshwater and dyed varieties represent the discount rack of the pearl world.

Steinbeck's *The Pearl* warned against the material symbols of love, but ZZ Top wailed, "She wanna pearl necklace." When your lady hollers for one, step into higher end jewelry stores, not mall outlets hawking cheap beads. Get acquainted with the basics: pearls are rated in quality like muni bonds, from AAA to A and below. Price increases according to size (7 mm is the average diameter), luster (deep, smooth coats of nacre make a radiant inner glow), and shape (perfectly round pearls are as rare as perfect gentlemen). Color is not a matter of quality, but a consumer taste issue, and mild imperfections are expected even on pristine pearls. Furthermore, necklaces are individually knotted to avoid a free-fall marble catastrophe, but gravity stretches the silk cord over time, requiring restringing service now and then. Pearls aren't meant for frequent wear, as everyday elements eat

♥ ◆ ♥ **CELEBRATION** ♥ ◆ ♥

♥ ◆ ♥ **Light rum** ♥ **Grapefruit juice** ♥ **Splash gin** ♥ **Dash grenadine** ♥ ◆ ♥

at the jewel; a pearl-laden lady should steer clear of solvents, perfumes, alcohol spills, and swimming pools.

SPOTTING FAKES

Obvious costume jewelry aside, be wary of peddlers unloading inexpensive natural pearls or "Kultured" or "Faux" pearls. These acrylic-painted glass balls are worth neither a velvet box, nor the zirconium-like distaste from a mate who will likely equate your cheap baubles with third-rate love. To test authenticity, rub the pearl along your upper front teeth— real jewels have a grainy texture, whereas fakes are slippery smooth. Real pearls also feel heavier in the hand, with smooth and sharp (not ragged or chipped) edges around the drilling holes.

Incidentally, go for baroque without going broke. Asymmetrical or free-form pearls (called baroque) are the perfect complement to a quirky kitten who doesn't fit the standard mold. These gems are more prevalent and less expensive than symmetrical pearls yet no less a mollusk feat. If you insist on round perfection around the neck, oblong pearls make lovely studs or ring stones.

DADDY DETOX

[habitual vice]

Get your mind and body ready for the big swim. When the baby is born, the father's phenotype is on view, and everyone knows where the blueprints came from. A healthy baby is a validation of self, and the daddy detox is the first showing of parental responsibility before the oomph of conception. Your wife has prepared her body for pregnancy, so ensure the seeds you're planting aren't tainted with toxicity or marred by poorly managed wellness. Why toy with the percentages for the short-term luxury of recreational drugs, alcohol, and sundry vice? Should pre- or postnatal problems arise, your lifetime of compounded guilt isn't worth an extra month of menthols, J&B guzzling, or Thai Stick fascination.

Prior to conception, wean yourself off major vices and take a two-month hiatus; if you can't do it for two, why are you asking mom to do it for nine? Get yourself in decent shape. Quit moonlighting as a plutonium rod polisher at the nuclear power plant and cut back masturbation at least 40 percent to increase the volume, potency, and purpose of your semen.

❤ ◆ ❤ ═ DETOX ═

❤ ◆ ❤ **Peach schnapps** ❤ **Cranberry juice** ❤ **Vodka** ❤ **Layer in order** ❤ ◆ ❤

Vitamins, supplements, and yoga are recommended, but don't go tinkering on the inside with exotic grapefruit diets, political hunger strikes, or full-body prison tattoos that leach ink into your vas deferens. The result of the daddy detox is pristine sperm, the cream of your crop. After easing back into vice, you'll return a little wiser and tempered for the road to parenthood.

RIGHT PLACE, RIGHT TIME

Make conception a meaningful act. Sperm is sperm, but for luck beyond biology, conceive during tender, intimate sex to avoid the imprint of fetish on fertilization. Do you want to tell your daughter she was conceived on the bar sink of Ronnie's Roadhouse with Kiss blasting on the jukebox? If you've been fired, depressed, or fighting at home, now's not the time to spark new life. Time your coupling with we-cycle highs and declare yourself ineligible if your spirit isn't in the right space.

NEW DAD

[baby buggy]

[4WD]

For many, fatherhood requires little more investment than dinner, a movie, and a room key. The gentleman, on the other hand, acknowledges that daddyhood begins when the child opens her eyes and doesn't end until papa permanently closes his. Presumably, that aphorism was originally coined before the advent of prenatal care, which means that fatherhood these days also includes forty weeks of spring training.

"And wed" is a fitting anagram for "new dad," since the classic wife and husband scenario remains the smoothest path for new parents and the best chance for your child to prosper. An unwanted junior in a rickety marriage, however, is misery compared to a love child raised by an accountable though unwed mom or a progressive two-dad partnership. That said, it is advisable to either formalize your union at city hall or otherwise confirm long-term resolve before a new little person calls your neo-urban commune bluff and proves that raising a child takes a father, not just a village.

BABY BROADCAST

When you first find out, no need to go public right away, although watchful friends catch on quickly as your bubbly-guzzling lady refuses her first drink in recorded history. Like the engagement announcement, the secret on your tongue should be enjoyed for days or weeks before you break the news to family and intimate friends. Anything can happen in the first trimester, and the only thing worse than a miscarriage is reliving it as friends out of the loop drop by to see how the pregnancy is going. When making rounds with the happy report, compassionately downplay your exuberance in front of unwed husband-shoppers or frustrated couples in hock for in vitro.

IT'S A ?

Some insist that knowing the baby's sex beforehand simplifies gift-giving and nursery-painting conundrums, while others advocate the coin toss draw of fate that makes a birth so exciting. With so many sure things in the world—you can always count on Old Faithful to gush every ninety minutes or so and the cursed Red Sox to implode every October—why not infuse the affair with some mystery? There's also the office pool to think about, whereby contestants buy their way into the game with their declared guess of gender, birth date, and weight (like the Monday Night Football over-under, closest to exact time makes an ideal tiebreaker).

MYRTLE OR MACKENZIE

Once the old wives' tales of gender guessing settles down ("she's carrying it high—it's a bambino"; "her feet are colder than before pregnancy, you know what that means . . ."), the name caucus begins. Your child is an unconquered wilderness, and each family wants to stake a colonial claim with ancestral names. Meanwhile, glossy mags trumpet the yearly baby name hit parade that later results in flocks of dopey fourth graders named Dakota. To eliminate name naysayers who squawk at any proffered label ("No, no, I dated a slut named Madison once"), keep mum until the birth certificate is signed and notarized. Better, throw the hordes off the scent with a dummy name that your kin can squabble over ("In honor of the fallen rapper, we're naming the boy Grand Master Flash").

Incidentally, if you affix an esoteric religious or obscure literary moniker like Agamemnon, buffer it with familiar middle name like Charles. The alternative name will spare your child school-yard teasing should he major in football rather than Greek mythology.

MORNING SICKNESS

A husband proves his mettle at 6 A.M. when his lady is suffering over the toilet bowl and negotiating but a tablespoon of cereal. Gestation lasts nine months for good reason, since it takes that long to adjust to the new lifestyle. Activating your compassion gene is vital; with her uterus doing carnival tricks, it's up to you to bear down as wicked epithets of "You did this to me!" are hurled your way. When a lover is blue or turning green, it's your job to dash to the all-night pharmacy as things get liquid. Remind her how sexy she is even during the acne and bloated-feet phase. Don't be another discomfort: harping on your few inconveniences is insensitive given her lion's share of the embryonic workload.

SHARING TEMPERANCE

An expecting mother wants to know that the husband shares in the sacrifice. Fathers who have successfully completed the daddy detox for conception should maintain a low vice profile during pregnancy. Strict abstinence from booze and such is unreasonable, but moderation isn't lost on a nauseous partner who cannot order a sirloin, scotch, and cigar. Since you can't carry her belly, cutting back on recreational use is a wordless act of support; combine with daily foot rubs and weekly flowers for best results.

PRENATAL WARM-UP

Most medical checkups are but brief visits to monitor weight and fetal heart rate, but the critical first round of comprehensive exams establishes rapport with the doc and demonstrates your willingness to participate. Missing the sonogram also means missing first hints of your child's life, and besides, you'll feel like a champ in a waiting room crammed with preggies but precious few hubbies. Keep up with the recommended reading list and do the Internet homework so that Bradley Method, Hypno-Birthing, Braxton Hicks, and mucus plug aren't foreign terms. Prenatal yoga and new-parent classes settle nerves and demystify the labors ahead.

Incidentally, turn the baby shower into a unisex event so that dad can mine the patriarchs for parenting tips while mom collects the loot. For traditionalists who insist on a girly event, direct the gents to a simultaneous Sperm Appreciation brouhaha. While the ladies munch on tea sandwiches, the boys clink pilsners at a nearby saloon and toast to healthy seminal vesicles everywhere.

CERVIX SERVICE

Due to supercharged hormones, lucky daddy-o's will enjoy an insatiable mom into the thirty-ninth week of pregnancy. However, if an aching mother closes the bedroom for renovations, don't bug her with blue balls. This is the time for cuddling and coddling, so climb in the sack if only to spoon. Pregnancy's awkward gaseous emissions shouldn't put the kibosh on Sunday morning antics, though an extra thirty pounds of woman will change the logistical dynamism of *Kama Sutra* positions and trampoline tricks. Remember, she can't be doubly pregnant, so let it fly during these precious months when birth control is irrelevant. Fortunately for horny dads looking to pitch in, hormones in semen help soften the cervix for labor, making hot sex cool comfort for the expectant mom. Both of you ought to stock up during the blissful second trimester, since the waning days before birth and subsequent months will find your genitals in dry dock and your hungry eyes scanning adult pay-per-view features. (Later, with a newborn, don't think that you've lost a step just because the box springs are quiet; nursing releases prolactin, a hormone that inhibits sex drive, purportedly to discourage a quick second pregnancy or nights in smoky clubs instead of pink-painted nurseries.)

NESTING

In the final weeks, you'll return home to find the mom-to-be at the foot of a closet, folding and organizing, preparing for the stork. Nesting is a prenatal mammalian trait that serves to both quiet the mind and adjust the living quarters for the new roommate. Get into the groove by adding your own personal touches to the nursery. After assembling the crib and changing table, undertake the other chores that cannot be done with a four-day-old in your arms: pay the bills, complete forestalled projects, thoroughly scour the house, and charge your batteries with an abundance of sleep.

Nice touch: Fill the icebox with a month's worth of nourishment. At homecoming, no one feels like cooking, yet healthy foods are just the tonic after a hospital stay. Stock the freezer with homemade goodies divided into portions for quick defrosting. A ready supply of lasagna, soup, and casseroles keeps the kitchen clean while taking minimal time away from the newborn.

DOULAS & MIDWIVES

Next to pristine prenatal health and a tubful of folic acid, there is no single greater gift to the parents and unborn baby than a doula and a midwife in the birthing room. The medical staff handles clinical precautions, but these women do all the other things you'd do for the mother if you had the knowledge and experience of a New York cabbie with two-dozen backseat births on your résumé.

From the Greek word for "servant woman," a doula (rhymes with hula) is a woman who provides emotional and physical support—but not clinical advice—during labor and after childbirth. For $300 to $500, you commission an angel whose sole duty is to nurture the mother and expertly guide her through waves of contractions and pleas for an epidural. Doulas know an array of body positions that relieve pain and they employ a bag of natural remedies to aid mom's widening cervix: birthing ball, massage, tub and shower, and focused breathing. Labor is a full-time gig for mama, but when a doula is on hand, dad can take a time-out from the beeping fetal monitor for journaling, photography, and updating the waiting room floor-pacers.

The certified midwife (CM) and certified nurse-midwife (CNM) are accredited specialists, counseling women from conception to afterbirth. For those leaning toward natural delivery, midwifery is a vital health care component. CMs and CNMs are licensed to write prescriptions, so moms looking for holistic care can also count on anesthesia as needed. As for home births, friends should collect the requisite number of doctors' signatures in order to commit naïve first-time parents who entertain thoughts of a serene, trouble-free birth in their home bathtub far from emergency care.

GETTING OVER GRODY

Not all boys are raised to appreciate uterine gymnastics and the mystical properties of placenta, and the birthing room is just the place to break through any phobias instilled by hard-core medical filmstrips during fifth grade health class. Instead of reeling at the sight of the crowning child as scenes from *Alien* flash across your mind, embrace the primal beauty of a mother's guttural groans as she pushes vernix-covered life into your arms. Volunteer to announce the sex and cut the umbilical cord so that you're not watching a movie but joining in a human moment. Vaginal births are not for the faint of heart or full of stomach, however; if you're easily squeamish, stay at mom's head, not her thighs, and maintain eye contact through the delivery. Especially beware the Act II: The Afterbirth, whence the steaming, sanguineous placenta hunk is delivered. Hard-core placentophagists might ask the doc, "Can we get that to go?" and ceremoniously sup on this nutritive ambrosia, paired nicely with a pungent, aromatic, Alsatian white.

Not so nice touch: Perfervid new dads equipped to capture breaking news photos of the five-minute-old babe shouldn't record and transmit every intimate scene. Spare your email list the graphic bedside tableau boasting a worn-out mother, puffy-eyed newbie, and meconium-flecked diaper.

FIRST MOMENTS ALONE

Before the family is alerted and a videographer sets up the boom mic, huddle with mother and child alone. If drugs were administered, mom may be loopy, in which case you can enjoy your first father-child heart-to-heart as the babe is cleaned and Apgar scores are recorded (the only standardized test without a prep course).

Spend the first hour together, not separated by a bullying medical staff who insists on poking and prodding immediately. Also, for pro-foreskin folk or those who already booked a mohel (and ordered the lox), have the nurse mark the card "No-Circ" (no circumcision), lest your child return with less than he started with. Phineas supports a neat salami, while Tesauro, though a cut man himself, favored the intact model with pita-pocket intrigue for his own son.

HOMECOMING

Everyone wants to see the baby, but it takes work to host even the most well-meaning relatives. Put up the velvet ropes and enforce a strict door policy that limits visiting to essential helpers; keep other friends in a holding pattern until you break into the second box of diapers. Put the family to task. After being gone for a few days, there are suitcases to unpack and laundry to wash. Send out a brother to fetch the new mom a pastry favorite and coax the proud grandpappies to spring for a simple lunch on paper plates. Get sis-in-law working the phones to spread word through the grapevine and put the grandmums to writing and sending birth announcements. Come December, clear the mantel—an "It's a Boy" mailing pushes your subsequent holiday card take up 20 percent, yet thanks to junior's overstuffed stocking, your pile of presents shrinks by nearly as much.

FIRST 100 DAYS

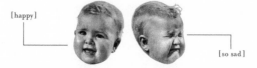

[happy]

[so sad]

The first two weeks are a REM-less blur. The third week is marginally better, but once you endure the first month, your body adjusts to sleep-lessness, and the afterburners kick in. Mother Nature set it up perfectly so that just when you reach the end of your rope, the baby comes alert, starts to smile, and provides the heart-melting impetus to muster more serenity. At that point, despite your hypochondriac mother-in-law's doomsaying germ theory, get out of the house. Until the baby puts on a few ounces, leave the stroller home and enjoy swathing the babe in your arms as the three of you saunter in the sunshine.

Baby advice abounds from nosy passersby and any kinfolk with offspring, yet for once, you can tell them all to buzz off without apology—they'll just chalk it up to sleep deprivation. Get your hands on the in-depth child guides before the babe comes home, since the only thing you'll read for a while afterward is the instructions for the bouncy seat. To help sort out the commonest ills, here are our daddy-tested and mother-approved fatherhood recommendations.

DIAPER DRAG

Treat mama tenderly. Like understanding the lethal combination of menstrual cramps and displaced anger, commiserate with a partner in the throes of postpartum baby blues. The condition is no joke, but it is temporary, as the body reorganizes the newfangled configuration of hormones. Moreover, a salve of compassionate words heals a new mother's distorted body image, especially regarding a C-section scar or an episiotomy.

There is no need for two insomniacs. If your household has the privilege of a nursing homemaker, it is most efficient for her to handle the 4 A.M. feedings and changes without waking the breadwinner, who needs to be fresh for the morning commute. This isn't about splitting kitchen jobs or sexist ideals, rather a workable solution during a difficult time. However, when you're home, corral bonding time with the child through bathing, bottle-feeding, and coddling a colicky baby to sleep.

An infant works in minishifts and so must you. Unless you bring in outside help, large blocks of your free time will disappear. To compensate, sharpen your one-minute managing skills, and instead of futzing with the remote during downtime, jet wash the bathroom or pen a letter. When the babe is idle and happy, take him with you to the computer while you pay bills, read email, or download files.

Nice touch: Before leaving the birthing center, ask an attendant to teach you "the swaddle," a series of folds that turns child and blanket into a cozy baby burrito.

MACK DADDY

Your baby is a magnet that draws sexy moms and doting grannies to the stroller, plus the occasional veteran dad. Better than a swinging bachelor's jog with a pup in the park or a cruise down the boulevard in a low-rider, your tot attracts smiles from fellow parents who know the drill. To experience this phenomenon in full force, head to the deli counter on a weekday afternoon when the mom to dad ratio is nine to one, and enjoy insider chat about diaper brands and nipple sensitivity as you exchange pleasantries ("Sleeping through the night yet?"; "Sweet minivan").

Worried that you'll slip in social status? Gather the gang at your pad instead of skipping invitations to deafening bars. Entertaining at home affords you all the baby-changing comforts while maintaining community spirit over potluck dinners and parlor games. When a sitter is holding down the fort, recall your hip personas and stow the baby minutiae before venturing out to a dinner party; like nitrous-free dentistry, there are few things more excruciating than enduring party chatter with new parents who prattle incessantly about diaper rash, gassiness, feeding schedules, or hypoallergenic detergents. Lastly, after three months, must you count the baby's age and everything else in pediatric-style week-measured increments? ("After the little one goes off to day care at twenty-eight months, I'll be returning to my MFA program in another fourteen weeks.")

Incidentally, want her called Josephina, not Jo-Jo? Put your foot down regarding nicknames before they stick (though "my little monkey" is fine until age five). Hand washing and overstimulation are your call, too. Visitors ought to get in the habit of washing up before handling the infant, and after five consecutive games of peekaboo turn laughter into tears, pull the plug on stimuli.

SOP ON POP

Fatherhood is an aqueous undertaking. Before nestling with a milk-filled infant, shed your tie and three-piece to cut down on needless dry cleaning bills. With the onset of spilled sippy cups and limbs sticky with strained peas, delay the purchase of new living room sets and say goodbye to the backseat leather sheen of your shiny Bimmer. As for feedings away from home, casual settings like shopping plazas, diner booths, and friends' pads render an unobtrusive breast-feeding under the receiving blanket justly decorous. At formal events and table-clothed trattorias, though, mom should step away to the lobby or retire to a settee in the ladies' lounge. Once the little one is put to bed, sample the goods yourself and put a little cream in the coffee. Whether out of the bottle or hot from the tap, revisit the taste of breast milk, the official sports drink of regression therapy.

NIPPLE CONFUSION

In the first hundred days, there's a temporary aversion to undue breast groping and aggressive foreplay. The areolae used to be beacons of eroticism, but now they're bull's-eyes for the ever-hungry, pinchy tot seeking sustenance. Tender and chafed from a string of vigorous feedings, her breasts deserve extra-ginger treatment; when in doubt, proceed directly to third base. Walk a mile in her nursing bra: after twenty-four hours of labor, a three-day hospital stay, and twelve weeks of interrupted winks, if you still think she's into fellatio, think again.

Allen, Ed and Dana Allen, *Together Sex: The Playful Couple's Key to Better Sex Parties.* Momentpoint Media, 2001. Paints a realistic picture for sexy trailblazers, from politics to propositions to party preparations. The naked truth about swinging manners, jealousy, and the playpen, plus a fabulous appendix.

Brame, Gloria, *Come Hither: A Commonsense Guide to Kinky Sex.* New York: Simon & Schuster, 2000. With her PhD in clinical sexology, Dr. Brame strips SM to its essentials for both doms and subs. "The Glossary of Scene Slang" is indispensable for kinky conversationalists.

Brazelton, T. Berry, *Touchpoints: Birth to 3.* New York: Perseus Publishing, 1992. While mom reads Dr. Spock in the third trimester, study up on what the first weeks will bring. Prepare for challenges, from the creamy coos to the pukey goo-goos, and confirm that your child is right on course.

Buscaglia, Leo, *Love.* New York: Fawcet Books, 1972. The workingman's Dale Carnegie and the godfather of soulmates. Under his watch, love became a personal rallying cry and the cornerstone of a 1970s cottage industry. With doses of humor and histrionics, Leo was hot, especially during his groundbreaking "Love Class," a hit on PBS back in the day.

Dempsey & Carroll Society Stationers, *Marriage.* New York: Dempsey & Carroll Society Stationers, 1901. Focused on the correct forms for wedding invitations, announcements, and receptions, this thin book is also endowed with wonderful engravings, love poems, and quotable gems on "Managing a Husband" and "Marrying for Money."

Duvall, Sylvanus M., *Before You Marry.* New York: Hill & Wang Pub., 1959. A terrific book in Q&A form that provides hysterical anachronisms while promoting spouse-to-be debate on vital topics. An old school snapshot of the Xs and Os of the marital institution, recalling the days when matrimony was a social merger, not necessarily a love connection.

Fox, Susan, *Rookie Dad.* New York: Pocket Books, 2001. For papas afraid of breaking their tot, this fun guide highlights exercises and games that encourage playfulness, fitness, and bonding.

Gottman, John M. et al, *The Mathematics of Marriage: Dynamic Non-Linear Models.* Cambridge, MA: The MIT Press, 2002. A postgraduate treatise that explains the marital dynamic through empirical models and scientific data collected at the Love Lab. The book's positive and negative predictors of marital bliss are fascinating. Not a beach read for the faint of mind.

Hopkins, Martha and Randall Lockridge, *Intercourses: An Aphrodisiac Cookbook.* Memphis, TN: Terrace Publishing, 2003. Decadent recipes and gorgeous photography that will make you swoon at the sight of ripe figs. A juicy gift for a saucy recipient.

Hopton, Dr. Ralph Y. and Anne Balliol, *Bed Manners and Better Bed Manners: How to*

Bring Sunshine into Your Nights. New York: Arden Book Company, 1948. Comedic, wry look at missteps in the boudoir from cold creams to cold feet. Enlightening rules of bediquette written before marrieds lived together first.

Humphrey, Charlotte Eliza ("Madge of Truth"), *Manners for Women.* Whitstable, England: Pryor Publications, 1993 (originally published 1897). Madge casts an acerbic tongue on the subjects of formal grace. Far ahead of her time, she dispels fashions out of vogue while trumpeting a sharp sense of decorum that wouldn't be out of place on today's thoroughfares.

J, *The Sensuous Woman.* New York: Lyle Stuart, 1970. The companion guide to the mysterious M's *The Sensuous Man.* A brassy how-to guide written at the peak of sexual exploration. "The birds and the bees" meets 70s porno. Buy a used hardcover or examine a public edition at the Library of Congress.

Muir, Charles and Caroline Muir, *Tantra: The Art of Conscious Loving.* San Francisco: Mercury House, Inc., 1989. Handbook for exploring the sexual/spiritual connection, deepened monogamy, and sexual healing. With five chapters devoted to lovemaking techniques, this is for soulmates who exhale love, not fuck buddies with whiskey breath.

Nabokov, Vladimir, *The Annotated Lolita.* New York: Vintage Books, 1991 (originally published 1955). Extravagant modern novel (with helpful explanatory notes) full of lofty themes, dazzling wordplay, and challenging viewpoints. De rigueur for rounding out one's mature sexual and literary boundaries.

Napheys, George H., A.M., M.D., *The Transmission of Life: Counsels on the Nature and Hygiene of the Masculine Function.* Philadelphia: J. G. Fergus & Co., 1874. Presented in the scare-you-straight tone of a gruesome driver's ed film, virility, celibacy, and marriage are examined through the eyes of a doctor who points to the unnatural crime of solitary vice or "self-abuse" as the frequent cause of insanity.

Viorst, Judith, *It's Hard to Be Hip Over Thirty and Other Tragedies of Married Life.* New York: Signet Books, 1968. An epic poem on the vagaries of marriage from honeymoons to mothers-in-law, from sex to suburbia. Nearly forty years old and yet absolutely fresh and sardonic.

Whitman, Stacy and Wynne Whitman, *Shacking Up: The Smart Girl's Guide to Living in Sin without Getting Burned.* New York: Broadway Books, 2003. One part *Cosmo* article, one part legal advice from two sisters who know that anything can happen when suitcases and checking accounts collide within four walls and 500 sq. ft.

Wurdz, Gideon, *Eediotic Etiquette.* New York: Frederick A. Stokes Co., 1906. Billing itself as "a Complete Catalogue of the Social Dues—and Most of the Don'ts," this diminutive manual ranges from Kisses to Christenings and Picnics to Proposals with tongue-in-cheek wit and cartoonish drawings.

INDEX

PHINEAS MOLLOD (right) received a BA from Drew University and his law degree from Vanderbilt. He lives in New York and occasionally tolerates the clamor of the courtroom, all the while pining for the vintage ding of his manual typewriter. As for his *Mod Lov* credentials, he has attained mastery of "The Evolved Bachelor," currently living in sin at a new pad boasting exposed brick and a slinky blonde. JASON TESAURO (left) also graduated from Drew and, in lieu of the LSATs, pursued wine school and a U.S. design patent for the elliptical backgammon board. He and his wife, the Fair E, share a toy box boasting a custom croquet mallet, feather masks, and their leather anniversary gifts. By day, he lives in Richmond, Virginia, serving as marketing director for Barboursville Vineyards. By night, Tesauro travels with his saber and ascot, performing wine and etiquette seminars. Having again drawn lots with Phineas, Tesauro pulled the short straw once more and was nominated to proffer a Y chromosome for the sake of chapter 8's "New Dad," and thus was born little gent Sebastion. Messrs. Mollod & Tesauro joined *Men's Health* in 2003 as monthly manners columnists.